DATE DUE

GAYLORD			PRINTED IN U.S.A.

CRIME, DRUGS AND SOCIAL THEORY

Dedicated to my parents, Brenda and Bernard

Crime, Drugs and Social Theory

A Phenomenological Approach

CHRIS ALLEN
Manchester Metropolitan University, UK

ASHGATE

Published by
Ashgate Publishing Limited
Gower House
Croft Road
Aldershot
Hampshire GU11 3HR
England

Ashgate Publishing Company
Suite 420
101 Cherry Street
Burlington, VT 05401-4405
USA

Ashgate website: http://www.ashgate.com

British Library Cataloguing in Publication Data
Allen, Chris
    Crime, drugs and social theory : a phenomenological
    approach
    1. Drug abuse and crime - Great Britain
    I. Title
    362.2'9'0941

Library of Congress Cataloging-in-Publication Data
Allen, Chris, 1969-
    Crime, drugs and social theory : a phenomenological approach / by Chris Allen.
        p. cm.
    Includes bibliographical references and index.
    ISBN: 978-0-7546-4742-3
    1. Drug abuse and crime. 2. Crime--Sociological aspects. 3. Drug abuse--Social aspects. I. Title.

    HV5801.A39 2007
    364.2'5--dc22

                                                                    2006033558

ISBN: 978-0-7546-4742-3

Printed and bound in Great Britain by MPG Books Ltd, Bodmin, Cornwall.

Contents

Acknowledgements

This book has benefited from the labour of the following people who gladly undertook the arduous task of reading earlier drafts of the manuscript: Dave Cowan, John Flint, Nigel Sprigings, Mike Hodson and Colin Wisely. Their willingness to read and comment on earlier drafts of the manuscript, in the context of very busy lives, demonstrates their incredible generosity of spirit for which I am dearly grateful. Their insightful comments and suggestions were of immense help to me at the various stages of re-drafting.

Although all of the above have had a fundamental impact on the content of the book, I am also grateful to my family for being supportive throughout each stage of its production. I am indebted to my partner Kate Drewett, who has shown incredible patience as I toiled away from early until late on far too many occasions. Thanks also to Fraser for getting me out of the office to play football and cricket in the back garden, and Charlie for being born about one month from the end of the writing of the book. They put things in perspective and ensured that some semblance of sanity was retained despite the pressures of needing to bring the book to its conclusion. The book is dedicated to my Mum and Dad who embody everything that is decent in the world and who deserve so much more than a mere mention in the acknowledgements of an academic book.

Introduction

On the Question of Being and Crime

This book is essentially about the form of being that emerges out of close proximity to economic necessity (poverty, dispossession and so on) and that, in many cases, results in crime and drug use. It is therefore about 'problematic drug use' rather than 'recreational drug use', which is only analysed insofar as it precedes the former. My motivations for writing this book are twofold but interdependent. First, the form of post-modern thinking that is driving welfare policy (especially crime and drugs policy) is based on an unacceptable level of intolerance towards the practitioners of these activities and needs to be challenged. Second, social science epistemologies that have conventionally been used to explicate the relationship between crime, drugs and urban deprivation conceptualise the phenomena in the same inadequate way as policy makers and therefore run the risk of exacerbating the intolerance and prejudices propagated by the dominant mode of policy thinking in this area. I will now address these two issues in turn.

Policy Thinking and the Social Production of Intolerance

There are good political reasons for wanting to write about the nature and extent of the relationship between crime and drugs. The Blair Government, for example, has sought to attach the crime to drug users in a way which is typical of its tendency to pronounce in haste but, sadly, without seeking to understand the social phenomenon of crime and drug use at leisure. Such are the benefits of the class privileges that, when invested by their inheritors in order to secure political privileges, are too often used to marginalise those that are already marginalised. Despite New Labour's claim that it 'understands' the link between urban deprivation and problematic drug use, then, its political programme of labelling drug users as 'dangerous criminals' has simply provided justification for an increased police focus on 'eliminating' the 'drug problem' (e.g. the 'street crime *initiative*') by catching offenders and then forcing them into treatment. This coercive strategy demonstrates a woeful lack of understanding of the lives of problematic drug users living in deprived urban areas. Unfortunately, this lack of understanding is only to be expected given that it is a consequence of the new economy of power that underpins the 'joined-up' forms of governance (Allen 2003).

The principles of this new economy of power can be detected in *New Labour* rhetoric which lays the blame for previous welfare failures on the fragmentation that characterised the *modern* welfare state ('institutional silos', professional boundaries, *etc.*), which was therefore culpable for its inability to address welfare recipients' problems that are multi-dimensional in nature. However, the gradual shift towards a joined-up welfare system over the last 30 or so years has resulted in (what has become under the Blair Government) a chronic emphasis on 'holistic' welfare practices that can 'see everything, know everything and do anything'; these 'holistic practices' are often presented as 'helping' and 'supportive' (Allen 2003). The shift towards a holistic system of welfare provision has therefore resulted in the production of a political discourse that exhibits growing confidence in the problem resolving capacity of the welfare system, which is increasingly seen to be infallible. Given that a holistic welfare system can 'see everything, know everything and do anything', then, the blame for welfare failures can now be passed onto the recipients of welfare who are consequently thought to be culpable for failing to capitalise on the context/resources/opportunities that the holistic welfare system has provided to enable them to resolve their problems and issues (Allen 2003; Crawford 1999). However, that is not the end of the matter. Of key import here is that welfare recipients' enduring 'failures' and 'shortcomings' are then used as justification for recourse to coercive approaches to welfare provision. This brings me to the crux of the problem with New Labour and the political establishment more generally. Although the Blair Government has 'acknowledged' that 'holistic' measures are required to tackle drug use (for example, in regeneration programmes and drug treatment regimes) its *primary* focus has actually been on these recalcitrant individuals. This has resulted in initiatives such as the Drug Intervention Programme which involves the targeting of drug using offenders who are then coerced into treatment regimes (e.g. Drug Treatment and Testing Orders) that, as coerced, are ethically questionable and ineffective for reasons that are discussed in Chapters 1, 7 and 8.

The point to make here is that the infallibility of holistic practice and imperative towards coercion that it produces obviates the practitioners of holistic discourse from the need to understand why welfare recipients find themselves in a position that apparently requires their exposure to a more coercive approach. They are simply assumed to have shortcomings which justify the amount of attention that is given to the need for a coercive approach. Such is the nature of the political logic that results in the social production of abhorrence towards marginal and excluded groups such as problematic drug users. In other words, the Blair Government might *understand that* urban deprivation results in the social and economic production of a range of social ills (crime, drug use, hopelessness, *etc.*) and that this therefore demands a holistic approach that necessitates a focus on drug issues in regeneration programmes and a focus on 'social' issues in treatment regimes. However, the logic that underpins holistic thinking means that, when they are confronted with drug users that present continuous problems, they do not have to trouble themselves with going out of their way to *understand how* it is that these problems persist and whether and how, therefore, a different approach might be required. Conversely, the only imperative is to 'crack down' on such recalcitrant individuals that have allegedly wasted the resources that have already been poured into them. I hope that what follows in this book shows that such a strategy is primitive, punitive and unnecessary.

Scholarly Thinking and the *Implicit* Problematisation of Drug Users

My purpose for writing the book is not simply borne of a desire to counter the inadequacies of understanding possessed by the mainstream political elite. Academic concerns are also pertinent. This reflects my belief that understandings of crime and drug misuse produced through academic research also possess key deficiencies. Only some of these limitations are a result of the 'policy relevant' nature of criminological research in this area. Other limitations are of a more scholarly nature.

Clearly, much criminological research is commissioned by 'policy funders' and this is true of work in the field of crime and drugs. A number of scholars have noted that much criminological research has followed the policy agenda and has therefore been concerned with the causal links between drugs and crime (Hunt and Barker 2001). The purpose of this research has been to establish a causal link between drugs and crime that can be used to justify a policy approach towards drug users that is ultimately coercive (Hunt and Barker 2001). Now, much of this policy funded research has been hypothetic-deductive in nature (e.g. 'to what extent is drug use linked with acquisitive crime?') and claims to have established that 'drugs cause crime'. It even looks convincing at first sight. However, it falls apart when placed under closer critical scrutiny. Although a large volume of research claims to have 'demonstrated' causal links between drugs and crime, then, this has been counterbalanced by a wealth of research findings that raise questions about whether the causal relationship between drugs and crime is straightforward, for example by demonstrating that criminal careers tend to precede drug careers. Drugs and crime might tend to coexist, then, but such findings suggest that it is not possible to say, with empirical certainty, that 'drugs cause crime'. The danger with this empirically uncertain situation is that it has left many scholars stranded in the epistemological quicksand (do drugs cause crime or don't they?).

As Chapter 1 shows, the solution to this uncertainty has largely been defined in methodological terms (i.e. what other ways are there to establish whether 'drugs cause crime'?) rather than epistemological terms (i.e. what should the research questions be now?). One need only note how different methodologies – and types of research design and study focus – have been employed over time in pursuit of the accumulation of indisputable facts that will 'speak for themselves'. The result, however, has been a less than satisfactory production of yet more mixed evidence about the causal relationship between drugs and crime. Meanwhile political elites, buoyed by their confidence in the infallibility of the holistic welfare system, have been able to continue on their merry way towards the use of coercive approaches to welfare provision – largely unopposed by the public. A key reason for this is the 'mutually tolerable ignorance' (Fuller 2000) that exists between social science and the public which means, of course, that the public are generally unaware of the empirical uncertainty that surrounds the crime-drugs link. Given their tolerable ignorance of the empirical uncertainty surrounding the drugs-crime link, the public has had no reason to doubt in the intuitive appeal that the dominant 'holistic welfare' discourse has for them and which, ultimately, justifies a coercive approach to confronting the drugs problem.

Given this context, it is not surprising that some criminological research has switched attention away from attempts to prove the causal links between drugs and crime, and towards identifying the extraneous social factors ('third variables') that might cause drug use and crime to coexist. However, the notion that social research can identify the 'third variables' (e.g. family disruption, poverty, *etc.*) that result in crime *and* drugs, through the use of hypothetic-deductive research approaches, is equally questionable and has simply resulted in more disputes over what those third variables might be. Some claim evidence for the existence of 'third variables' such as family disruption. Others question the explanatory power of those 'third variables' and put other third variables forward instead.

Herein lies a key problem which Fuller (2000) describes as the problematic imperative for knowledge producers to 'get it right'. Specifically, the social scientific search for indisputable 'facts' about drug use and crime (which are assumed to be autonomous of the epistemology of social science) has taken place on the basis that they are 'there' to be discovered. There is, in other words, a 'right answer'. Given this perceived emphasis on the need to 'get it right' (which is a possibility that is regarded as epistemically unproblematic) the production of mixed evidence tends to be interpreted as a consequence of 'something going wrong'. When empirical problems have been encountered, then, these are seen to be a consequence of the failure of social science to capture 'the facts' that are 'out there'. Hence the level of investment in devising new research methodologies that are believed to be better equipped to capture the 'facts'. However, the result of this is misrecognition of the epistemological status of criminological knowledge, which is that the 'facts' about crime and drugs are 'out there' to be discovered. This means, of course, that the social processes involved in the production of criminological knowledge come to be regarded as more or less unproblematic. This is an undemocratic state of affairs and one which this book is centrally concerned with.

First, I have already sought to highlight how the claimed ability of the holistic welfare system to 'see everything, know everything and do anything' results in a high level of intolerance towards welfare recipients that do not conform to the demands that are placed on them. By the same token, a 'policy-oriented' research agenda based on a search for the 'facts' suggests intolerance towards the notion that criminological knowledge is actually produced from competing 'points of view'. Yet this is exactly what 'holism' and the empiricist research agenda that underpins it are constituted on. Both represent 'points of view' that masquerade as 'right' in their essentials. Yet they are neither 'right' nor 'wrong' in their essentials. They are each socially produced 'points of view' that are expressive of the contemporary relations of power and domination that exist between the producers of political discourse (and the criminological enterprise that supports it) and those that are the subject of that discourse. The important thing here is that the force with which this dominant point of view is put forward – and misrecognised – as the 'right' point of view proscribes others (notably welfare recipients) from their own right to possess a 'point of view'. Such is the undemocratic nature of the holistic point of view and much of the empiricist research agenda that is parasitic upon it. And, as we have seen, the mutually tolerable ignorance that exists between social science and the public ensures that this undemocratic dominance endures relatively unscathed even in the face of the conflicting evidence produced by the former.

Second, sociologists and criminologists that recognise the arbitrary nature of the dominant holistic and empiricist points of view have sought to recover the crime-drugs research problematic from its descent into issues of research design and methodology and, instead, formulate it as an epistemological issue. Whereas empiricist researchers have sought but failed to substantiate *hypotheses that* 'drugs cause crime' or *that* some other 'third variable' causes them both, thereby plunging crime and drugs research into the epistemological quicksand, these sociologists have been more interested in *understanding how* urban deprivation, crime and drugs concur in order to extract it from the quicksand. Chapter 2 shows how this has resulted in the production of a variety of theoretical points of view on the crime-drugs problematic.

Unlike the hypothetico-deductive reasoning that underpins empiricist research, which is premised on the need to 'get it right' and discovery of universal facts that 'speak for themselves', sociologists that have taken the crime-drugs problematic into the realm of epistemology have explicitly done so from points of view that have been derived from a variety of traditions in social theory. These points of view, and the accounts of crime and drug use that they articulate, are not presented as 'factual'. Conversely the criteria by which this work seeks to be judged concerns its 'relevance' to the situations in which the research was undertaken (its 'explanatory power') rather than its ability to prove itself inherently and universally 'right'. And given that they are explicitly articulated from a theoretical point of view that represents a version of 'truth' (cf. Foucault 1979), they seek to render the dominant (holistic, empiricist) point of view as arbitrary thereby undermining its claim to legitimacy. Whereas the stale abstract empiricism of policy funded research plunged crime and drugs research into the epistemological quicksand, then, these sociologists have opened up a democratic debate that is characterised by the diversity of epistemological positions from which the understanding of drugs and crime has been articulated. Participants in this debate therefore regard their detractors as entitled to their point of view rather than as, simply or straightforwardly, right or wrong. Further, the manner in which this has engendered a process of dialogue between those holding different theoretical positions can be seen in the way in which these different theoretical positions have exerted a mutual influence on each other. This can be seen in Chapter 2 which discusses how the various theoretical approaches to crime and drugs (the most obvious example being 'social network analysis') have been influenced by ideas that have their origins in other theoretical points of view of crime and drugs, for example, symbolic interactionism, socialisation theory, social constructionism.

Of course this is welcome. However, this book has emerged out of a concern that these theoretical points of view are plagued by some of the limitations that have plagued the holistic point of view; that is, by a form of epistemic ignorance that results in an inability to understand the experiential point of view of drug users. So, how does this happen? The theoretical points of view outlined in Chapter 2 have sought to *understand how* social conditions foster crime and drug use and have led to a rich and democratic debate about how to understand drug use as an urban phenomenon. However, they have done this in a particular way that has enforced the same type of closure on democratic debate as holistic epistemology. We have already seen that epistemic arrogance of holistic epistemology emerges from its infallibility (which is a consequence of its ability to 'see everything, know everything and do anything') which means that it does not even recognise itself as an epistemological position. It claims to speak the *only truth* rather than a truth that is produced from a particular point of view (cf. Foucault 1979). A similar form of epistemic arrogance can be detected in scholarly accounts of crime and drug use. Although these accounts are more democratic in the way they acknowledge differences with each other, they fail to recognise that scholarly points of view (from whatever theoretical position) are exactly that, i.e. scholarly points of view. So, although there are differences between different theoretical approaches to understanding crime and drug use, there are also some key similarities between them that tend to go unrecognised. These similarities emerge from a collective failure to recognise that the social and epistemological conditions in which scholarly research takes place are radically different to those in which everyday life takes place, thereby resulting in a 'scholarly point of view' that is different to the 'everyday point of view'. When unrecognised, then, this leads to a lack of reflexivity concerning the differences between the scholarly and everyday practical points of view which, Bourdieu (1977) argues, has profound epistemological consequences:

> The practical privilege in which all scientific activity arises never more subtly governs that activity (in so far as science presupposes not only an epistemological break but also a *social* separation) than when, unrecognised as privilege, it leads to an implicit theory of practice which is the corollary of neglect of social conditions in which science is possible ... Science has a time which is not that of practice. For the analyst, time no longer counts: not only because ... he cannot be in any certainty as to what may happen, but also because he has the time to totalize, i.e. to overcome the effects of time. Scientific practice is so 'detemporalized' that it tends to exclude even the idea of what it excludes: because science is possible only in a relation to time which is opposed to that of practice, it tends to ignore time and, in doing so, to reify practices. (Which is to say, once again, that epistemological reflection is constitutive of scientific practice itself: in order to understand what practice is and in particular the properties it owes to the fact that it unfolds in time it is therefore necessary to know what science is and in particular what is implied in the specific temporality of scientific practice.) (Bourdieu 1977: 1 and 9)

The purpose of Chapter 3 onwards is to examine the epistemological issues that Bourdieu has presented us with above. My argument is that scholarly epistemology is based on a spatial and temporal distance from everyday practice, which means that social scientists tend to objectify the field of everyday practice in a way that those engaged in it do not. This point is illustrated in Chapter 3 which shows how social scientists tend to assume that the subjects of their attention similarly objectify their own practices and that, as such, that they are capable of providing what Bourdieu (2000) refers to as 'reasoned reasons' for what they do. The problem here is that research participants often cannot provide 'reasoned reasons' for what they do. Yet when presented with respondents' silence, in the face of questions that assume such an objectifying distance, the stock in trade response of the social scientist is to ask another, probing, question rather than to seek an understanding of the silence that confronts them. For example, confronted with a blank response to a simple question such as 'why do you wear jeans?', the typical social scientific response is to return with a probing question such as 'by that I mean, some people wear jeans whereas some people prefer not to. Why do you think that you are one of those people that prefer to wear jeans?' Since the first question failed to elicit a 'satisfactory answer' (because there is no 'satisfactory answer' for the interviewee who 'just wears them'), then, the probing question makes an explicit demand for the subject to objectify the field of fashion and articulate a reason for why they chose to wear jeans rather than, say, trousers. This second question may elicit a response such as 'because I don't like trousers'. The problem with this is that it overlooks the interviewee's first answer (that they 'just wear them') which is arguably their 'real' non-reasoned reason for wearing jeans.

Merleau-Ponty (1962) is also instructive for me here. Merleau-Ponty distinguishes between 'second order' and 'first order' language. Second order language is a reflexive form of articulation that orients itself to the question at hand (which is the social scientist's stock-in-trade) rather than everyday practice. Conversely 'first order' language is a primordial form of language that emerges from within the thick of practice. Scholarly adherence to second order language has profound consequences and, in many ways, reflects the social relations of domination within which the education system and scholarly researchers are situated. Bourdieu and Passeron (1977) have analysed the internal workings of the education system and convincingly argued that it is an instrument for the reproduction of legitimate culture as defined by the dominant classes that populate the education system. For Bourdieu and Passeron (1977), then, middle class inheritors of *bourgeois parlance* (whose distance from economic necessity facilitates their artistic and literary culture of consumption) are those that are best equipped to work with pedagogic communication and, via their mastery of it, reproduce both it and the basis of their own domination. The working class inheritors of *common parlance* are those that exist at such close proximity to necessity (which is characterised by their dispossession and therefore comparative lack of 'interest' in artistic and literary forms of consumption) that they are far less well equipped to receive and work with pedagogic communication. Chapter 4 shows how this resulted in my respondents' self-elimination from the education system at their earliest opportunity. The most interesting aspect of this self-elimination was that it was a consequence of their tendency to misrecognise the dominant status of pedagogic communication as culturally legitimate rather than arbitrary. Thus, Chapter 4 also shows how my respondents interpreted the 'linguistic gap' that existed between pedagogic and working class language (which resulted in their poor exam performance) as a consequence of their own 'stupidity' or being 'thick'. In other words, as a form of communication whose dominance they misrecognised as culturally legitimate, my respondents attributed the existence of this linguistic gap to their own 'shortcomings'.

A key problem here is that my respondents used a primordial and unselfconscious form of language (that reflected the dramatic consequences of their dispossession and proximity to necessity) rather than the more sanitised form of bourgeois parlance that academics use in such a take-for-granted way, demonstrating their contempt for primordial forms of language that they regard as primitive, crude and even rude. For example, the dominant tendency is for middle class academics to use disengaged terms such as 'my understanding of the issue is ...' whereas they tend to be dismissive of forms of pronouncement that are articulated from a close proximity to the issues at stake and therefore through a more emotional form of expression, for example 'This is fucking wrong and you know it ...'. Indeed academic colleagues have asked me, on several occasions, to omit swear words such as 'fuck' from quotations in research reports for policy makers for these very reasons. Purveyors of the dominant form of sanitised pedagogic communication that are intolerant of any form of communication that is underpinned by an interlocutor's proximity to the issues at stake tell me that such language is 'unnecessary'. However, acquiescing to their demands to abide by pedagogic forms of communication would only serve to justify the legitimacy of that form of communication which, this book seeks to show, is arbitrary and therefore in need of critique. The absence of a critique of pedagogic communication would only serve to excuse the scholars that *do not understand* from *ever having to understand* why articulation occurs through forms of language other than bourgeois parlance. In other words, it would justify the class biases possessed by scholars who are ill-equipped to describe and analyse the experiences of people living at close proximity to necessity. Furthermore, it would justify the apparently acceptable form of cultural discrimination practised by those academics who appear to be able to censor the 'unnecessary' use of profane speech by those whose dispossession actually demands its use in order to express the gravity of their condition. The acceptability of this form of discrimination is exemplified by the almost complete absence of controversy that meets attempts to censor speech forms that simply deviate too much from pedagogic and bourgeois standards. Given these circumstances, then, it has been necessary to write this book because:

> Working class people require intermediaries in the realm of culture to relay their condition: that is, people committed to expressing their condition through the instruments offered by the field of cultural production. It is, in a sense, a matter of translation, but not from a foreign language: rather it is a translation from a different mode of being: a translation of indeterminate, embodied experiences of forms of domination and exclusion into a language that allows for respect of the experience, that captures it without doing violence to the nature of that experience.
>   (Charlesworth 2000: 13)

The book seeks to achieve this by critically examining the epistemic demands of my research sponsors as well as aspects of my own research practices that sometimes invited respondents to articulate themselves within a second order form of language that was oriented to the policy or scholarly point of view (which was constituted at a social and spatial distance from their practices) rather than their own experiences. For example, Chapter 4 discusses the limitations of my questions that asked respondents to 'look back' in order to provide me with 'reasoned reasons' for their involvement in crime and drug use. I show how respondents' tendency to misrecognise the cultural legitimacy of this form of questioning, and therefore answer them in the same second order form of language ('looking back now, I can see that ...') linguistically violated their primary orientation to crime and drug use that came out in other parts of the interviews when they talked about these practices 'as they happened'. They would then describe their involvement in crime and drug use through non-reasoned language such as 'it just happened' or 'came naturally' to the 'likes of us'. The temptation here, of course, is to employ the stock-in-trade response of the social scientist which is to issue a 'probing' question ('what do you mean when you say that it just happened?'). Since this would replicate the problem, by ignoring the epistemological legitimacy of the first answer given, I seek to provide a sociological understanding of the range of 'first order' discourses that my respondents provided me with to articulate the gravity of their social condition (as it presented itself to them 'in the thick' of everyday life) and how this was related to their involvement in crime and drug use. I suggest that this assignment of articulatory authority to my respondents (whose language bore all the hallmarks of an imminent relation to the world that was characterised by the pain of their dispossession, and verbalised though a form of impassioned speech that described their condition in terms such as 'fucking shit' and so on) leads us to a form of explanation that provides us with a more adequate insight into the nature of involvement in crime and drug use in deprived urban areas.

This captures a key difference between this book and much of the work in contemporary criminology: Most books about crime and drugs are written by 'specialists' within these fields of sociology and criminology. The starting point, and direct focus of interest, is with the activities of crime and drug use. Sociological theory is drawn upon to provide a context that may go some way to explaining crime and drug use. My own interest, and starting point, is with understanding the form of being in the world that exists in close proximity to economic necessity and that is a result of a life exposed to urban deprivation, dispossession and their consequences, for example crime, drug use, *etc.* A key aim of the book, then, is to understand how the pain and suffering that results from the experience (and constant exposure to the consequences) of urban deprivation inscribes itself into the being of people living in deprived urban areas *and only then* how this affects involvement in crime and drug use. Nevertheless, this only really covers the first part of the book which concludes at the end of Chapter 4. The second part of the book suggests that the subjective relation to the world (being) is not simply governed by the mundane brutality of the everyday experience of economic dispossession and constant exposure to the consequences of urban deprivation. As Heidegger points out, being is capable of undergoing a process of 'modification'. This means that we cannot treat the relation between being and crime (or drugs) as uni-dimensional. The implication of this, of course, is that the social democratic maxim that 'poverty causes crime' is far too simplistic because the being-towards of people living in close proximity to necessity is variable.

Starting with Chapter 5, the second part of the book addresses itself to the question of modified being by introducing a series of concepts that have been derived from my phenomenological reading of my data. Drawing influence from the work of Heidegger, Chapter 5 argues that the subjective relation to the world that I have referred to as 'imminent' or 'immersed' is only sustained through what I refer to as 'confirming encounters', that is, social encounters that reinforce the self-evidence of an already doxic relation to the world that 'just happens' to produce language and practice. This doxic relation to the world (or 'worldliness') is evident in the way practice is described through the public language of 'we' and thus typically expressed in terms such as 'everybody was doing it'. Disturbing encounters, on the other hand, transform this imminent relation to the world (and therefore 'worldliness') into a problematic that, as such, becomes the focus of thematic attention. The important thing to note here is that disturbing encounters have an existential basis and are prompted by the *specific* 'relevance', 'appeal' or 'meaning' that they have to a form of being-in-the-world. For Heidegger, this induces an individualised relation to the world and, in turn, ethic of being-towards-care which I show to be expressed in a much more private language of 'I', 'me', *etc.* For example, a cannabis user with a doxic relation to drug use ('we just do it, everybody does it') might be 'warned off' heroin as a consequence of disturbing encounters with heroin users in their 'circle' which results in the now individualised subject taking a critical distance from the object ('I would never do that'). The implication of this is that universal appeals to 'care', such as through a political discourse of individual responsibility (i.e. 'do not do that', e.g. the government publicity campaign to 'Just say NO to heroin') will simply fall on 'deaf ears' because, quite simply, they are not recognised as having any existential relevance to lives-being-lived.

Although Chapter 5 draws on the concept of 'disturbing encounters' to explain various states of being-in-the-world (i.e. the 'doxic' and 'care' relations) the concept is fluid in the way it manifests itself, which is situational. Specifically, disturbing encounters that project *problematic* others onto self (e.g. 'I could be like that heroin user if I don't watch it') are simply one manifestation that induced an individualised relation to being-in-the-world and resulted in my recreational drug users' initial desistance to drugs such as heroin. However, Chapter 5 discusses 'disturbing encounters' within existentially different situations, specifically, when *normalised* others were projected onto the self. Leder's (1990) phenomenological concept of dys-appearance is helpful here. Leder argues that our mundane experience of ordinary everyday life, which we tend to take for granted, is characterised by the *disappearance* of the body-subject. For example, we might not ordinarily be aware of the social characteristics of our comportment or even regard our comportment as socialised at all. Since comportment is not something that we are immediately aware of in the course of conducting our everyday lives, it can therefore be said to disappear. In Heidegger's (1962) terms, the body-subject is something that we do not need to pay attention to because it is 'ready-to-hand', that is, 'fit for purpose'. This disappearance of the body-subject is, however, ruptured by experiences and encounters that disturb our taken-for-granted attitude towards the body-subject. This might be, for example, social responses to an acquired disfigurement (Hawkesworth 2001) or simply the way in which the generalised manner of our comportment is 'out of place' in an unfamiliar situation (Skeggs 1997, 2004).

The second part of Chapter 5 explains how this is what happened to respondents who had suffered from sexual abuse. For these respondents the abused body appeared as a thematic focus of attention but, as a dys-state of awareness of not 'matching up' to normalised others, this was a socially and emotionally painful experience. However, in the same way that universal appeals to 'care' ('Just say NO to heroin') fall on *deaf ears* if they do not have existential 'relevance' to the being-in-the-world of the body-subject, the body-subject is equally *blind* to universal 'calls' to care (e.g. availability of counselling services and so on) that have no existential relevance, appeal or meaning to its being-in-the-world. Conversely, the phenomenal body-subject has a disposition to see and grasp what is 'there for it' which, in this case, is drug use which 'just happens'. I refer to this as a dys-state of being-towards-care ('I just need to forget, block it out, not think about it') because it captures this blindness to universal calls to care (e.g. counselling) and disposition towards what is 'there for it' (i.e. drugs) which, in the case of my respondents, opened the door to *moderate* levels of serious drug use (e.g. small amounts of heroin, *etc.*) that 'numb the pain' (i.e. dys-care).

The other form of 'disturbing episodes' that I discuss in Chapter 5 is the experience of bereavement. This chapter develops a phenomenological interpretation of insights from the sociology of death and dying literature in order to understand more about the 'disturbing' nature of bereavement. I argue that the sequestration of death (which has become hidden behind the walls of hospital, mortuaries and so on) enables us to deny our mortality on an everyday level and thereby maintain a sense of meaningfulness. This enables us to invest our efforts in enterprises, such as establishing a career, which ordinarily appear to be important. However, hiding away from death only means that the experience of bereavement is even more traumatic when it comes. Bereavement undermines the sense of meaning that we establish on an everyday level which means that the effort we invest in our projects, such as career building, suddenly appear all too trivial. That is to say, the things we ordinarily hold dear suddenly lose their sense of value and meaning. Middle class people might be familiar with the feeling that the effort invested in a career suddenly appears to be trivial because life suddenly appears to be trivial. This is why bereavement and depression often coincide (Hockey 1990). The recreational drug users in Chapter 5 describe similar feelings. If their disturbing encounters with heroin users were an existential 'call' that initiated a 'being-towards-care', the pursuit of care was parasitic on their personal sense of meaningfulness which was evident in the way they made constant reference to 'I', 'me', *etc.* The sense of meaningless that is engendered by bereavement was similarly evident in the way they now referred to not caring about themselves, anyone or anything. We might say, then, that bereavement initiated a 'being-against-care' that, crucially and in contradistinction to the dys-appearing group, resulted in their immediate descent into serious heroin use 'big time'. Well, why not use heroin 'big time' when they no longer cared about anything.

In the same way that 'dys' and 'against' modes of care are described in the book as deeply sociological issues that can be illuminated via recourse to phenomenology, the same is true of subsequent levels of involvement in crime *and* the routes that my respondents had taken that resulted in their desistance from serious drug use. Chapter 6 shows that the dys-appearing group engaged in only moderate levels of heroin use which meant that this did not immediately affect their involvement in crime, which was largely restricted to petty shoplifting. However, involvement in crime grew as their habits grew over time. That said, they described their *a priori* revulsion of violence which was a consequence of experiences of abuse. This meant involvement in acquisitive crime was planned so that committal of violent crime, such as street robbery, was avoided. The contrast with the bereaved group was stark. Their mode of being-against-care meant that they consumed copious amounts of heroin which meant that there was an immediate change in the level of their involvement in acquisitive crime. They also talked about acquisitive crimes such as street robbery as a 'possibility' that was 'on the agenda'.

The lesson of Chapter 6 is that it is inadequate to decontextualise acts that are committed for the purposes of acquiring resources to procure drugs. Such acts are not driven by a pharmacological need for drugs, which is a key claim that is used to sustain the establishment argument (pedalled by the government, opposition parties and police) that drugs *cause* crime. Neither are these acts 'reckless' or whatever other label is placed on them by an establishment that wishes to denigrate the agency of drug users as somehow 'deficient'. A key purpose of the book is to show that these acts are best understood sociologically, which is to say that we would all probably do the same thing were we ever to find ourselves in such a position. Dys-appearance is a consequence of the power of the normalising judgement which is designed – whether maliciously or pastorally – to make one feel inadequate, incomplete or whatever other adjective is appropriate. Being-against-care is similarly a consequence of the failure of modern societies to come to terms with death.

What is clear here, then, is that society has a responsibility yet this is routinely denied by the political establishment as well as, sometimes deliberately and at other times inadvertently, the academic establishment which views drug use as a consequence of deficient agency. Now, middle class people might deal with the issues this presents by engaging in 'therapy' but that is because they might have a disposition to grasp therapy which is 'there' for them. Of course, this middle class strategy is presented as the 'responsible' thing to do. But people that have lived their lives at such close proximity to necessity as my respondents are not in the same position at all. Their dispositions have been formulated in entirely different conditions and as a consequence of exposure to symptoms of urban deprivation, such as widespread recreational and serious drug use. Although serious drug use was initially resisted by my respondents, for whom recreational drug use and crime 'came naturally', it is not surprising that they should cope with disturbing encounters and episodes by eventually turning to what was 'there' for them, that is, drugs such as heroin. There is nothing qualitatively different about this response when compared with middle class responses even though the political and academic establishment would have us believe that the former was responsible and the latter irresponsible. In actual fact, both are socially structured dispositional responses that involve grasping what is there, where what is 'there' for different social groups is clearly going to be different. This is another key purpose of this book, which is to show that phenomenology stands out from the collection of other criminological theories for its ability to illuminate this point about the universal principles that govern human agency which just so happens to manifest themselves in acts (e.g. drugs, therapy) that are consistent with the social conditions in which agency is formed (i.e. proximity, distance from economic necessity).

Chapter 7 makes the point that the same is true of the routes that my respondents took to desist from serious drug use. Again, the political and academic establishment often paint desistance from drug use as an issue (at least partially) of users taking some responsibility for their drug use and, ultimately, doing something about it. Unfortunately, it is not as simple as that and a phenomenological analysis shows why. Since the dys-appearing group possessed revulsion of violence, their eventual involvement in violent acquisitive crime (such as street robberies) resulted in what I call 'psychological low points' where they sought to put their drug use to rest 'for good'. This 'shock' resulted in urgency for treatment which created its own dynamic as the respondents sought immediate access to 'quick fix' treatments that often did not exist. The being-against-care of the bereaved group, on the other hand, meant that their involvement in violent acquisitive crimes was less of an issue for them.

This meant that they were less likely to encounter 'psychological low points'. The point at which they sought desistance from serious drugs use was at 'physiological low points' when their bodies could not take any more drug abuse. Again, this set in train its own dynamic as respondents sought ways to give their bodies a temporary break. This phenomenological analysis of my respondents being-towards-treatment highlights why the voluntarism that contaminates ideas about individual responsibility (peddled by the political and academic establishment and accepted by an ideologically seduced public) is so flawed.

The essence of the book when both of its parts are taken together, then, is that it is important to understand the nature of being that is a consequence of dispossession as well as changes in being-towards crime and drugs that are a consequence of disturbing encounters, episodes and so on. However, these are not simply matters of epistemology. The understanding that the book seeks to generate is also important because it provides a way of critically examining the currently dominant policy discourse (holism, joined-up thinking, *etc.*) that is presently being used to justify the ultimate imposition of coercive measures to address the drug problems of 'stupid' people that have been involved in crime. This is why Chapter 8 also offers some observations about the conceptual and practical inadequacy of the current policy framework. Of course, it goes without saying that my own argument is neither 'right' nor 'wrong'. Following phenomenologists such as Bourdieu, Heidegger, Merleau-Ponty and Charlesworth, my argument is intended to represent (as closely as possible) a 'point of view' that was articulated to me from a particular (dispossessed) position within the social relations of power and domination. That said, it is only reasonable to expect that some scholars *and* drug users will disagree with all or part of the argument. That is to be expected. If we agree with Fuller's (2000) argument about the need for a more open dialogue about research, it is to be welcomed.

Empirical Origins of the Book

The material used to develop the argument in the book was drawn from an analysis of interviews with 77 problematic drug users living in deprived neighbourhoods across Greater Manchester in the North West of England. These 77 drug using offenders were selected for interview because they had been involved in violent acquisitive crime *and* because they were either heroin users *or* poly drug users that usually combined their use of heroin with drugs such as crack cocaine or cocaine powder. Mention was also made of the occasional use of drugs such as cannabis, mushrooms, ecstasy, LSD, amphetamines (speed), *etc.* Contact with these offenders was established during the conduct of three interrelated research projects, undertaken by the author in Greater Manchester between 2002 and 2005. First, contact with drug using offenders between the ages of 20 and 50 was established through a variety of drugs services and drugs projects throughout the Greater Manchester area, as well as through a variety of Probation Service Offices and probation hostels in the Greater Manchester area. Second, contact with younger offenders (i.e. below the age of 19) was established through HMYOI Hindley and a criminal solicitors' practice in Manchester.

Participants were self-selecting in that they volunteered to be interviewed in exchange for £10 vouchers, which were given out prior to the interviews. This provided me with an opportunity to make two points to participants to minimise the effects of the power relationships that surrounded the interview. First, I used this opportunity to tell them that the provision of the voucher in advance of the interview meant that it was in no way contingent on their provision of answers that they might think would 'please' me. I also told them that they could terminate the interview at any time whilst retaining the voucher. None of the interviews were terminated unusually early. Second, I made the broader point that interviews were a chance for my respondents to 'tell it like it really was' and would be undertaken in confidence, according to ethical standards set down by the British Sociological Association whose purpose and impartiality was explained. I explained that 'in confidence' meant that I would be the only person that would know what *they* had said within the interview.[1] I also explained that some of what they said might be used, in the form of quotations, within written reports of the research but that it would be reported in an anonymous fashion. Again, the purpose of this was to encourage respondents to use their interview as an opportunity to speak 'for themselves' rather than *to me* or *via me* to the service provider that had introduced us. That said, as a constructionist phenomenologist I entirely accept that the effects of an 'interview situation' can only ever be 'managed' but not eradicated (Allen 2005). This becomes clearer as the book progresses, when I discuss the limitations of my conduct of interviews from a phenomenological point of view.

Interviews took place in the offenders' own homes or within a private room at the various organisations that assisted us to make contact. The only persons present during interviews were myself and the interviewee. All interviews were taped and later transcribed, including those undertaken within prison. The format of the interview invited respondents to think and articulate themselves primarily through 'first order' language (which I regarded as a phenomenological necessity) that so often resulted in their production of 'non-reasoned reasons' ('it came naturally', 'it just happened') to explain involvement in crime and drugs. Specifically, they were encouraged to tell *their side of the story* about their involvement in crime and drugs *using their own words* and by explaining *how it really happened and how they felt* when they were 'in the thick of things'.

My research sponsors' request for 'reasoned reasons' for 'criminality' (which they took to be the only acceptable form of reason for such behaviour) meant that I was also obliged to ask respondents to articulate themselves through a second order language that reflexively made connections between their social history and situations (family

---

1   To safeguard the confidentiality of the interview, I asked respondents to talk *only* about how their drug use and involvement in crime occurred 'in the thick of it' *in general terms*. I asked them *not* to discuss *specific* details of their involvement in crime (i.e. in terms that specified nature of criminal act, dates, times, location, *etc.*) because this could compromise the interview, for example, by providing me with information that I may be obliged to pass to others. My reason for taking this approach stemmed from previous experience of interviewing sex offenders, when I obtained information that, I was subsequently advised, I was obliged to pass to the Probation Service. I was never provided with compromising information during the course of the interviews undertaken for this study.

background, area of residence, schooling, social networks, *etc.*) and involvement in crime and drugs. I therefore asked them to provide an autobiographical account of their involvement in crime and drugs within the context of their everyday experience of the neighbourhoods that they grew up in and currently inhabited. Subsequent questions were asked in relation to the story they were telling, for example by asking interviewees to expand on aspects of their story, to discuss aspects of their story in more depth, to think about connections between different parts of their story or to gain clarification about an issue. Although I was obliged to elicit second order responses as part of the condition of my research funding, my approach to interviewing was not simply a consequence of these external funding pressures. It was also a consequence of my own 'natural' tendency to adopt a scholarly view of my respondents at various points during interviews, which is something I became more aware of as I reflected on the content of the transcripts. I am referring here to numerous points during interviews when I voluntarily invited my respondents to 'look back' on things as I discussed earlier in this introduction and in further detail in Chapter 4.

It follows that my key analytical task in writing this book has been to identify (and understand the relationship between) my respondents' use of first and second order concepts when they were accounting for their involvement in crime and drugs. This comes through in the parts of the book when I am critical of the way I sometimes invited respondents to think about their involvements in crime and drugs by using second order concepts. At these points in the book I therefore seek an understanding of the epistemological status of these 'second order' answers by juxtaposing them with the types of account that my respondents gave to me when I encouraged them to talk about their involvement in crime and drugs using first order concepts (e.g. 'as it happened', 'in the thick of it'). In undertaking this analytical task it is important to note the ease with (and extent to) which my respondents articulated themselves through first order language (evident in their unselfconscious profanity and widespread production of non-reasoned discourses about drugs and crime) because this indicates that interviews were not overly compromised by my respondents' (often long) history of involvement with services to whom they are regularly required to make 'reasoned confessions'. That is to say, my respondents appear to have accepted my invitation to 'tell it like it was' and how they felt it to be rather than obliged to provide me with the type of 'acceptable answers' that service providers routinely demand from them.

When I had identified 'first order' and 'second order' accounts of crime and drug use in the transcripts, I undertook an in-depth comparative analysis of them. I assigned 'codes' to every empirical theme identified within each first and second order account so that the empirical consistency of each code could be judged. This enabled me to identify the *extent* to which first order responses such as 'comes naturally' and 'just happened' were used by respondents, as well as the situations in which they applied. It also enabled me to identity the *extent* to which second order responses such as 'looking back I feel stupid ...' were used by respondents as well as the situations in which they applied. The book is essentially a product of my analysis of empirical themes within the transcripts as well as my interpretation of how this analysis is situated in relation to other academic texts about crime, drugs and social theory.

Chapter 1

Crime, Drugs and Social Research

Introduction

Drug use is now 'normalised' across a wide range of social groups in modern societies (Williams and Parker 2001; Parker *et al* 2002; Duff 2005). This means that most people below the age of 50 have now tried drugs and that large numbers of people regularly use drugs (Pearson 2001; Williams and Parker 2001; Parker *et al* 2002). Further, the majority of the population appear to think that there is little wrong with the use of drugs, even cocaine and LSD, so long as they are taken within 'sensible' limits which they tend to be, for example at weekends (Parker *et al* 2002). Indeed, most users of illicit drugs have otherwise conforming social profiles (Williams and Parker 2001; Pearson 2001). However, some illicit drug users do not have such conforming social profiles. These users tends to live in deprived urban areas (Parker *et al* 1998) and have involvements in crime which, the state has long claimed, is connected with their need to support their drug 'addictions' (Bean 2002). This chapter is concerned with this 'official view' of the drugs-crime problematic and, in particular, the extent to which social research has been implicated in the problematisation of drug use by certain sections of the population. The chapter begins by charting the nature and extent of drug use in modern societies. This highlights how drug use by people living in deprived urban areas, or working class people more generally, has been problematised for its relation with acquisitive crime (Helmer 1977). This problematisation of the link between drugs and crime is, of course, a product of the political discourse from which it originates rather than a real or necessary empirical relationship. This will become more and more apparent as the book progresses.

Given that links between drugs and crime are the product of political discourse (rather than 'real' empirical relationships) the second part of the chapter examines how social research has been implicated in the political problematisation of the drugs-crime link. It does this by examining the social relations of funded research production, specifically, how 'facts' about the link between drugs and crime that are said to 'speak for themselves' are little more than products of a political discourse that manifests itself in the epistemology of a state funded criminological enterprise that *problematises* rather than *understands* the practice of drug use. This informs a discussion of the different types of research studies that have sought to establish the nature and extent of the link between crime and drugs. The discussion shows that much of this drugs research is based on ontological assumptions about the pharmacological properties of drugs (i.e. that they are addictive), and therefore a hypothetico-deductive approach that seeks to test the ensuing proposition that addiction is criminogenic because it perforce necessitates crime. Although the political and arbitrary nature of these ontological assumptions will be exposed as the book unfolds, for the purposes of this chapter I simply seek to demonstrate that they manifest themselves in a variety of research designs that seek to verify this proposition though which fail to do so when placed under closer scrutiny.

My discussion of hypothetico-deductive research into the proposition that 'drugs cause crime' will also show that counter-factual evidence of the internal relationship between drugs and crime (e.g. that involvement in crime precedes drug use) has been used in one of two ways by the criminological enterprise. First, some criminologists have used counter-factual evidence to suggest that the 'causal' relationship between drugs and crime is not necessarily straightforward, i.e. because drug use may only increase – rather than cause – involvement in crime. This does little to challenge the dominant political discourse that problematises people that engage in drug use and crime. Second, other criminologists have used counter-factual evidence to suggest that an eclectic range of 'third variables' (e.g. poverty, family disruption, delinquent peers, *etc.*) may cause involvement in drugs and crime. My argument will be that hypothetico-deductive testing of the range of 'third variables' that are thought to cause both crime and drugs is equally futile. This is because we are presented with a further round of research that either proves *or* falsifies the validity of the hypothesised 'third variables'. Verification and then subsequent falsification of various hypothetical 'third statements' about the 'causes' of drugs and crime simply causes confusion and therefore leaves us in the epistemological quicksand. This distracts from the production of a critical criminology of why the practice of drug use is not problematic in the way the dominant political discourse suggests. This sets the scene for Chapter 2 where I examine the various ways in which the relationship between drugs and crime has been explicitly theorised in order to develop critical understandings (*verstehen*) of drug use as social phenomena.

The Nature and Extent of Drug Use in Modern Societies

'Recreational' drug use is now endemic across a wide range of social groups in modern societies with young people between the ages of 16 and 29 reporting the highest levels of drug use (Bean 2002). The most convincing evidence of this has been accumulated by Howard Parker and colleagues who have undertaken longitudinal work that has plotted changes in drug use within a sample of young people for over a decade. Their evidence not only suggests that drug use is endemic within this population (with high and regular levels of alcohol, tobacco, amphetamine and LSD use) but also that the nature of drug use is becoming more serious (Parker *et al* 2002; Williams and Parker 2001). This is exemplified in recent findings about the changing nature and extent of drug using among their sample of young people. At the age of 18, most of Parker's respondents identified cocaine powder (along with heroin and crack) as drugs they would avoid because they were seen as too addictive and too expensive (Williams and Parker 2001). However, when surveyed at the age of 22 a significant minority of the sample had changed their minds, resulting in a steep rise in cocaine use. Although alcohol, tobacco and cannabis continued to be the most favoured multi-purpose and mixable substances among this cohort, then, stimulants like ecstasy and cocaine were now being used in the mix (Williams and Parker 2001: 410). These findings have been replicated in other countries and amongst other age groups. For example, recent work in Australia by Duff (2005) replicated Parker's methodology and found that over half of a representative sample of people between the ages of 18 and 44 were drug users and that over half of these drug users had now tried cocaine. Similar findings have also been attached to adults in their 30s and 40s (Pearson 2001).

Furthermore, this mixing of licit and illicit appears to be continuing unchecked with the boundaries between 'acceptable' and 'unacceptable' drugs eroding even at the extreme end of the drug use continuum, where drugs such as heroin are often located. One of the repeated findings of drugs surveys in the 1990s was that young people with increasingly diverse 'recreational' drug appetites rejected 'hard', addictive drugs such as heroin and crack cocaine as an unacceptable drug to even try (Parker *et al* 1998). Indeed, Aldridge *et al* (1999) point out that no representative youth survey in the 1990s recorded more than a 2 or 3 per cent lifetime trying of heroin (Aldridge *et al* 1999). Yet, anecdotal evidence collected by Parker and colleagues (Parker *et al* 1998) during the course of their work on new heroin outbreaks found that these outbreaks were not simply confined to the usual places, i.e. deprived urban areas. Serious recreational drug users with otherwise respectable and conforming social profiles were starting to use heroin as a 'chill out' drug within the dance scene.

Nevertheless, although the line between 'recreational' and 'problematic' drug use is becoming blurred within this social group of otherwise conforming young people (Williams and Parker 2001; Parker *et al* 2002), raising 'policy concern' about the likely health problems that this social group are likely to encounter at some stage in their lives (Pearson 2001), higher rates of 'problematic' substance use, specifically heroin and crack cocaine, are still thought to be overwhelmingly concentrated in deprived urban areas (Advisory Council on Drug Misuse 1998; Parker *et al* 1998; Aldridge *et al* 1999; Foster 2000; Hunt 2001; Bean 2002; Bernberg 2002; see also earlier studies by Preble and Casey 1969 and Dai 1970). Furthermore, the level of heroin use within 'socially excluded' populations 'coming from the poorest parts of towns and cities' has recently been increasing as the supply of heroin has increased (Parker *et al* 1998). In other words, as the supply of heroin has increased it has been soaked up by people living in deprived urban areas. The key political concern here has been less to do with the potential health problems that this may cause and more to do with how this low income population is likely to engage in acquisitive crime to sustain serious drug use (Bean 2002; Allen 2005a). It is within this political context that a plethora of social research into the relationship between crime and drugs has been undertaken. Much of this research has been commissioned by state agencies ('policy funders') that are concerned about the links between drugs and crime. The next part of the chapter examines the highly politicised nature of this research which has sought to problematise serious drug use by employing hypothetico-deductive approaches that seek to verify the proposition that there is a link between drugs and crime.

Research Funding and the Social Production of Criminology

The notion that social relations influence the process of knowledge production is becoming increasingly accepted within the social sciences (Allen 2005b; Beaumont *et al* 2005) where there has been a longstanding debate about the social production and epistemological status of social science. Social scientific interest in the political and social relations of knowledge production began in earnest when Kuhn (1970) argued that a key test of scientific validity concerned the level of correspondence between individual works of social science and its own established paradigms, rather than with social phenomena itself. This led researchers such as Woolgar and Latour (1979) to develop a critical 'sociology of science', although their attention was on the 'natural' rather than 'social' sciences. While this missed Kuhn's point, which was also pertinent to the social sciences, there has since been a 'turn' towards examining the social relations of knowledge production in the social sciences from a variety of theoretical perspectives (see Coffey 1999; Harding 1991; Bourdieu 2000).

Since Elias (1966), Kuhn (1970) and Woolgar and Latour (1979) wrote about the social relations of knowledge production in the natural and physical sciences, an increasing number of social scientists have turned the 'critical gaze' of social science upon itself. Some social researchers have analysed how social interactions *within the field* consciously influence process of knowledge production (see Coffey 1999). Other social researchers have examined how the 'habitus' that researchers carry with them *into the field* produces 'background thinking' that can *unconsciously* affect the process of knowledge production (see Harding 1991; Bourdieu 2000). This 'background thinking' is thought to result from the social positioning of the researcher, for example, because their social class background, gender or some other aspect of their identity and experience has provided them with a particular but unacknowledged set of beliefs that tacitly influence their understanding of social phenomena (Allen 2005).

Although illuminating, much of the literature on the social relations of knowledge production demonstrates an oversight towards one key variable which places criminologists in an even more complex position. Specifically, criminology is an applied social science (Moyer 2001) and criminological research has historically been 'bound to the service of the state' (Hillyard *et al* 2004) which has used the state funding of research to steer the criminological enterprise since its inception (see Lee 1997 for a historical overview of state funding regimes for criminological research). There is nothing controversial about this suggestion, of course, because knowledge production tends to be 'bound to the service of the state' in one way or another, irrespective of whether or not it has been 'bought' (see Bauman 1987; Foucault 1977) and, furthermore, key architects of the welfare state, notably the Webbs, placed great emphasis on instrumental role that the 'intellectual aristocracy' of social science should play in contributing to the development of an 'enlightened state' (Lund 2002).

That said, the extent to which criminologists have been 'bound' to the state has intensified as a result of the restructuring of research funding (and higher education funding more generally) over the last two or three decades (Hillyard *et al* 2004; Allen 2006). The key change has been a shift of emphasis away from the system in which social science councils provided 'research grants' in order to 'steer' the criminological enterprise towards the service of the state, that is, by concentrating funding on researchers that came up with research projects that councils' deemed to be 'relevant' (Lee 1997). Although social science councils still exist to provide 'research grants' (and indeed now place even more emphasis on steering social research to ensure its 'relevance': Allen 2006) social research undertaken from the early 1980s onwards has been *mostly* conducted 'under contract' to government departments (Lee 1997; Hillyard and Sim 1997; Walters 2003; Hillyard *et al* 2004) suffice it to say that 'contract research' has a much longer history than its recent elevation in importance suggests (see Horowitz 1967 especially the chapter by Blumer 1967). The purpose of switching emphasis to a 'contract research' model has been to take key research tasks (such as conception and objectives of research, formulation of methodology, *etc.*) out of the hands of scholars and place them directly into the hands of policy makers, who provide scholars with a 'written specification' that outlines a timetable of tasks to be completed 'under contract' (Hillyard and Sim 1997; Allen 2005). 'Steering groups' comprising 'stakeholders' in the 'policy community' oversee their conduct of tasks to ensure that they are conducted in a way that is consistent with the demands of the written specification (Allen 2005).

Now, the career trajectories of academic staff are increasingly contingent on their successes in obtaining 'contract research' (Delanty 2001; Walters 2003; Allen 2005) largely because such staff are valuable to universities that have experienced reductions in their core funding for decades and are now more reliant on income generated through contract research and other 'enterprising' activities (Lee 1997; Hillyard *et al* 2004). The extent to which 'income generation' pressures within universities have created a growing body of 'entrepreneurial' academic staff (Walters 2003; Hillyard *et al* 2004; Allen 2005) is evident in the proud proclamations of some universities which now claim that their 'largest single source of income comes from contract research'. Some universities are now even making formal position statements that curiosity driven research has 'no strategic value' within their walls because it does not attract external funding. So, in addition to the influence that factors such as social class, gender, fieldwork experiences, *etc.* have on researchers' understandings of the phenomena they investigate, criminological researchers are also moulded by the social relations of state funded research production (Lee 1997; Hillyard and Sim 1997; Walters 2003; Hillyard *et al* 2004). A good example of how social researchers are moulded by the social relations of state funded research production is provided by Allen (2005) who has analysed how his career of constant exposure to the 'disciplinary gaze' of research funders produced a level of 'docility' that resulted in an intuitive and taken-for-granted way of doing things that was primarily moulded to the needs of his research funders rather than the demands of seeking to understand the field. Hillyard *et al* (2004) have identified how the same:

> ... intimate relationship between criminology on the one hand, and the demands of the state and private interests on the other, has seriously infected the character of British criminology. For us, such trends are the key context for understanding how the massed ranks of policy-driven academic criminology have swollen with such alacrity in recent years. These processes – the marketization and commodification of knowledge – have

touched criminology as much as any other discipline in the social sciences, with significant effects for those who work within the discipline and, concomitantly, the work they produce ... The subordination of research workers to the imperatives of the market has played a crucial *disciplinary* role in the drive to fashion the academic, self-regulating subject, while simultaneously attempting to normalise those individuals and, indeed, institutions who might dissent from these imperatives, or at least harbour serious doubts about the moral and political discourses that underpin them.   (Hillyard *et al* 2004: 374 and 377-8)

Although policy makers now write the 'contract specifications' that govern contemporary criminological research, then, it is important to note that scholarly production has always tended to conform to the realities of power over the longer term in one way or another – so much so that 'official' definitions of what constitutes crime have more or less always been taken for granted by criminologists who use them to define and frame the criminological enterprise (Hillyard *et al* 2004). For Mauss (1991: 188), this is nowhere more apparent in substance 'abuse' research where 'social scientists have generally accepted the definitions of politicians as to what constitutes the most serious "social problems" of the day, especially with the growing dependence on federal research funding'. Martin and Stenner (2004) have similarly argued that drugs researchers have adopted a 'docile' relation to 'policy concepts' that are used to frame social research into drug use. They cite 'addiction' and 'habit' as politically loaded terms that are unproblematically used by drugs researchers that tend to adopt an uncritical relation to the way that:

A good deal of research in the drugs field – and most research funding – is aimed either at preventing drug use or minimising the harms associated with it. The rationality of this enterprise is taken for granted: accumulated knowledge and a better evidence base will enable us to develop more effective responses to drug-related problems.

(Martin and Stenner 2004: 395)

For Hunt and Barker (2001), then, the stimulus for research questions into drug use has increasingly come from (an uncritical acceptance of) government agendas infused by moral concerns tied to the 'war on drugs' rather than from critical developments within academic disciplines. They argue that research situating drug use within its proper context is rare and that there has been a tendency for disciplines such as sociology, anthropology and criminology to forgo one of their most important tasks which is to chart the normal everyday use of drugs within their social and cultural contexts (Hunt and Barker 2001: 171). Indeed, far from viewing drug users as active agents situated in a complex social structure, Hunt and Barker (2001) argue that criminologists often construct them as isolated, passive and decontextualised 'others':

[T]he extent to which representations of the 'other' hides social relations of power, one can but wonder how it is that anthropologists in the alcohol and drugs research fields have failed to question the way in which a problem perspective contributes to the drug user or problem drinker being defined as a disreputable and stigmatised 'other'. Such an approach is particularly troubling when we remember the tendency within the field of substance use research to study members of disenfranchised groups as opposed to examining the class culture of the professional ... In uncritically adopting societal notions of acceptable and unacceptable behaviour, anthropologists take for granted a professional and middle class view of the world ... This tendency to examine the cultural practices of the working class and ignore those of the middle or upper class is well exemplified in anthropological accounts of alcohol and drug consumption.   (Hunt and Barker 2001: 182)

There are now two things to note about these observations on criminological research production. On the one hand, my outline of crime, drugs and social theory in Chapter 2 will show that critics of criminological research into drug use, such as Hunt and Barker, slightly overstate their case. The critical work on the context of drugs use by anthropologists, sociologists and criminologists outlined in Chapter 2 might be in the minority, but there is a rich tradition of it. What is significant about this work is that much of it has been produced by researchers that have not been subjected to the 'disciplines' of state funding and whom have, instead, followed the principles of 'intellectual craftsmanship' outlined by Mills (1959):

> Any working social scientist who is well on his (sic) way ought at all times to have so many [of his own] plans, which is to say ideas, that the question is always, which of them am I, ought I, to work on next? And he should keep a special little file for his master agenda, which he writes and rewrites just for himself and perhaps for discussion with friends. From time to time he ought to review this very carefully and purposefully, and sometimes too, when he is relaxed. Some such procedure is one of the indispensable means by which your intellectual enterprise is kept oriented and under control. A widespread, informal exchange of such reviews of 'the state of my problems' among working social scientists is, I suggest, the only basis for an adequate statement of the 'leading problems of social science'. It is unlikely that in any free intellectual community there would be and certainly there ought not to be any 'monolithic' array of problems.   (Mills 1959: 198)

The Chicago School of Urban Sociology was able to make its key contributions to the development of the urban ecological, urban ethnographic and symbolic interactionist perspectives outlined in Chapter 2 through its commitment to postgraduate supervision rather than funded research (Deegan 2001); subcultural ethnographies of drug use that have emerged since the pioneering efforts of the Chicago School have similarly been produced by postgraduate researchers rather than by funded researchers (Hunt and Barker 2001; Hobbs 201); finally 'critical criminologists' conducted much of their pioneering work in the 'heyday' of critical criminology, which was in the 1970s and therefore prior to the explosion of the contract research culture in the 1980s (van Swaaningen 1999; Hillyard *et al* 2004). The remainder of the critical work cited in Chapter 2 has been produced by a minority of more contemporary researchers that are well known for engaging with funding whilst exhibiting resistance towards the 'disciplinary effects' that research funding regimes have had on the vast majority of criminologists (Hillyard *et al* 2004). Their work, in other words, has been produced despite (rather than because of) research funding.

That said, the arguments of Hunt and Barker provide an instructive introduction to the *vast majority* of the long history of criminological research that has been undertaken into the political problematic of whether drugs cause crime (cf. Bean 2002). Bean (2000) argues that much of this state sponsored research has been underpinned by (what are clearly 'well disciplined' researchers that have exhibited) an uncritical acceptance of the pharmacological assumption that drugs are addictive which means that users require money to support their habits. Bean also argues that these assumptions assume particular pertinence for certain (notably 'socially excluded') populations because they are thought likely to have no other option than to support their 'addiction' through involvement in acquisitive crime:

> The British literature on drugs and crime tends to be dominated by epidemiological considerations aimed at establishing the extent of drug use in a particular cohort or at showing that drug taking and crime go together, whether before or after the user is arrested.
> (Bean 2002: 14)

Suffice it to say that hypothetico-deductive research into the proposition that 'drugs cause crime' has sometimes produced counter-factual evidence (i.e. contrary evidence that involvement in crime tends to precede drugs). Yet, criminologists seduced by the dominant ideas that construct drug users as a 'problem' have interpreted this to mean that the drugs-crime link is not straightforward (i.e. that drugs might increase, rather than cause, involvement in crime) rather than in terms of a need to produce critical discourse challenging the notion of the drug user as a problem to be explained. Other criminologists have examined whether an eclectic series of 'third variables' (e.g. poverty, unemployment, family disruption, delinquent peers, *etc.*) cause the coterminous 'problem' of crime and drugs. However, this simply leads to arguments about the comparative validity of different third variables which distracts from the construction of a critical discourse about drugs and crime 'problems'. It is this that plunges criminology into the epistemological quicksand.

Establishing Links between Drugs and Crime

Since the 1920s, there has been a wealth of government funded research into the nature and extent of the links between drugs and the committal of crime, reflecting long-standing political concern about the drugs issue (Bean 2002). Although these studies have employed different research designs (e.g. studies of arrestees, studies of treatment participants) two characteristics are common among them. First, many of the research studies have been underpinned by ontological assumptions about the pharmacological properties of drugs, i.e. drugs are addictive (Hunt and Barker 2001: 175). Second, the research studies have generally followed a hypothetico-deductive approach, and therefore sought to 'test' the associated hypothesis that 'narcotic addiction causes, or contributes very strongly to an increase in [acquisitive] crime ... Heroin addiction is criminogenic' (Nurco *et al* 1985: 96). Given the hypothetico-deductive nature of this research, the 'results' that have been produced have concealed as much as they have revealed. For every study claiming to have 'discovered' that drugs produce an 'economic necessity' to commit acquisitive crime (Anglin and Perrochet 1988; White *et al* 2002), there is seemingly another study that suggests the drugs-crime link is not entirely straightforward. The point here is that the strength of the historical link between the state and criminology, with respect to the drugs problematic, has meant that most criminologists have been unable (in thought and deed) to construct a critical alternative drugs discourse which, in turn, has meant that they have been unable to do anything other than tenuously suggest that the causal relationship between drugs and crime is not simple and straightforward. To put it another way, most criminologists' failure to develop an 'alternative' conceptualisation of drug use (which is a consequence of its historical bind to the state which has plagued the discipline with epistemic and methodological limitations) has ensured that drugs-crime research has been plunged into a state of epistemological paralysis when faced with variable evidence.

Statistical Associations between Drugs and Crime

A plethora of European and American studies into the relationship between drugs and crime have mostly found a significant statistical association between the two variables (Bean 2002; Nurco *et al* 1985). First, some researchers have undertaken *'penal studies'*, which involves an examination of the drug consumption of individuals in contact with the criminal justice system (e.g. new arrestees and incarcerated prisoners) and concluded that there is a statistical association between offending behaviour and drug misuse. For example, the NEW-ADAM programme of research into the relationship between drugs and crime, funded by the Home Office, found that 31 per cent of *new arrestees* tested positive for opiate use whereas 22 per cent of arrestees tested positive for cocaine use (Holloway and Bennett 2004), and that heroin and cocaine using arrestees reported annual illegal incomes that were four times higher than the annual illegal incomes of arrestees not using illicit drugs (Holloway and Bennett 2004; Holloway *et al* 2004). Similar results have been found in incarcerated populations by a plethora of other researchers (e.g. Anslinger and Thomkins 1953; Ford *et al* 1975; Weisman *et al* 1976; Kozel *et al* 1972; Edmunson *et al* 1972) who have found that between 15 and 40 per cent of their respondents reported using heroin prior to incarceration and that even larger percentages reported using other illicit drugs.

Second, other researchers have undertaken *'treatment studies'*, which involve an examination of the offending behaviour of drug users undergoing treatment, with a large number finding that drug users are regularly engaged in crime (Meyer 1952; Defleur *et al* 1969; Voss and Stephens 1973; Stephens and Ellis 1975). For example, research into the offending behaviour of 100 treatment participants by Best *et al* (2001) found that 56 had been involved in acquisitive crime such as shoplifting[1] in the previous month, whereas a study of 245 opiate users in methadone treatment, by Ahmed *et al* (1999), found a high proportion using acquisitive crime to fund their habits. The findings of Inciardi and Chambers (1972) are even more suggestive of a 'drugs causes crime' relationship because they found that *all* 38 of the (male) narcotic users that they interviewed whilst in treatment had engaged in crime, mainly robbery and other property crimes. In a very different type of study that examined the social consequences of a heroin outbreak in a defined urban area, Parker and Newcombe (1987) similarly found that burglary rates increase when heroin use increases. On the

---

1   These were mainly crack and heroin users and spent more on drugs than the others in the sample.

basis of a similar study, Garb and Crim (1966: 44) felt able to claim that offenders 'became criminals because of the addiction; they did not become addicts because they were criminals'.

Statistical Associations between Heroin and Types of Crime

The penal and treatment studies, cited above, suggest a clear and unambiguous statistical relationship between drug misuse and crime, which has probably been best expressed by Nurco *et al* (1985), who found that the mean crime days per year of addicts was 255/365 during periods of addiction and 65/365 during periods of non-addiction, i.e. a 75 per cent decrease in criminality from the addiction to the non-addiction periods. Nevertheless, studies have not only demonstrated a *general* statistical relationship between drug use and crime. Some studies have also shown that particular types of drugs (e.g. heroin) are associated with particular types of crime (e.g. property crimes rather than crimes against the person).

A classic study of heroin users and property crime was conducted by Ball *et al* (1981), who followed heroin users for more than ten years and reported remunerative property crime to be six times higher when users' habits were at their peak level than when they were abstinent. These findings have been confirmed by a wide-ranging review of research studies into the links between heroin and crime by McBride and McCoy (1982: 142) who found that 'the [research] literature suggests a statistical relationship between heroin and robberies or other property crimes'. Thus, researchers such as Inciardi and Chambers (1972) and McBride (1976) have found heroin users to be over represented in property crime categories (in terms of their proportion to the total population studied) and under represented in crimes against the person. Indeed, McBride (1976) found that heroin users commit five times more property crimes than crimes they commit against the person. These findings substantiate those of Finestone (1957), whose research in the 1950s showed that crimes against the person decrease, and crimes against property increase, as rates of heroin addiction increase in a given geographical area (see Chein 1964, for similar findings). Nurco *et al* (1985) have thus claimed that drug addicts commit over 50 million crimes per year in the USA, whilst Hough (1996) has suggested that, in 1992, the overall cost of crime committed by dependent drug users was between £58 and £864m in the UK. For McBride and McCoy (1982: 142), then, 'the reasons for the heroin and property crime connection have generally been perceived as due to the expense of heroin'.

Statistical Associations between Crack Cocaine and Types of Crime

Research by Collins *et al* (1985) has shown that levels of weekly use of crack cocaine is more highly associated – than levels of heroin use – with criminal activity, whilst other studies have shown that the reduction of crack cocaine usage in some American cities has coincided with reductions in crime rates (Golub and Johnson 1997; Baumer *et al* 1999). For example Best *et al* (2001) found that crack cocaine users report a higher mean income from shoplifting and handling stolen goods than heroin users. Perhaps more significant, however, are studies that have shown crack users to be more likely, than heroin users, to engage in violent crimes and crimes against the person. For example, Grogger and Willis (2000: 523) used various sources of data, including FBI reported crime rates from 27 metropolitan areas (taking account of the year in which crack arrived in each area) and emergency room admissions data collected by the National Institute on Drug Abuse (NIDA), and found that 'the arrival of crack had a sizeable and significant positive effects ... [It] caused murder rates to rise by 4.4% per 100,000 population'. Later on in their article they calculate that 'in the absence of crack, our models predict that the crime rate would have been ... 10% lower' (page 526). They summarise their article by stating that:

> ... the arrival of crack cocaine led crime to rise substantially in the late 1980's and early 1990's. The most prevalent form of violence – aggravated assault – rose significantly.
>
> (Grogger and Willis, 2000: 528)

Statistical Associations between Drug Treatments and Crime

The final and most damning evidence that drugs cause crime appears to emanate from studies of the effectiveness of drug treatment programmes which have generally been shown to lead to reductions in the levels of criminal activity committed by opiate addicts (Nurco *et al* 1985; Ball and Ross 1991; Hubbard *et al* 1989; Strang *et al* 1997; Gossop *et al* 1998). For example, Dole *et al* (1968) studied the effects of methadone maintenance on criminal behaviour and found that, prior to treatment, 91 per cent of their 912 sample studied between 1964 and 1968, had been incarcerated but that, since entry into treatment, 88 per cent showed arrest free records. In a similar study, Gearing (1970) found that the number of arrests following treatment increased for 'detoxification' patients whereas they decreased for patients on methadone. Gearing (1972) replicated these findings in later study that found methadone users to be the only group of patients to show a decrease in arrests compared to three other groups (drop outs from the methadone programme, discharges from the methadone programme, those who had only received detoxification). These studies therefore suggest that methadone maintenance is the most effective method of reducing crime. In Britain, Bennett and Wright (1986) found that the number of crimes reported by opiate users for the year prior to their receiving a prescription was significantly higher (over 80 per cent) than the number reported during the year of prescription (32 per cent).

The Drugs Cause Crime Hypothesis as Complex

Some criminologists argue that the concurrence of drugs and crime does not necessarily mean that 'drugs cause crime'. It simply means that drugs and crime tend to co-exist and that the causal sequence may even be vice versa, i.e. involvement in crime may precede drug use rather than the other way around (Newburn 1999). This point has been made by Johnson *et al* (1985), who found an association between opiate use and crime but made the qualification that one important determinant of whether or not a person used on a given day was whether or not they had the funds, which depended on their success in committing crime. So, rather than stealing to obtain a constant amount of heroin, some users adjusted their heroin intake within the limits of the funds that they had generated from their involvement in crime. For Johnson *et al* (1985), then, the funds that came from crime sometimes better predicted drug use, than drug use predicted the level of involvement of crime. Hammersley *et al* (1989) drew a similar conclusion from their research when they argued that:

> Day-to-day crime was a better explanation of drug use than drug use was of crime ... All drugs tend to be associated with crimes. This may in part be due to the 'need' for drugs leading to crime [for heavy users] but it is also, probably in greater part, due to the income from crime leading to greater expenditure on drugs.   (Hammersley *et al* 1989: 1040-41)

Drugs Increase Rather than Cause Involvement in Crime

In order to provide a sterner examination of the hypothesis that 'drugs cause crime', a large number of researchers have undertaken 'sequencing' studies. Criminological researchers have been undertaking '*sequence studies*' since early in the twentieth century, in order to establish the temporal relationship between involvement in crime and drugs and have cast doubt on the simplicity of the proposition that onset of drug use or addiction is a significant predictor of crime. For example, Lukoff (1973) found that 44 per cent of the 765 clients of a methadone clinic studied had been arrested before engaging in the regular use of heroin; Cuskey *et al* (1973) found that 52 per cent of a sample had been arrested prior to heroin use; Gordon (1973) found that 48 per cent of his sample had been convicted of crime prior to heroin misuse. Gordon's study also distinguished between heroin and other drug users and found that the extent and pattern of crime for both groups was similar. In a similar vein, Rosenthal (1973) found that the majority of a sample that had committed robbery, burglary, or shoplifting during addiction had committed the same crime prior to addiction. Rosenthal also found that there was no absolute increase in crime after addiction with respect to either frequency or seriousness and that, therefore, there was a high degree of continuity in criminal patterns before and after addiction. More recently, Apospori *et al* (1995) found that deviance predicted subsequent drug use but that drug use did not predict deviance for any ethnic group in their multi-ethnic sample of teenagers in Florida. Finally, making reference to a wide range of *sequencing studies* Hough and Mitchell (2003) have shown that the average age for the onset of a criminal career tends to precede the average age for the onset of a drug career whereas Bean and Wilkinson (1988) have referenced a wide range of studies in Britain and America which show that about 50 per cent of drug users are criminal before they start using drugs.

Such findings are not new, but have been emerging from studies since as early as 1925, when Kolb (1925) found that, among 225 opiate addicts, the majority had been arrested for disorderly conduct and that – in every case – the arrest had occurred prior to addiction. In the 1930s Prescor (1938) similarly found that three-quarters of a sample of over one thousand male hospital patient addicts had a criminal record prior to addiction but that those who did were for minor offences. Finally, a study in the 1950s by Chein and Rosenfeld (1957) also found that three-quarters of the heroin users they came into contact with via court and hospital records had been deviant prior to drug misuse. In the light of this substantial weight of evidence concerning prior criminality, then, some researchers have argued that, insofar as there is a relationship between drugs and crime, this could be due to drugs being a reason for maintaining and increasing – rather than initiating – involvement in criminal behaviour. One key proponent of this view is Tim Newburn (1999) who has argued that the available evidence indicates that heroin users usually have a prior and extensive involvement in criminal activities and that their heroin use might, therefore, be associated with criminal activity in the following ways:

- increases in criminal activity
- sustenance of criminal activity
- changes in the nature of criminal acts commissioned.

Newburn (1999) refers to this mutually reinforcing crime-drugs-crime cycle as a 'web of causation'. Other researchers would even question this and, instead, have used their findings to argue that crime not only precedes drugs but that crimes committed after the initiation of drug use are sometimes unrelated to their drug use (McBride and McCoy 1982).

Involvement in Crime Persists Despite Drug Treatment

The notion that there is not a simple causal link between drugs and crime is supported by a number of studies that have questioned the effectiveness of drug treatments and, indeed, the methodological reliability of the previously cited studies that have claimed to establish its effectiveness. For example, Barton's (1999) study of the effectiveness of a coerced treatment programme in Plymouth, UK, found that 59 per cent of offenders were stabilised after 12 weeks on the programme and that 24 per cent were stabilised to complete their probation orders. However, he also suggested that these findings could not be taken at face value for a number of reasons. First, he claimed that the threat of breach of probation supervision, which carried with it a custodial sentence, provided an impetus for patients to persist with their treatment and therefore artificially enhanced its effectiveness. Second, he suggested that changes in criminal involvement were probably due to social as well as pharmacological factors. This is because the drug users that were in treatment were 'often marginalized or excluded by their family and suffer[ing] feelings of social isolation ... [They therefore benefited from] the attention and concern [of the drug workers] as to the offenders well being' which may have impacted on their motivation to desist from involvement in crime (Barton 1999: 154). Third, he noted that reductions in local crime were probably due to a range of extraneous factors and that the treatment programme may have even had perverse effects on the crime rate. This was because some clients had committed crime with the intention of arrest so that they could access the treatment programme which was only available to people within the criminal justice system!

Although Barton found reductions in crime among those in treatment, but then assigned this to a range of treatment and non-treatment factors, other researchers have been less circumspect. Following a wide-ranging review of evidence from treatment effectiveness studies, Rothbard *et al* (1999) concluded that retention in methadone treatment only had a slight effect on reducing crime, especially where there was a prior criminal history. Following the earlier lead of Hammersley *et al* (1989), they argued that methadone treatment *per se* is not sufficient to produce positive outcomes because a range of studies have shown that heroin use is an expression of a more enduring criminal orientation:

> It is entirely possible that drug abuse and crime are but two manifestations of an underlying lifestyle. In this event, the elimination of drug-seeking behaviour, with nothing else, would have an uncertain effect on crime, (e.g. it could conceivably *increase* the energy and time available for the commission of certain types of crime which are unrelated to illegal drug use itself).   (Rosenthal *et al* 1973: 8)

These arguments have resonated with researchers such as Stephens and Ellis (1975: 487) who have suggested that 'narcotics addicts are increasingly drawn from population groups highly susceptible to both crime and addiction'. They also resonate with Tim Newburn (1999: 610) who has similarly suggested that 'associations between crime and drug use ... probably exist because of shared antecedents of drug using and delinquency, rather than because drug use "causes" offending behaviour in any simple sense'. Chein (1964) would even claim to have produced 'hard evidence' to support this proposition: virtually all of the 3,500 cases of drug users that he studied over a seven-year period were similar to non-drug user criminals in terms of a variety of extraneous social variables. For Greenberg and Adler (1974: 259), then, this would suggest that 'it is necessary for [treatment] programme administrators to have detailed knowledge of the [social] characteristics of the population their programme is serving'.

In Search of the 'Third Variable'

Given the hypothetico-deductive nature of much research into the link between crime and drugs, many criminologists have responded to evidence of the shared antecedents of drugs and crime (which appear to suggest that drug use does not straightforwardly foster criminality or vice versa) by hypothesising that crime and drug use are *both* the result of an eclectic range of 'third variables' that can be associated with 'an underlying lifestyle'. Criminologists such as Bean (2002) have therefore formulated new hypotheses about what 'might be', which therefore need to be subject to empirical tests:

> [Drug use and criminal involvement] might have more to do with the background and personal circumstances of the user than anything else. For example, ecstasy use is not usually associated with crime, and it is reasonable to suggest that this is because of the socio-demographic features of the population taking it (i.e. ecstasy users are more likely to be occasional drug users, employed, of higher social class and single or restricted multiple drug users – i.e. taking similar types of drugs but not the heavy end of the drugs

scene). They will not likely have a criminal history or a subsequent criminal career. This is in contrast to the heroin user, who is usually working class, unemployed (probably unemployable having never had a job), homeless and a poly addict (taking heavy amounts of all drugs including cocaine). Drugs and crime are strongly associated with this group (especially if a street user), but, again, the socio-demographic background of this group of users puts them at a higher risk of criminality in the first place.   (Bean 2002: 12)

Some criminologists have actually sought to empirically test such hypothetical propositions, in order to identify a 'third variable', by collecting information about the social characteristics of drug users involved in crime. In doing so, Newburn (1999: 620) found that 'rates of family disruption were high, educational achievement was minimal, association with delinquent peers was very common and, perhaps most significantly of all, the age onset was extremely young and frequency of drug use was particularly high'. He moves on to conclude that 'effective interventions need to target more than one risk factor [and] involve the delivery of more than one service .... Drug-focused work needs to be embedded within other work with young offenders ... [and] successful drugs work needs to be inter-agency or joined-up' (1999: 621). In other words, Newburn wants interventions to focus on helping drug using offenders to tackle the 'problems associated' with their drug use and offending. A similar line is taken by Lane and Henry (2001: 220) who studied the impact on crime of a number of community development initiatives and concluded that a 'multi-problem solving approach' based on a:

> *combination* [of initiatives] was essential for achieving change. That is, the perceived and apparent reduction in violence and crime in the area were due to a combination and integration of strategies – money for specific, locality based social projects; changes to the physical environment which created 'defensible spaces' along with increased use of public areas; and skilled, broadly based, community development which brought resources and strategies together to achieve desired outcomes. We see here an integration of situational, developmental and socio-cultural approaches to the prevention of violence and crime – modifying physical environments; providing opportunities for young children and youth; addressing underlying social problems and injustices.

Conclusions: The Criminological Legacy

Social research is always undertaken from a 'standpoint' (Harding 1991) or 'point of view' (Heidegger 1962) which is a product of social positioning where, for example, the class, gender, *etc.* positions that frame experience also frame the perspective that researchers throw onto the objects of their interest (Allen 2005). The extent to which social research is funded by producers of the dominant political discourse about the 'evils of drugs', and whom use research as a means to mobilise and assert their own moral authority (e.g. by creating a 'war on drugs'), simply makes the issue of social positioning even more problematic. Yet this is seldom acknowledged by many of the social researchers that study relationships between drugs and crime using a hypothetico-deductive approach and that present their research in terms of a search for 'facts' that 'speak for themselves' (Kemeny 1995). This is not only problematic in itself but also because, amazingly, some of these researchers criticise the partiality and bias of industry funded studies even though the drugs and alcohol industry is simply in the business of using research to sell their products, whereas policy makers are in the business of manufacturing social problem definitions and therefore research that facilitates the consumption of these problem definitions (Hunt and Barker 2001; see also Kemeny 1992; Jacobs *et al* 2003).

This chapter has shown that a mere cursory look at the research evidence from these hypothetico-deductive studies is sufficient to create and sustain radical doubt in the propositions that they are designed to support. There is little credible evidence to suggest that there is a clear and unambiguous relationship between drugs and crime. Indeed, for all the empirical evidence that suggests drugs do cause crime there is a seemingly equivalent amount of empirical evidence that drugs do not cause crime. Even researchers that have sought to move beyond the idea that there is an internal and necessary relationship between drugs and crime, for example, by identifying the shared antecedents of crime and drugs have failed to take us anywhere new. We are simply taken on another search, this time for the 'third variable' that causes both drug use and crime and an ensuing debate about what that third variable might be. There is only one way to resolve this debate, of course. A hypothetic-deductive approach is required to examine the comparative validity of the various 'third propositions' that have emerged, only to produce an equally confusing picture with claim and counterclaim being made for each third variable. Herein lies the problem of social research that seeks to buttress hypothetical propositions with 'facts' but only succeeds in generating confusion and plunging social science into the epistemological quicksand. The alternative to this would be for social science to seek to generate a critical understanding (*verstehen*) of phenomenon, from whatever 'point of view' that understanding may come from. In the next chapter I examine drugs and crime research that has been informed by social theory and therefore explicitly undertaken from a variety of epistemological standpoints and 'points of view'. The purpose of this is to establish whether the rich tapestry of drugs and crime research that has been informed by contemporary debates in social theory can take us any further forward in terms of advancing our critical understanding of the drugs and crime phenomena.

Chapter 2

Crime, Drugs and Social Theory

Introduction

Chapter 1 has shown that copious amounts of research effort have been invested in examining the links between drug use and crime. It also showed that some effort has also been invested in tracking the changing nature and extent of drug use in modern societies, for example, the last chapter also discussed the work of Howard Parker and colleagues which has provided detailed descriptions of the changing nature of recreational drug use in Britain. However, notwithstanding Parker's work which has sought to explain the 'normalisation' of 'recreational' drug use in modern societies, we have so far come across precious little work that has sought to theoretically understand (*verstehen*) why 'problematic' drug use occurs in deprived urban areas and how it is linked to crime. Hunt and Barker (2001) argue that this is because most criminological research is conceptually limited and therefore tends to decontextualise drug use from the social situations within which it emerges and proliferates. Bean (2002), on the other hand, argues that this is because '[t]here is little by way of trying to establish links with established sociological theory or other theoretical propositions. Only a very small number of theories have been offered ... What is interesting about these models is how little they are connected to the main theories of the sociology of deviance. They seem to have developed outside mainstream deviance sociology ... For example, control theory is not mentioned, nor is labelling or differential association theory'.

Although Chapter 1 has shown that the vast majority of criminological research into drugs and crime has been conceptually limited, this chapter shows that this is not entirely true of *all* social research in the field of drugs and crime. For example, Mike Hough (1996) has identified scholars with three theoretical approaches to explaining drugs and crime. The *structure model* emphasises how people seek to achieve their goals through illegitimate activities when they are denied legitimate opportunities to achieve social goals. This model is therefore inextricably bound up with sociological theorising about the social and economic consequences of post-industrialism, post-modernism and the end of organised capitalism (see Lash and Urry 1987, 1994). The *coping model* explains drug use and crime as a palliative to poor quality of life and is thus intimately tied to the ecological theories of deviance developed within Chicago School of Urban Sociology (see Heidensohn 1989; Moyer 2001). Finally the *status model* identifies the positive social value attached to drug use and crime in subcultural contexts and therefore draws inspiration from symbolic interactionism and subcultural theory within sociology (see Lalander 2003).

This chapter provides an outline of these (arguably minority) perspectives of drugs and crime as well as some other theoretical perspectives that are not covered by Hough (1996). The chapter begins by examining social constructionist and social creationist perspectives which contend that the ontological status of crime and drug use as problematic activities has no basis in reality *par excellence* since they cannot be understood outside of the power/discourses that are mobilised against 'what goes on' in certain groups and urban areas, in order to problematise them. The remaining theories discussed in the chapter (with the exception of subcultural ethnographies) take the problematic nature of crime and drug use for granted and, instead, seek to account for the social contexts within which these activities emerge and proliferate. First, the chapter examines the influence of the Chicago School of Urban Sociology. Two key ideas are explored from this school. These are the idea that crime and drug use can be understood by reference to the ecology of urban growth with 'problems' concentrating in certain 'distressed' areas (the ecological approach), and the idea that crime and drug use emerge in the search for an identity that is formed with reference to feedback from the local environment (symbolic interactionism). Second, an overview of ethnographic perspectives shows that crime and drug use can also be explained in terms of their emergence from subcultures that have their own norms, rituals and codes and which are defined as 'successful accomplishments' rather than problematic activities. Third, an overview of social network and socialisation theories shows that crime and drug use can also been explained as an outcome of social influences on individual behaviour which, in turn, is contingent on the social composition of each individual's social networks. Finally, post-modern perspectives highlight how crime and drug use are a consequence of the way in which some people respond to changing 'opportunity structures' in post-industrial urban areas where, for example, there are fewer legitimate opportunities to enable them to get by. The overview of these social theories of crime and drug use will provide us with something to return to in Chapter 3, when we will identify and examine epistemological problems that are common to each of these theories and which, I will argue, demand a new theoretical approach to criminology and the sociology of crime and drugs.

Social Constructionist and Creationist Perspectives

Social constructionist epistemologies (Berger and Luckman 1967) have informed the development of a 'critical criminology' (Scraton and Chadwick 1991) and found their most popular expression in 'conflict theory' (Quinney 1970). Quinney echoes Foucauldian theories of knowledge and power (Foucault 1977, 1979) when he contends that human behaviours such as 'crime' and 'drug misuse' are nothing more than social products that have no ontological validity outside of the discourses and definitions that are mobilised by the institutions of modern societies (e.g. legislators, police, welfare professions, *etc.*) in order to marginalise and problematise the behaviours of some social groups but not others. Definitions of social practices such as 'theft' and 'drug use' are not only formulated and imposed by the institutions of modern societies, but reflect the way in which powerful social groups can translate their interests into public policy. The intensity of conflict between these powerful social groups and other segments of society is thus reflected in the proliferation of legal discourses that identify the social practices of certain social groups as criminal. It follows that social groups without influence are more likely to have their social practices and ways of life more generally (e.g. as thieves, drug users, *etc.*) problematised by definitions of what is considered to be criminal (Hillyard, Pantazis *et al* 2004). However, the authors of these problematised practices only become 'offenders' when criminal definitions are applied by those who have the power to enforce prohibition and administer the law, that is, when the network of practitioners (police, youth workers, *etc.*) that are charged with enforcing criminal definitions close in on people that are engaged in practices that are defined as illegal. For Quinney, then, social practices such as 'theft' and 'drug use' are not 'inherent' behaviours but social constructs that can be understood in terms of the following formula: 'the greater the number of criminal definitions *formulated* and *applied*, the greater the amount of crime' (Quinney 1970: 16).

Insofar as 'critical criminology' emphasises how the social practices of socially and economically marginalised groups are criminalised, it resonates with 'Marxist' and 'radical' criminologies. The key difference between 'critical criminology' and these other perspectives is that the latter also articulate a 'political economy' of crime. The political economy of crime is based on the contention that social practices such as 'theft' and 'drug use' need to be taken seriously (rather than treated as ontologically vacuous) because they are a consequence of structural location within capitalist societies (Walklate 1998). That is to say, social practices such as crime and drug use are visible expressions of the brute pain of alienation and therefore have 'real' effects outside of the political discourses that are mobilised against them. This is a view that Quinney (1977) later came to espouse when he began to adopt more of a Marxist stance on whom, exactly, the powerless (and powerful) groups were.

A good example of 'critical criminology' in the field of crime can be found in the work of Estrada (2001) who studied juvenile violence as a social problem in Sweden and argued that the 'youth problem' was nothing more than a media construct. Following the murder of the Swedish Prime Minister in 1986, Estrada shows that the media manufactured anxieties about the level of juvenile violence by changing the way it portrayed young criminals, from victims of poor social circumstances to 'super predators' that assaulted other people out of choice. This led to more regular reporting of juvenile offences by the public which, in turn, were reported by the media and so the problem was socially constructed. Yet, 'in reality', Estrada shows that there was no evidence to suggest that the problem of juvenile violence was any worse than in any other decade and that, therefore, there could not be said to be a 'real problem' with juvenile violence as measured by actual prevalence of the problem (see Jacobs *et al* 2003, for a similar perspective on the rise of the 'single parent problem').

A wide range of researchers have used ideas from 'critical criminology' to explain the emergence of drugs and crime as a social problem. One of these researchers is Helmer (1977) who has examined the social construction of drug use as a problem behaviour via the political definitions that are formulated to define it as an 'illegal activity', and the subsequent network of practices (e.g. police activities) that grow out of the need to apply those definitions. For Helmer (1977), then, heroin use was a non-issue until the end of the 1920s when, following its spread from the middle class to the urban working class, it was illegalised and brought under the control of the medical profession. Following Quinney, Helmer argues that the illegalisation of narcotics was in the interests of the medical establishment, which wanted to monopolise control of drug use to secure its privileged status as a 'profession' (see Wilding 1982 for a discussion of the sociology of the professions). From that point onwards, the problem can be constructed as follows:

> when police action reduces the supply and market prices rise ... there is a correlative increase in the amount of crime to finance purchase ... The most common source of funds is dealing in the drug, with the result that prohibition can have an indirect multiplier effect on the size and profitability of the illegal drug trade. As police action succeeds temporarily in making drugs scarcer and trade riskier, adulteration and prices increase, the level of profit rises, more users become traders and marketing becomes more diversified, stimulating more demand, which in turn can be reflected in more arrests.   (Helmer 1977: 413)

Unsurprisingly, then, heroin addicts are more likely to be arrested for drug law violations rather than any other type of offence (Stephens and Ellis 1975). The 'drugs problem' is therefore a social construct that followed rather than preceded prohibition.

Greenberg and Adler (1974) provide a similarly 'critical criminological' explanation of the social construction of the drug use and crime 'problem' in America by taking a historical approach. Drawing on research findings from as early as the 1920s, and going through to the 1960s, they show that heroin addicts prior to 1952 were predominantly non-criminal. This was because heroin was largely inexpensive and so criminal behaviour was not required to support the habit. However, the situation was reversed for heroin users that became addicted in or after 1952 (Greenberg and Adler 1974: 233). This is because, in the early 1950s, the federal government enacted a series of stringent drug laws that were strongly enforced and which resulted in price increases and subsequently crime to pay for the increased expense of heroin use (ibid: 234).

For Greenberg, Adler and associates, then, the *drugs problem* is a social construct rather than empirically real. Others scholars have taken this form of analysis one step further and argued that the *social consequences* of the social construction of the drugs problem are also constructed rather than empirically real. For example, some proponents of the 'radical' social constructionist perspective have argued that the 'problem' of 'drug related' violence is not a consequence of the pharmacological properties of drugs and therefore empirically real, as some would claim. Conversely, they argue that drug related violence is also a social construct that is a consequence of the political definitions that are mobilised to illegalise drug use as a practice, as well as the network of policing activities that emerge out of the need to enforce this legal prohibition. Thus, Resignato (2000) has argued that drug prohibition not only means that dealers will compete on the black market ('turf wars') but also that there are no legal property rights to drugs which means that, first, there is more likely to be violence because there is no recourse to the law and that, second, the only way to seek justice is through retaliation. This is to say nothing of the value of the goods that drug dealers carry with them which is a consequence of post-prohibition price increases and which necessitates that dealers arm themselves. The outcome of this is a spiral of violence (see also Goldstein, 1987 for similar arguments about the spiral of violence; also Topalli (2002), for a discussion of the culture of retaliation amongst drug dealers). Indeed some scholars would go even further than this and argue that the social production of this spiral of violence creates a renewed focus on law enforcement which, in turn, means that more resources are put into law enforcement of the drug trade and fewer resources into controlling other types of crime thus lowering the probability of arrest for other types of crime (Benson and Ramussen 1991, and Benson *et al* 1992). For Resignato, then:

> ... where there is a higher allocation of police resources to drug crime relative to total police resources allocated to crime, there is a higher murder rate and violent crime rate ... According to these results there is a stronger relationship between systemic factors and violence than that of psychopharmacological/economic compulsion factors and violence ... Policies ranging from legalization to decriminalisation... should [therefore] be considered for all drugs. (Resignato 2000: 687-8)

The defining feature of the social constructionist position, then, is that the drugs problem, and the consequences of the drugs problem, are highly problematic social constructs rather than empirically real and therefore ontologically unproblematic. The key issue for these researchers is to understand how the drugs problem, and its consequences, are socially constructed via the mobilisation of legal definitions (that are in the interests of powerful groups such as the medical establishment) and networks of practice that emerge out of the need to enforce those definitions.

'Chicago School' Influences and Ecological Perspectives

The University of Chicago was established in 1892 as a new foundation and had a disproportionate influence on social science through the 'Chicago School of Urban Sociology' which dominated debates in sociology between the years 1914 and 1940 (Moyer 2001). A defining feature of the Chicago School was its development of an 'ecological' perspective of urban growth which was best elaborated in Park, Burgess and McKenzie's (1967 [1925]) work on *The City*. In this book, Park and his colleagues noted that there had been numerous studies of the physical expansion of the city from the standpoint of the city plan but little in the way of an analysis of the social consequences of urban growth. They argued that the social consequences of urban growth could be illustrated by a series of concentric circles that identified successive zones of urban expansion and that these zones became socially differentiated from each other during the process of expansion. Specifically, they identified a tendency for:

> ... any town or city to expand radially from its central business district (I) .... Encircling the downtown area that is normally an area in transition, which is being invaded by business and light manufacture (II). A third area (III) is inhabited by workers in industries who have escaped from the area of deterioration (II) but who desire to live within easy access of their work. Beyond this zone is the 'residential area' (IV) of high-class apartment buildings or of exclusive 'restricted' districts of single-family dwellings. Still further out beyond the city limits is the commuters' zone – suburban areas. (Park *et al* 1967 [1925]: 50)

This analysis of *The City* provided other Chicago scholars with a 'heuristic tool' with which to analyse the social distribution of deviance (e.g. Morris 1957; see Heidensohm 1989). Notable in this regard are Shaw and McKay (1931, 1942) who created 'spot maps' to show the spatial distribution, by place of residence, of juvenile delinquents at various stages of the criminal justice system as well as school truants. They were then able to note that the highest rates of delinquency were found in areas in or adjacent to the districts zoned for industry, these being the areas of physical deterioration characterised by low rents and low family income. They were also able to show that an inverse relationship to delinquency could be found in zones characterised by higher rent levels and home ownership (Shaw and McKay 1972). Taken together, this enabled them to develop an 'ecological' perspective of crime and deviance based on the notion that the atrocious physical and social conditions endured by the urban poor, which were a consequence of the process of urban growth, 'pushed' them into a life of crime. This urban ecological perspective enabled members of the Chicago School to argue that crime did not occur as a result of the innate inferiority of 'the criminal class'. Furthermore, it has influenced a number of social researchers that have sought to make sense of why people living in distressed neighbourhoods also turn to drugs.

Surveying the research scene in the early 1980s, McBride and McCoy (1982) were able to claim that the crime and drugs 'problems' literature had been dominated by a concern with the 'isolated individual' and that ecological explanations had received only scant attention. One of the exceptional cases, at that time, was one of the earliest and well known urban ecological studies conducted by Dai (1970) who found that rates of known opiate use were higher in areas that were characterised by poor housing and transient populations mainly composed of disrupted families of low socio-economic status. Dai (1970) used these findings to argue that deviance was the product of a constellation of variables in the urban environment and that opiate use and crime were attempts to adapt – or respond – to such environments.

Since the 1980s, the ecological approach has provided the conceptual influences for a plethora of studies into crime and drugs 'problems' as researchers have sought to get to grips with understanding the consequences of de-industrialisation. These recent ecological studies have shown that individuals living in poor neighbourhoods that have borne the brunt of de-industrialisation tend to experience a greater number of negative life events than individuals residing elsewhere (Fang *et al* 1998; Massey and Shibuya 1995) and that substance use is often used as means of coping with or alleviating stress (Lindenberg *et al* 1994; Rhodes and Jason 1990).

Perhaps one of the best known of these recent ecological studies was conducted by Foster (2000) who was concerned with understanding the 'devastating impact' of de-industrialisation and unemployment on the life chances of people living in economically marginalised urban areas (Foster 2000: 318). She was specifically concerned to understand why crime and drug use tended to concentrate in these areas as well as with how they subsequently became 'mutually sustaining' activities. Her observations led her to conclude that 'long term' social exclusion had resulted in a precarious existence that residents experienced as 'deadening'. Foster argued that this 'deadening experience' was having a devastating impact on their social attitudes and expectations leading to a sense of hopelessness and fatalism. She referred to this as an 'escalating cycle of despondency'. Drugs were used to 'fill the void' and were seen as a way of imposing some sort of meaning upon an otherwise empty time and space. In a nutshell, they made life bearable and enabled people to establish some sense of 'normality' (Foster 2000: 322-3). Storr *et al* (2004) have taken the types of ecological analysis produced by Foster and associates one step further by suggesting that the proliferation of drug use does not merely serve as a palliative. In common with the post industrial perspective discussed later on in the chapter, Storr *et al* argue that drugs also offer illegitimate economic opportunities which contribute to the further proliferation of the drugs and crime problem:

> An array of community and neighbourhood conditions is associated with higher levels of drug use. Some of these conditions are shaped by economic conditions (poverty, deprivation, unemployment, type of housing, and housing stability) ... disadvantaged communities with visible drug problems may [then] fall prey to a criminal drug market that offers economic advantages to otherwise resource-poor neighbourhood residents.
>
> (Storr *et al* 2004: 254-5)

Nevertheless, some researchers that are sympathetic to the ecological perspective have qualified its explanatory strength. For example Bronfenbrenner (1979) employed the ecological construct of 'nested contexts' to provide a theory-based framework for examining drug use in deprived urban areas. The concept of 'nested contexts' continues to recognise the impact of variables such as 'neighbourhood stressors' in the usual way, but also takes account of factors such as the strength and quality of family ties which may work to counter or alleviate these stresses. This 'nested' approach, which has some parallels with the socialisation and social network perspectives discussed later on in the chapter, forced her to qualify her attachment to the ecological model because it enabled her to find that:

> ... poor urban black female adolescents are less dependent on drug use to deal with stress, are more attached to family, are more likely to be highly discriminative in peer associations and assume the role of parent when social cost is low. Persistent poverty induces psychosocial distress but prompts the development of resilient capacities ... poor families develop effective strategies that aid in managing many of the social consequences of economic disadvantage.
>
> (Bronfenbrenner 1979: 439)

Nevertheless, research is context specific and Bronfenbrenner conducted her work in the 1970s, before the consequences of de-industrialisation had taken root in working class urban areas to the extent that they have today. This is important because de-industrialisation has resulted in the break-up of the type of kinship support networks that Bronfenbrenner refers to (Crow 2002; Sprigings and Allen 2005). It is also important because Scheier *et al* (1999) recently conducted a similar analysis that also accounted for the intervening influence of psychosocial characteristics and life events but found that perceived neighbourhood stress still uniquely predicted alcohol use. The ecological perspective is therefore alive and well in its original form.

'Chicago School' Influences and Symbolic Interactionist Perspectives

The epistemological value of the ecological perspective is that it has provided a frame through which researchers have been able to identify the spatial distribution of crime and drug use. However, in doing so, the ecological perspective simply illuminates the *context within* which crime and drug use occurs. Insofar as the ecological perspective presents itself as an explanation of these phenomena (i.e. crime and drug use occurs *because* the individuals involved live in deprived urban areas) it tends towards a form of social determinism that treats residents as passive victims of urban circumstance (Heidensohn 1989). For this reason, researchers such as Shaw and McKay (1972) later came to view the ecological perspective as unacceptable.

In their earlier work, Shaw and Mckay (1931) felt that the ecological map served as a formal index for locating delinquency, thereby enabling them to make distinctions between different areas of the city. However, they later came to argue that the traditions, standards and moral sentiments that characterise neighbourhood life may be more important in *explaining* distinctions between these various urban areas (Shaw and McKay 1972). Their argument was that children living in middle class areas are insulated from direct contact with delinquency *and* have the advantage of being exposed to neighbourhood traditions, values and behavioural norms that contrast with:

> ... low income areas where there is the greatest deprivation and frustration; .... where there exists the greatest disparity between the social values to which people aspire and the availability of facilities for acquiring these values in conventional ways, the development of crime as an organised way of life is most marked.   (Shaw and McKay 1972: 319)[1]

Since residents living in low income areas are exposed to a wide diversity of norms and standards of behaviour, then, explanations of delinquency have their 'roots in the dynamic life of the community' (Shaw and McKay 1972: 315). These claims provided the foundations from which a symbolic interactionist perspective of crime and drugs could develop. Symbolic interactionists are critical of the ecological notion that social action can be 'read' as 'effects' that occur in a given social situations, for example a need to 'cope' with urban deprivation where drug use is one way in which this can be achieved. This is because it fails to take account of the wider processes of interpretation that occur in given social situations and which inform the decision to use drugs.

For symbolic interactionists such as Charles Horton Cooley (1902) and Herbert Mead (1930) individuals develop an *image of the self* from the perspective of others or continually see a reflection of self as they believe others view them. This shapes who and what the self becomes. It follows that the *self acts* with reference to these others (and not simply according to its own coping needs) by 'taking the role of others' and conceiving of themselves through the responses, attitudes and expectations of both 'significant' and 'generalised others' which communicate with the self via symbols such as gestures and language (Mead 1930). This notion of the 'generalised other' therefore controls processes of interpretation and informs social practice via the expectations that are formed about the likely reactions of others to the self. So the process of developing a self is merely the product of the creative process of learning to assume the role of others. Cooley (1902) refers to this as the 'looking glass self'.

---

1   There are links here with the 'opportunity structure' argument that post industrialist theorists espouse, see below.

Now the relation between self and society is usually considered in terms of the 'objective situation' of the individual, which usually refers to the values of the society *writ large* to which the individual belongs. Symbolic interactionists, on the other hand, seek to understand how individuals interpret their 'subjective situation' (i.e. their 'local situation') since this will influence their attitudes and how they respond to the objective situation (i.e. how they behave towards society). This is important because 'struggles for existence' (Park 1972: 118) within the 'immediate' social setting provide individuals with an image of how they are perceived by others which is modified during the course of social interaction: 'a person's identity is formed from feedback provided by the [local] environment' (Dunlap *et al* 2002). Symbolic interactionism therefore focuses on the local processes of individual change from conformity to career deviancy rather than on the structure of society or the city. All in all, then, symbolic interactionists reject societal determinism and contend that social structure can only be admissible insofar as it enters into interpretations of actors who pursue purposes as emotionally charged human beings in local social situations.

Suffice it to say that symbolic interactionism is not a unified body of thought (May 1996). One school of interactionist thought stresses the creative process of self formation which is generated over time through interaction rather than imposed (the social constructionist perspective). However, they argue that once individuals have developed their identity, and the process of social learning is 'complete', people will act according to habit in the 'normal circumstances' of day-to-day life until they are confronted by a crisis (May 1996; Moyer 2001). In other words, these individuals subsequently tend to become victims of their social environment and self-image and thus no longer act with 'free will' (Moyer 2001: 161).

This perspective comes through clearly in the work of Dunlap *et al* (2002) who have studied the intergenerational transmission of conduct norms for drugs, sexual exploitation and violence in the American inner city. Dunlap *et al* compare life in the inner city to life in a 'total institution' (cf. Goffman 1968) which means that residents are almost entirely 'cut-off' from the outside world. Subjected to the limitations of low income neighbourhoods and ostracised from involvement in 'mainstream society' (other than through humiliating experiences such as seeking employment without success due to their address, *etc.*) life is experienced as degrading. Dunlap *et al* argue that this 'closed' inner city environment allows alternative conduct norms to flourish: drug, sexual and violent behaviours are practised against women with little risk of censure from representatives of mainstream society; young people use substitute markers of success (being well-dressed, having money however obtained, *etc.*). They exemplify this argument by using a case study of one family and conclude that:

> Young girls learn (unhappily) to accept violent physical and sexual assault, substance abuse and sales, and unstable households as the effective conduct norms in their households whilst growing up. In essence, their sense of self and any possible hope and preparation for a mainstream lifestyle seem to die in the face of the realities of their households. This socialises them to internalise the prevailing conduct norms, accept and expect abusive relationships, and treat their children no better than they had been treated as children ... Dolita, Read, Tea and Phoebe never had much of a chance to enter the mainstream of conventional society. They were socialised to and accepted their situation and made

the best of it. Their early protests against their mistreatment went perhaps unheard at the time and certainly unheeded. In many respects the totalitarian asylum of the inner city and their severely distressed households have been insulated from the outside world and conventional norms of behaviour. Instead, the conduct norms [described] ... permeate each generation's experience.   (Dunlap *et al* 2002: 17)

Activities such as drug taking cannot be explained in terms of a need to find 'ways of coping', then. Conversely, the tragedy in this account is that individuals that had developed their identity, and whom had begun to act in habitual ways, were in no danger of being confronted by the type of existential crisis (cf. May 1996) that could have been initiated by integration into mainstream society and which would have demanded a reflexive response to their social situation.

A second school of symbolic interactionist thought is based on the notion that self formation and the management of self-identity is a constant process that is managed within the changing context, circumstances and occurrences that permeate the life course (Mead 1930) thereby demanding the use of 'life history' methodologies (see Heidensohn 1989). This perspective has influenced a number of crime and drug 'problem' researchers who argue that understanding the changing context within which identities are *constructed* and *managed* is fundamental to understanding movement in and out of deviance, including substance use (Anderson 1993; Ray 1968; Pearson 1987; Waldorf *et al* 1991). Drug use here is understood to escalate as the motivations to change identity increases and participation in contexts that provide opportunities for drug use present themselves.

A key proponent of this approach is Anderson (1998) who discusses how traumatic events and experiences such as sexual abuse have negative and self-alienating effects that become central to the description of the self because they produce a sense of 'personal identity dissatisfaction' whereby the individuals concerned feel bereft of a positive sense of the self. These *micro level* factors are said to provide respondents with the motivation to create drug use identities, although this can only occur if the *macro level* context is conducive to such a response. Two *macro level* concepts are of key import here: a *social climate conducive to drug use* is required to provide the opportunity for drug use whereas *social appraisal sources* (i.e. intimate others, friends, *etc.*) make the activity of drug use appear desirable. This is because it provides the individual concerned with a sense that the opportunity exists for them to acquire a newly created identity that is positively regarded and socially approved. So Cooley's (1902) 'looking glass self' is very pertinent to this perspective whereas Anderson (1998) argues that any comparisons between this symbolic interactionist perspective and the subcultural theories discussed below should be avoided because subcultural forms (e.g. rules, styles, rituals, language) are absent from her symbolic interactionist analysis.

The defining feature of the symbolic interactionism perspective, then, is that drug use is best understood as a social behaviour that primarily occurs because of the significance it carries to an individual life in the local context within which that individual life is being lived. Drug use is therefore an outcome of the manner in which individual lives uniquely relate to their local situation. Of course, this notion that drug use is a contingent social behaviour means that it cannot be treated as empirically real or ontologically unproblematic, and therefore subject to the types of measurement and mapping that ecologists and the like prefer to undertake.

Ethnographic Research and Subcultural Perspectives

Ethnography requires a commitment to personal observation, interaction and experience of the 'natural setting' as the only way to acquire accurate knowledge about deviant behaviour (Adler 1985). Unfortunately ethnographic research in the crime and drugs fields seldom receives government funding (Hunt and Barker 2001) so such studies tend to be conducted by 'undisciplined' postgraduate research students at or near the beginning of their academic careers (Hobbs 2001). And in the same way that ethnographic research is associated with the entire range of theoretical perspectives in the social sciences (see Atkinson *et al* 2001) this is also apparent in ethnographies of deviant groups. For example, Paul Willis's (1977) celebrated work *Learning to Labour*, which involved ethnographic work with the 'subordinate culture' of male teenagers ('the lads'), is based on a narrative that comfortably fits a 'conflict theory' perspective as well as a subcultural perspective. For Willis, then, the 'subordinate culture' of deviance expresses a conflict between 'the lads' and the dominant 'middle class' culture of the school. Ethnographic work undertaken as a community worker in Liverpool by Howard Parker (1974), on the other hand, comfortably fits into an ecological framework and rejects subcultural theory. The deviance of 'The Boys' in Parker's study was narrated as in terms of an accommodation to their urban situation, focused upon the structural constraints and social inequalities of the 'Roundhouse Estate', rather than a rejection of or resistance towards dominant values. Nevertheless, our concern in the remainder of this section is with ethnographic research that has been influenced by subcultural perspective of crime and deviance since the conflict, ecological and other perspectives that have influenced deviance ethnographies are covered elsewhere in the chapter.

Now, most ethnographic research into crime and drug use undertaken from a subcultural perspective has been stimulated from a desire to counter professional and academic descriptions of drug users as social-psychological failures driven to socially deviant behaviour by the need for narcotics. According to Michael Agar (1973) the authors of these professional and academic descriptions assume the social-psychological status of the addict as a problem to be explained and are therefore:

> ... not as interested in [providing] a description of the [drug] culture as they are in operationalising variables derived from various substantive theories ... [T]hey have been interested in addict culture mostly for the purpose of isolating and abstracting measures for the variables in a hypothesis. Consequently their statements are of little use in constructing an ethnography of *the life*. (Agar 1973: 3-4)

For Agar 'such characterisations offer valuable information concerning the addicts' failure to adapt to traditional society; they have nothing to say about his success in adapting to life in the streets' (Agar 1973: xi-xii). What is required is that 'such a priori judgements be temporarily suspended and drug users studied ethnographically as a legitimate community with an alternative culture, different but equally valid if compared to other American subcultures' (Agar 1973: 1-2). These forms of ethnography seek to describe crime and drug subcultures as the skilful accomplishments of participants who employ a complex set of rules, rituals, communicative codes in order to create a sub-universe that provides them with a sense of belonging and meaning as well as a life lived successfully. Agar, whom is one of the most widely quoted ethnographers in the field of drugs research, therefore defines the purpose of ethnography as:

> ... essentially a decoding operation. Beginning with the observation that some group successfully intercommunicates in a manner not understandable to an outsider, the ethnographer asks what knowledge is necessary to interpret correctly the verbal and non-verbal messages.
> (Agar 1973: 11)

There are numerous examples of this form of ethnography in the drugs literature. An ethnography by Fiddle (1967), for example, refers to the heroin addict as an 'existential man' for whom addiction is a method of assigning meaning to life: 'heroin gives symbolic significance, a meaning to life. Events, persons, objects, places – all can be characterised in the light of the need for heroin' (Fiddle 1967: 65, quoted in Agar 1973: 6). Preble and Casey (1969) similarly concern themselves with the meaning of life for the addict and articulate 'the quest for heroin [as] the quest for a meaningful life, not an escape from life. And the meaning of life does not lie primarily in the effects of the drug on their minds and bodies; it lies in the gratification of accomplishing a series of challenging, exciting tasks, every day of the week' (Preble and Casey 1969: 3). For example, one of Preble and Casey's participants describes his feelings following a successful day of shoplifting in terms of those of 'a man coming home after a hard day's work'.

One of the most recent ethnographic studies of heroin users was conducted in Sweden by Philip Lalander (2003) and funded by the Institute of Public Health. Lalander's study was located within a post-industrial landscape of urban deprivation in Norrkoping, Sweden. The purpose of the ethnography was to 'analyse the rationality that makes it possible to try, and to continue using, heroin' (Lalander 2003: 7-8). Lalander addressed himself to this question by undertaking 'an analysis of how a subculture, with its own particular logic and special rules of play, identities and rituals, develops and grows. However, the subculture can neither arise nor exist in a vacuum in relation to society in general. That which occurs within the subculture can describe how it is to live in our times' (Lalander 2003: 8).

There appear to be a number of elements to Lalander's ethnography, although he does not present it in these terms himself. The first concerns the *context* that provides the opportunity for the subculture to develop. Since the post industrial landscape of unemployment in Norrkoping provided little incentive for working class pupils to engage with their secondary school studies, participants in the study had begun to 'separate' themselves from school culture and, instead, build their own informal culture which emerged as they began to 'hang out' in the city centre (Lalander 2003: 12; cf. Willis 1977). The second concerns the *attraction* of 'the group', which is that it provides its 'separated' participants with a feeling of belonging and sense of companionship in an otherwise arid urban landscape. This is reinforced by the drug taking activities of the group which are undertaken secretly and follow collectively defined rituals which serve to strengthen bonds within the group. Thus, there is a symbolic (as well as pharmacological) aspect to heroin use which is that it is always used *together*, in a 'flat sitting' context. Furthermore, the 'preparatory work' of locating, purchasing and preparing the heroin is described as a skilful accomplishment because it is undertaken as a group and therefore in a co-ordinated fashion with each member of the group making a 'specialist' contribution. This too is said to 'strengthen social bonds' within the group (Lalander 2003: 51).

The third key element of Lalander's ethnography is that this togetherness is reinforced by the '*common perspective*' that is held by the group. The group perspective is the 'vision of the world' that is created when its members put their heads together and agree on how to see life in general (Lalander 2003: 31). In this case, the group perspective is partly a reflection of its 'separation' and therefore rejection of mainstream values but, also, partly a consequence of their embrace of heroin use. The group demonstrate resistance to mainstream values of 'deferred gratification' and, instead, have made a 'lifestyle choice' to 'live in the now' which involves 'taking things as they come': They are all said to have 'membership' of 'Drifters Association' (Lalander 2003: 18-19 and 123). And as a group that rejects mainstream values and 'lives in the now' rather than the future, it embraces crime and drugs because the illegality of these activities provide its members with an instant sense of excitement (Lalander 2003: 21-3). Furthermore, the group also exhibits expansionary ambitions, as if this was some sort of attempt to 'win over' others to the world view held by the group. Specifically, Lalander describes how the use of 'techniques', such as smoking rather than injecting, 'hasten the recruitment process' because they de-dramatise heroin and make it appear 'more like hash' (Lalander 2003: 43-4).

Taken together, then, these subcultural ethnographies show that individuals do not become heroin users by accident and, furthermore, are not simply pushed into heroin use by 'evil pushers' (Lalander 2003). Conversely it takes a certain level of socialisation into a particular subcultural perspective to make it possible for drug dealers to select people as possible consumers (Lalander 2003). They also show that:

> Previous characterisations of such groups [which] featured concepts such as 'disorganisation' or 'deprivation' ... encode the implicit biases of the subculture of the professional community who describe the groups ... The portrait of a *street junkie* in [these] stud[ies] contrasts with the usual stereotype of a social-psychological failure lacking the appropriate values, goals and rules of behaviour. Although this negative stereotype is part of the *junkie's* self-concept when his behaviour is measured against mainstream standards, there is another aspect of the junkie – a system of knowledge that differs from the mainstream model, but a system that enables the junkie to function and attain social success in the street context. (Agar 1973: 126-7)

Far from being social and psychological failures, subcultural ethnographic studies provide narratives that illuminate the skilful dexterity of heroin users. Heroin users 'learn the game' and how to interpret the world and situations. The life of the heroin user is dramatic, with heroin users constantly engaged in the social production of events that provide a sense of adventure and that act as an antidote to the humdrum of everyday modern life. It requires considerable skill to 'successfully' produce this drama, i.e. without being 'caught'. Finally, they create rituals and ways of being together that provide them with an illusion of sameness and therefore sense of belonging in an otherwise lonely post-modern world (cf. Bauman 1991). This is the defining feature of ethnographic and subcultural perspectives that seek to understand drug cultures 'in their own terms' rather than from the external perspective of a critical discourse analyst, urban ecologist, symbolic interactionist or any other such 'outsiders', however well-meaning or censorious.

Social Network Theory and the Socialisation Perspective

Proponents of social network theory have a multitude of problems with the perspectives discussed so far. Their key problem is that the perspectives of crime and drug use discussed so far all allude to the important contextual factor of urban poverty, in one way or another. Although social network theorists acknowledge the spatial concentration of crime and drug use in deprived neighbourhoods and, indeed, begin from this premise, they pose the contingent question: 'Why do some people living in deprived areas become involved in crime and drugs whereas other people do not?' (Fishbein and Perez 2000.)

A key departure point for social network theory can be found in the ideas of Sutherland (1937) who developed the concept of 'differential association'. The concept of Differential Association (which is similar to social disorganisation theory) is based on the idea that when two types of culture impinge on a person, or a person has associations with the two types of culture, the differential nature of that individual's group associations can explain criminal behaviour (Sutherland 1937). This conflict of cultures is the basic explanatory principle of social network theory, which is based on the core idea that 'individuals are influenced by the people they have contact with and that individual positions within larger social structures can determine behaviour' (Valente 2004: 1686). This means that it has some overlap with Bronfenbrenner's (1979) 'nested contexts' approach to ecological analysis, and that it draws some influence from the symbolic interactionist and subcultural perspectives.

Social network theory operationalises the abstract idea of differential association at different levels of generalisation. At the highest level of generalisation, social network theorists categorise people in terms of the character of their associations *and* the degree to which these associations are connected to one another. The suggestion here is that 'dense social networks' can reinforce behavioural norms once a behaviour is accepted by the majority (Valente 2004). Social network theorists argue that people who misuse substances are often surrounded by friends, family and associates that also misuse substances or tacitly approve of them. The best predictor of substance is thus said to be a function of the proportion of friends that are users, where drug use behaviour is a product of conformity with the peer group (Bauman and Ennett 1996). Numerous studies show that peer involvement in illicit drug use among adolescents is associated with the nature and extent of one's own use (Rai *et al* 2003; Windle 2000; Latkin *et al* 1995) whereas there is further evidence that the number of friends that use illicit drugs is positively associated with one's own illicit drug use (Jenkins and Zunguze 1998; Kandel and Davis 1991; Fraser and Hawkins 1984a, b). Hence it is possible that some people living in deprived areas will become involved in drug use whereas other people, with different types of social networks, will not.

Social network theorists have, however, had some difficulties in identifying the exact influence of social networks on behaviour, that is whether involvement in networks results in drug use or whether drug use is the reason for the emergence of the network. For this reason, Ennett and Bauman (1994) and Bauman and Ennet (1996) argue that it is necessary to distinguish between *influence* and *selection* of networks. It could be, for example, that sensation seeking individuals look for friends that are the same as themselves and who are more likely to want to experiment with drugs (Donohew *et al* 1999). Bauman and Ennet (1996) also highlight the important role of *projection*, which is when individuals project their own drug use behaviour onto their peers in order to arrive at judgement of peer behaviour. The trouble here is that these projections often overestimate the extent of peer use. This is a problem because the peer group pattern of use is then considered to be the cause of the respondents' behaviour when, in reality, it is simply the respondents' behaviour projected onto the peer group and therefore a consequence rather than a cause of respondents' level of drug use. Each of these factors provide reason to mediate our perception of the influence of the peer groups:

> Many theories specific to the use of drugs or related behaviours and more general behavioural and social theories include social influence as a component. Although these theories recognise peer influence as a determinant of behaviour ... [p]eers are sometimes included among a constellation of significant others, including parents, who influence adolescent behaviour. Our review is consistent with these theoretical perspectives in suggesting that the centrality often awarded to peer influence on adolescent drug behaviour should be tempered by integrating it with other causal factors and recognising that the importance frequently ascribed to peer influence may have been in part due to the other factors emphasised in this review ... [C]onsideration of selection effects and the use of peer reports of friend behaviour in the context of the relative worth of socialisation and social control theories to understanding [drug] use is particularly instructive in this regard ... [P]eer influence for drug use initiation may be overestimated.
>
> (Bauman and Ennet 1996: 192)

Middle range approaches place more emphasis on *network context* as opposed to simply the character and workings of networks. In doing so they are able to overcome some of the shortcomings of the generalist approach to social network analysis. Two examples of middle range perspectives will suffice. First, researchers such as Webster *et al* (1994) contend that the influence of networks is contingent on *perceptions* of neighbourhood context. Specifically, the experience of living in a deprived neighbourhood may engender feelings of powerlessness and helplessness for some people but not others (i.e. that they have little control over their local environment) and that those with low perceived control may be vulnerable to peer pressure within the neighbourhood to use substances (Webster *et al* 1994). Using this approach but also factoring in a gender dimension, Lambert *et al* (2004) were able to show that African American young people who:

> ... perceived greater disorganisation in their neighbourhoods – in terms of safety, violence, and drug activity – were more likely to use substances than those who did not have such negative perceptions of their neighbourhoods ... Neighbourhoods characterised by high levels of disorganisation tend to have higher rates of youth delinquency and adult participation in deviant activities. Males residing in these neighbourhoods may have greater opportunities to associate with delinquent peers and/or become involved in delinquent activities such as substance use. Consequently affiliation with deviant peers and level of participation in the neighbourhood are important to consider as possible mediators of the association between neighbourhood perceptions and male substance use.
>
> (Lambert *et al* 2004: 214)

Second, 'primary socialisation theory' points to three sources of socialisation within social networks; family, school, and peer clusters (Oetting *et al* 1998). In this theory, adult social ties are important to the degree that they create obligations and restraints that impose significant costs for submitting to peer pressure and translating criminal propensities into action. Key proponents of this approach are Fishbein and Perez (2000) who have studied the comparative socialising effects of social bonds with parents, peers and societal institutions. Their work focuses on the extent to which individuals bond to pro-social family and peers and school which, in turn, act as protective factors against crime and drug abuse. Their work shows that lack of commitment to institutions such as family, school and police, and negative peer influences, were significantly predictive of all offences of drug use as well as property crimes and offences against the person. Conversely, a positive relationship with fathers decreased the probability of property offences and drug involvement although this relationship did not hold true for offences against the person (e.g. fighting, violence) or where there was a good relationship with the maternal parent.

During periods when offenders live with spouses or attend school or work, evidence suggests that they commit fewer crimes (MacKenzie and De Li 2002). For example, Sampson and Laub (1993) analysed Glueck and Glueck's (1950) data and found support for their proposal that childhood anti-social behaviour and deviance can be modified over the life-course by adult social bonds. Similarly, Horney *et al* (1995) found that changes in circumstances that strengthened or weakened social bonds influenced offending over relatively short periods of time. Individuals with high propensities to offend have fewer social bonds compared to those with lower propensities to offend, yet they are still influenced by short term changes in social bonds. Thus, although high propensity offenders may be less likely to attend school, to work or to live with spouses, sometimes they do live with spouses, work or attend school and, at such times, they are less likely to commit serious crimes. Sampson and Laub (1993) similarly suggest that marital attachment is significant predictors of adult crime. This has been suggested in other work which has shown that the presence of a partner is inversely associated with the frequency of drug injecting, largely because the drug user may spend less time with drug using peers (Pluddemann *et al* 2004; Latkin *et al* 1995). For Fishbein and Perez, then, social development models and primary socialisation theory highlights:

... the important role of peer influences, paternal relationships and adherence to norms and values of society ... Youths likely to be considered at risk by virtue of their neighbourhoods are more likely to harbour anti-social values and engage in deviant behaviour when they lack these attachments, relative to youngsters in the same neighbourhoods who report more bonding to prosocial units.   (Fishbein and Perez 2000: 473, 475)

They conclude from this that:

Programmes that operate to strengthen social bonding may have potential to reduce drug abuse and delinquency ... For example, improving parental relationships, particularly with the father, may have direct and positive effects ... that may be 'protective' against the development of negative behavioural outcomes ... Another potential direction for approaches to treatment and prevention includes interventions that focus on peer influences. Negative peer influences have consistently been found to be among the strongest predictors of delinquency and drug use amongst youths. Programmes that enhance self-efficacy, decision making, judgement and social skills potentially reduce the impact of these influences ... In effect, a successful prevention strategy should be comprehensive in its focus, contain a multi-dimensional approach, and target underlying individual and social mechanisms that contribute to negative behavioural outcomes.

(Fishbein and Perez 2000: 476)

The antidote to all of this, however, is provided by Latkin (1995) who argues that individuals 'whose drug sub-networks are enmeshed in their other networks have fewer non-drug associates to counteract the influence of their drug sub-networks ... Having family members in one's social network many not be, as theorised, an indicator of ... social control' (Latkin *et al* 1995: 7).

Prior to concluding our discussion of social network theory it is worth noting the epistemological distinctiveness of network theory as well as the nature of its differences with the other theoretical perspectives cited in this chapter. This is necessary because social network theorists often allude to the influences of these other theoretical perspectives which can make the differences between them hard to spot and create confusion. For example, Latkin *et al* (1995: 1) state that 'social networks influence behaviour of individuals and group norms through social comparison processes [symbolic interactionism], fear of social sanctions [control theory, rational action theory], ... and socialisation of new members [socialisation theory]'. Valente *et al* (2004) cite a similar range of epistemological influences when seeking to understand the mechanisms underpinning network clustering: symbolic interactionism is important because patterns of association are a consequence of the modelling of behaviour on 'significant others', however, this fails to distinguish between the importance of relationships in an individual's life which is an empirical matter and even results in questions about the appeal of symbolic interactionism because drug use may not come from strangers or impersonal influences after all. This then leads Valente *et al* down another epistemological avenue: reasoned action theory might be useful because it suggests that the willingness to comply with peer norms and expectations is a function of the costs and benefits of engaging in the expected behaviour (links with control theory and rational action theory). So now it definitely has nothing to do with the symbolic interactionist premise that crime and drug use occurs because people wish to establish a meaningful identity and therefore imitate the behaviour of their peers. Social network theory is therefore alone in the perspectives discussed so far in that its proponents are open about their variety of influences and thus 'epistemological pragmatism' (cf. Turner 1992) which, of course, is the source of all the confusion regarding its differences with other perspectives. In practice, however, the influence that this wide variety of epistemological traditions has on social network analysis is often rhetorical. In reality, socialisation or social learning theories tend to predominate in social network analysis. The links and similarities and differences between social network theory and other theoretical perspectives outlined in this chapter can thus be summarised as follows:

- Although a wide range of influences are cited by social network theorists, primary socialisation theory provides a key explanatory tool. This focuses on social learning in terms of the transmission of societal beliefs rather than the formation and management of self-identity (symbolic interactionism). Furthermore, a fear of sanctions ensures that what is learned is translated into practice (control theory, rational action theory). This is the distinctiveness of social network theory, which provides more of an insight into social restraint and less of an insight into the motivation to use drugs.
- Symbolic interactionism is based on the premise that the process of self formation occurs within given social situations and thereby influences social behaviour. Thus it is concerned with the relationship between the self and society rather than the intricate dynamics of how social networks function. Symbolic interactionists therefore associate crime and drug use with the formation and management of self-identity. It therefore provides a sociological insight into the emotional motivation for crime and drug use but much less insight into the intricate particularities of individuals' social relationships.
- Subculturalism is based on the premise that groups develop as a reaction to the mainstream values. These groups develop their own sub-universe which is governed by shared rules, rituals, *etc.* Drug taking is a collective enterprise that reflects the subcultural values of the group and provides a sense of belonging. Since subcultural theorists analyse the process of 'social separation' that provides the context within which subcultures develop, then, they share network theorists' interest in the connections between social relationships and behaviour. The difference between the two perspectives is that subcultural theorists are more concerned with understanding drug use as a behaviour of social groups that have separated themselves from mainstream society, than with understanding the structure and relative influence of the various social networks that group members are enmeshed within, both within and outside the group.

Post-modern Social Theory and the Post Industrial Perspective

The same process of reflexive accumulation that gives rise to the service class also gives rise to what is becoming the bottom and excluded third of the 'two-thirds' society ... The new lower class represents a sort of structural downward mobility for substantial sections of the organised-capitalist working class .... The new lower class takes its place at the bottom of a restructured stratification ladder in which the hierarchy of capital and labour is replaced by a three-tiered ordering – a mass class of professional-managerials (alongside a very small capitalist class), a smaller and comparatively under-resourced working class and this new lower class.   (Lash and Urry 1994: 145-6)

Post-modern social theory avoids the simple and straightforward social democratic maxim that 'bad social conditions cause crime and drugs'. Conversely, it understands crime and drug use to be a result of the way excluded social groups *experience* and formulate a *response* to increasing social divisions. The increasing social divisions that characterise late modern societies arise out of the potent combination of de-industrialisation and mass unemployment that results in the creation of social 'out groups' in some urban areas *and* the coterminous rise of a culture of rampant consumerism (Lash and Urry 1994; Young 1999). For post-modern criminologists such as Young, then, crime and drugs are better explained as a consequence of a 'relative deficit' caused by the inflation of consumer expectations but, at the same time, the decimation of opportunities for 'this new lower class' or 'out group' to become 'successful consumers' (cf. Bauman 1987):

> It is not as simple as [poverty causes crime]. Lack of material rewards clearly does not mean absolute poverty; crime rose through the late 1960s with rising living standards: it is relative deprivation which is a potent cause of crime. So perhaps ... we should refer to a relative deficit: that is, the relative material standards of individuals compared one to another, a sense of inequality of unjust reward commensurate with merit. So as groups begin progressively to demand greater equality of reward, fuller citizenship, then their relative deprivation increases and, if no collective solution is forthcoming, crime will occur.   (Young 1999: 52)

A good example of post-modern theorising about crime and drugs can be found in the work of Rob MacDonald who has devoted considerable theoretical effort to understanding 'how multifaceted aspects of disadvantage cluster together in an area, sometimes experienced simultaneously and in combination by individuals from that area (e.g. poor housing, worklessness, poor health)' (MacDonald and Marsh 2001: 375). MacDonald examined the 'school to work' career experiences of what he describes as his *economically marginal* respondents in terms of a series of cyclical movements around various permutations of government schemes and college courses, low paid, low skill and often temporary jobs and recurrent unemployment. He describes these as common working class experiences in the areas he has studied rather than those of a numerically constricted underclass (MacDonald and Marsh 2001: 388). Now although MacDonald admits that this focus on post-industrialisation appears to be consistent with a structural explanation of social change, crucially, he argues that it is the *experience* of economic marginalisation that results in the formation of criminal and drug careers. For MacDonald, then, involvement in crime and drugs is not the social product of structural processes *or* an inter-generationally transmitted culture of deviancy but, rather, a consequence of disengagement from the limited 'school to work career' options available, especially when this combines with the availability of illegal opportunities. This point has also been made by Walklate (1998) who suggests that:

> There is more than one way in any society to achieve success. There are both legitimate and illegitimate pathways ... middle classes have greater access to the legitimate opportunity structure, with the lower classes [sic] having greater access to the illegitimate opportunity structure.   (Walklate 1998: 23)

MacDonald's post-modern explanation of crime and drugs therefore focuses on the issue of 'constrained choice':

> Although [people make] active choices to pursue [a] criminal career, these cannot be understood as a pure reflection of personal immorality or cultural estrangement ... we need to appreciate the context within which such choices are made; how the agency of people is bounded ... by the surrounding opportunity structure. 'Hard lads' would insist that they were the authors of their own life stories, would blame no one else for their wrongdoing and would oppose an analysis that positioned them as the unreflecting victims of social circumstance., nevertheless ... biography can only be made sense of with reference to the balance of opportunities presented by the local formal and informal economies.
>   (MacDonald and Marsh 2001: 383)

The issue of choice also emerges in the work of Benoit *et al* (2003) who focus on the ethics, as well as constrained nature, of choice-making. Benoit *et al* (2003) reinforce the points made by Macdonald and Marsh (2001) when they distinguish between 'street' and 'decency' codes. They argue that the absence of a formal opportunity structure can force economically marginal groups to adopt 'street codes', yet this does not mean that they reject values of decency. Indeed, they cite empirical examples from 'one of New York's poorest neighbourhoods' where strong adherence to 'decency codes' (e.g. the idea of sufficiency, providing for the children), paradoxically, results in the embrace of 'street code' of behaviour (e.g. drug dealing):

> In Dolo's version of the 'decent daddy' role, 'mainstream' values of self-sufficiency and paternal responsibility drive a lifestyle defined by 'deviant' street norms of conduct, mainly blunt use and crack selling. He can switch between codes of the 'street' and of 'decency' and lives by both simultaneously ... they therefore processed cognitive signals from their environments ... hold both sets of values simultaneously and switch according to situation – deviance even driven by adherence to mainstream norms.
>   (Benoit *et al* 2003: 521)

Benoit *et al* are therefore equally convinced that underclass explanations that focus on the transmission of deviant cultures are inadequate. Conversely, members of social groups that are economically marginalised are neither 'good' nor 'bad' citizens but, conversely, adhere to a complex and apparently contradictory apparatus of decency and street codes where the tendency towards:

> ... deviance or conformity depends on the 'balance of influences'; that is whether the variables informing one's behaviour tip towards one side or the other. The balance 'usually' exhibits some stability over time but it is not necessarily permanent; it can change with time or circumstance.   (Benoit *et al* 2003: 509)

The distinctive feature of post-modern accounts of crime and drug use is that it emphasises the post-industrial context of social division within which human beings make 'constrained choices'. Exclusion from participation in the culture of rampant consumerism, combined with the local availability of an illegal opportunity structure, has been shown to result in crime and drug use. There are, then, some parallels between post-modern forms of analysis and theoretical perspectives such as symbolic interactionism (the importance of consumer status) and social network theory (the opportunities that involvement in certain social networks presents). That said, the post-modern perspective is very different to the Chicago School's urban ecological analysis of the criminological consequences of industrialisation and urbanisation, which underplayed the role of human agency as Heidensohn (1989) and Shaw and McKay (1972) noted earlier in this chapter.

Conclusions

This chapter has shown that Bean (2002) and Hunter and Barker's (2001) contention that the crime and drugs literature has been by-passed by sociological theory is unfair. The research literature on crime and drugs might be dominated by the positivist perspectives outlined in Chapter 1, but there is also a rich minority of work that is conceptually sophisticated. This body of work has sought to enhance our understanding (*verstehen*) of crime and drugs as social phenomena, unlike much of the literature cited in Chapter 1. The ecological and symbolic interactionist perspectives of 'city life' that emerged from the Chicago School were groundbreaking at the time and have had a profound influence on criminology and the understanding of drugs and crime (Moyer 2001; Heidensohn 1989). Thanks to the work of urban ecologists we now understand much more about the spatial distribution of crime and drug use as well as the possible reasons for this. Thanks also to the symbolic interactionists we understand much more about how the formation of social identity takes place in urban contexts and how, therefore, practices such as crime and drug use are central to the process of identity formation in some urban contexts and not others.

Ethnographic and subcultural theories have also been invaluable in turning some taken-for-granted understandings of crime and drug use on their head. They point to the dangers of adopting the 'official view' of crime and drug use, which is that involvement in these practices is a symptom of social and psychological failure. Conversely, ethnographic and subcultural perspectives provide us with a rich insight into, and understanding of, the social worlds that are occupied by people involved in crime and drug use. These subcultural worlds are composed of a complex matrix of norms, rituals and codes and so participation within these worlds is seen as a skilful accomplishment. This has provided an understanding of crime and drug use as an expression of a different way of life that demands the same sorts of social skills that the so-called 'mainstream' way of life demands; otherwise these subcultures would not be able to sustain themselves in the coherent way in which they do. Socialisation and network perspectives turn this on its head again and assume involvement in crime and drug use to be a consequence of some sort of 'deficit' of socialisation. The important contribution to understanding here, then, has been the contention that crime and drug use emerge when the composition of a social network is such that socialisation favours the transmission of 'deviant' norms and values rather than mainstream norms and values. Finally, post-modern perspectives have been critical in enabling us to better understand how de-industrialisation has affected some urban areas much more than it has affected others. The consequence of this has been that different 'opportunity structures' emerge in different parts of the city. In parts of the city where there has been a reduction in 'legitimate opportunities', people are much more likely to engage in illicit forms of activity. This has resulted in a very uneven spatial distribution of crime and drug use that has proliferated in post-industrial urban spaces.

Although each of the perspectives outlined here have sought to contribute to the further development of our understanding of crime and drug use as social phenomena, they are not without their problems. In Chapter 3, I will return to examine what these problems are. I will point out that arguments between practitioners of each of the perspectives outlined, concerning *exactly* how the constitution of social and economic relations produce crime and drug use (e.g. through changing opportunity structures, deficient socialisation, *etc.*), conceal the fact that there is, in fact, much agreement between them. I will also point out that the basis of this agreement between the perspectives is hard to decipher because it is implicit rather than explicit in the debates that take place. This implicit agreement is based on the 'scholarly view' (cf. Bourdieu 2000) that each of the perspectives throws onto crime and drug use and which leads them to understand these practices *from the distance at which they are observed* rather than *from within practice as it occurs*, though without acknowledging that this form of observation constitutes an arbitrary view. This applies equally to the ethnographic perspectives cited that, contrary to the claims that are made for them, also objectify practice from a distance and without acknowledging that this is what is being done.

Chapter 3

Being and Crime (and Drugs)

Introduction

In this chapter I examine the epistemological limitations of social theories of crime and drug use outlined in Chapter 2. I will be arguing that the limitations of these established perspectives emanate from the epistemological relation that social scientists have to the crime and drug use that they observe and seek to explain. I refer to this as the 'scholarly view' which I distinguish from a 'practical view' of crime and drugs. I show that the scholarly epistemology is based on a spatial and temporal distance from the social and economic worlds that the subjects of their attention inhabit, which means that social science tends to view the field of practice as a 'landscape' that can be read like a map. The important thing to note here is that social science implicitly assumes that the subjects of their attention (e.g. drug users) adopt a similar spatial and temporal distance from their own practices which they are therefore assumed to objectify. This results in the further assumption that they possess 'reasoned reasons' for what they do, that is, that they can answer questions about their practices in terms such as 'I do it *because* ...'.

I use this chapter to show that the scholarly tendency to (make demands on research subjects to) look at the social and economic landscape from above demonstrates an oversight to the notion that those landscapes constitute 'lived space' for those subjects who therefore see them from *within* rather than *above*. I also show that research strategies that seek to understand the logic of practice at an epistemic distance from practice demonstrate an oversight to the immediate and urgent way in which social practice occurs 'in the thick of it'. I argue that this suggests a need to better understand the practice from within the 'lived' context that it takes place. I do this by examining the *practical authority* of the subject, that is, *how* the subject 'goes about things' in the thick of everyday life and what this means for our understanding of how crime and drug use occurs. I also examine the *articulatory authority* of the subject, that is, *how* the subject talks about going about everyday life 'as it happens' and 'in the thick of it', which is different to the way subjects will talk about the same everyday practices when they are situated at an epistemic distance from those practices. This is exemplified in the unselfconscious manner of someone that is engrossed in the practicalities of 'doing' everyday life rather than with explaining it and which manifests itself in a primordial form of language that is emergent from practice (e.g. 'No reason in particular. It's what I always do') rather than reflective upon it ('I did it *because* ...').

Epistemological Distance in Theories of Crime and Drug Use

The weakness of studies cited in Chapter 1 was that they tended to treat the relationships between crime and drug use as internally related and therefore failed to situate these activities within a broader social context. The strengths of the perspectives in Chapter 2 were that they acknowledged extraneous sources of the relationship between crime and drug use which they therefore sought to contextualise. The important issue for us now concerns the adequacy of these attempts to situate crime and drug use within their wider social contexts. These are essentially issues of epistemology.

If we briefly return to the theoretical perspectives outlined in Chapter 2 we can see that their epistemological relation to the field of crime and drugs can be boiled down to a series of rather straightforward questions and answers which are outlined in Table 3.1. The important issue here concerns the way in which these questions present the relationship between human agency (the subjective dimension) and the context within which activities such as crime and drug use occur (the objective dimension). Since social constructionist and creationist perspectives posit that crime and drug use have no ontological validity outside of the discourses that are mobilised about them, questions about the subject-object relation are asked from the perspective of those responsible for imposing these definitions. In other words, these perspectives are less concerned with why people become involved in crime and drug use and *more* concerned with why they are problematised for doing so. Although immensely important, then, it is of marginal interest to our concerns here, which are with *why* people become involved in crime and drug use.

If we look across the range of other perspectives, however, we can see that the questions that are asked are suggestive of a significant level of subject-object distancing at the point of entry into criminal behaviour and drug use. Two dimensions to this subject-object distancing can be identified. First, the assumption seems to be that human beings take a 'point of view' on their objective situation *prior* to deciding on whether to become involved in crime and drug use. To arrive at this point of view, the subject is assumed to engage in an act of distancing from their objective

Table 3.1 Theoretical Perspectives

Theoretical Perspective	Nature of Questions and Answers
Social Constructionist/Social Creationist	Q: 'Who are they?' A: Criminals and Druggies
Ecological Systems	Q: 'How am I going to cope with it all?' A: Crime and Drugs
Symbolic Interactionism	Q: 'Who am I?' A: I am a criminal and a drug user
Ethnographic Subculturalism	Q: 'Where do I belong?' A: In the drug culture
Social Networks and Socialisation	Q: 'Who are my main influences?' A: Criminals and Drug Users
Post-modern Ethics	Q: 'What choices are left open to me?' A: Crime and Drugs

situation which they therefore attempt to see 'in the round'. That is, the subject is seen to stand apart from their social world, at a point in time, surveying it, analysing it 'in the round' and deciding what to do; albeit their decisions are considered to be 'constrained decisions'. Second, we cannot assume from this that the subject is necessarily taking his or her own 'rounded' point of view on their objective situation. Conversely, the questions that are asked during these acts of reflection are those of the researcher, rather than the subject, and reflect the different academic points of view on the objective situation of the subject. The subject is not, then, asking him or herself questions such as 'how am I going to cope with it all?', 'Who and what do I want to be?', 'Where do I belong?', 'Who are my main influences?', 'What choices are left open to me now?', *etc.* Conversely, questions of this nature are asked – in a variety of different ways – by researchers that adopt a particular epistemological relation to the field as proponents of a particular theoretical perspective. In other words, whatever the subject is asked to consider 'in the round' is contingent on the researchers' point of view concerning what, exactly, 'the round' consists of; for example neighbourhood stressors *or* relations with self *or* relations with others and so on. There is a feeling from reading these works, then, that we are viewing the scene from the point of view of a spectator, and therefore as a 'landscape' that is best viewed with the benefit of distance. The apparent justification for this is, quite simply, that you can see more of what is going on even if you do choose to focus on particular aspects of what is going on, as each of the theoretical perspectives do. And since distance allows us to see the landscape in its panoramic detail, we can draw aspects of this detail to the attention of the figures within it via a series of research questions. They are therefore asked to take a point of view that is the point of view of the researcher and therefore to examine the landscape from a distance which, unsurprisingly, is reflected in answers that also project distance between themselves and the landscapes that they are part of.

Epistemological Limits of Theories of Crime and Drug Use

The academic purpose of taking a distant and panoramic view of figures on the landscapes of which they are a part is to understand the nature of the relation between subject (the *figures*) and object (on the *landscape*). This 'rounded view' of things enables researchers to construct theories that explain the social nature of crime and drug use in a way that might not be acknowledged by the figures on the landscape. For example, sociological researchers that survey the scene in which their respondents are situated have developed ecological theories of drug use that make connections between urban conditions, social suffering and drug use from answers such as 'I started heroin 'cos I was fucking depressed with all of this shit'. Of course, researchers with different disciplinary backgrounds, for instance psychology, might receive and understand the same answer in an entirely different way and might therefore make something else of such an answer, for example lack of coping skills, personal deficiency, *etc.*

Herein lies the main grounds for dispute between different theoretical perspectives outlined in Chapter 2. The commonality between these *social* theories of crime and drug use is that they each seek to understand the nature of the subject-object relation by situating the subject *on* the urban landscape. Insofar as disputes arise between them these tend to be over matters of comparative validity and emphasis concerning which aspects of the urban landscape have the greatest influence on human behaviour, for example does the opportunity structure explain more than social networks and so on. The trouble is that these disputes over what researchers regard to be important *on* the social and economic landscape obscure the fact that they share the same epistemological relation *to* that landscape, that is, as *detached* observers that treat it as an object of enquiry. The result is a silence concerning the epistemological relation that social scientific observers have to the social and economic landscape which, in turn, results in an epistemically distant form of questioning that conceals the *involved* nature of the research subjects' relation to that landscape.

Specifically, the scholarly tendency to view the social and economic landscape as a 'present-at-hand' object of theoretical contemplation obscures the nature of the relation between the research subject and its landscape (Heidegger 1962; Merleau-Ponty 1964; Bourdieu 2000). This is because the unproblematic projection of distance between the scientific observer and their object of contemplation presupposes that existential questions (in this case concerning the positionality of scientific observers in relation to the urban landscapes they observe) are irrelevant. Yet, the social and epistemological break between scientific observers and the social and economic landscapes that they stand apart from does not mean that existential questions can be overlooked. Conversely, it opens up existential questions concerning 'knowing [as] a *founded* mode of access to the real' (Heidegger 1962: 246) because it draws our attention to the social space that social scientific observers have which, crucially, enables them to view the social and economic landscape from a spatial and temporal distance. That is, they are able to see the social and economic landscape in panoramic terms (spatial distance) whilst also having the benefit of time to consider the likely relationships between the social and economic landscape and the figures on it (temporal distance).

This raises two epistemological issues. First, the academic 'point of view' that regards the social and economic landscape as an object of theoretical knowledge and therefore human action within it as a reflexive accomplishment is exactly that; a point of view. This 'point of view' is a product of their ability to see the social and economic landscape from a spatial and temporal distance and is therefore ontologically founded, as Thiele (1995: 48) observes when he remarks that 'the primary relation is not that of observer to the observed. Rather, the human being illuminates its world by way of its holistic embeddedness', i.e. in terms of its temporal and spatial proximity to the object of its enquiry. As Heidegger (1962) points out, then, the social position from which knowing (or a 'point of view') is made possible consists of a mode of 'being-in-the-world' which, in our case, means that scholarly knowing (or a 'point of view') is a consequence of the social scientific way of being-in-the-world and that, therefore, this social scientific way of being-in-the-world does not simply uncover the being-in-the-world of others:

> Every act of knowing always already takes place on the basis of the mode of being of Dasein which we call being-in, that is, being-always-already-involved-with-a-world.
>
> (Heidegger 1985: 161)

For Merleau-Ponty, then:

> Analysis has no justification for positing any stuff of knowledge as an ideally separable 'moment' and that this stuff, when brought into being by an act of reflection, already relates to the world. Reflection does not follow in the reverse direction a path already traced by the constitutive act, and the natural reference of the stuff to the world leads us to a new conception of intentionality, since the classical conception, which treats the experience of the world as a pure act of constitututing consciousness, manages to do so only in so far as it defines consciousness as absolute *non-being*, and correspondingly consigns its contents to a 'hyletic layer' which belongs to opaque being.
>
> (Merleau Ponty 1962: 283; *italics added*)

Yet, as we have seen, this is seldom acknowledged by scholars that accept different theoretical perspectives about *relations on the landscape* to constitute a 'point of view' but whom do not acknowledge that their shared *relation to the landscape* constitutes a 'point of view' (cf. Heidegger 1962; Merleau-Ponty 1962, 1964; Bourdieu 1977, 1990, 2000). This is crucial because it constitutes an epistemological blindness that fails to acknowledge how the social production of social scientific forms of objectification – of whatever theoretical form – is constituted upon a spatial and temporal distance between the observer and observed. The result is epistemological silence concerning the social scientific way of being-in-the-world as distant from that world (Heidegger 1962; Merleau-Ponty 1962, 1964; Bourdieu 1977, 2000) and therefore towards the validity of social scientific activity *in general*.

Second, the 'scholarly error' that arises from this failure to recognise the social and epistemological separation between social scientists' ('distant from') and acting subjects' ('involved with') relation to the social and economic landscape (cf. Bourdieu 2000, 2001) has consequences for the way in which research questions are asked and answers interpreted. Bourdieu (2000) devoted much of his career to this epistemological problem and, to exemplify his argument, pointed out that social surveys always tend to ask questions that require respondents to engage in reflexive acts of contemplation, for example 'What do you think about ... ?', 'In your view has ... a lot, a little, not at all?'. We could equally argue that most qualitative research texts and qualitative researchers in the crime and drugs field adopt a similar epistemological relation to their respondents-in-the-field. They therefore tend to demand 'reasoned reasons' for human action (e.g. 'I did it *because* ...') and so are seldom satisfied with responses such as 'it came naturally' or 'it just happened' which were the 'non-reasoned reasons' that, Chapter 4 shows, many of my interviewees gave for their involvement in crime and drugs. Indeed, far from being satisfied with the articulation of 'non-reasoned reasons', responses such as 'it just happened' or 'it came naturally' usually 'demand' the formulation of a 'probing' question ('When you say 'it just happened', what do you mean by that?'). Yet, in doing so, they do two things that result in the production of a very partial (i.e. social scientific) understanding of practices such as crime and drug use (cf. Merleau-Ponty 1964). First they project the social scientist's distant view of the social and economic landscape into the heads of the acting subject (Bourdieu 2000). Since the acting subject does not necessarily relate to the social and economic landscape as a distant object of enquiry ('How am I going to cope with this?', 'What choices are left open to me?') but as the object of their involvements, the projection of distance into the head of the subject obscures the involved nature of its relation to the social and economic landscape which 'takes place within a certain horizon and ultimately *in* the "world". We experience perception and its horizon "in action" rather than by "posing" them or explicitly "knowing" them' (Merleau-Ponty 1964: 12; see also Heidegger 1962; Bourdieu 2000). Second, they dismiss and therefore overlook the original answers to their questions (such as 'Don't know', 'it just happened' or 'it came naturally') which bear all the hallmarks of this involved – as opposed to distant – relation to the social and economic landscape[1] (Bourdieu 2000). Merleau-Ponty argues that we need to understand (rather than dismiss) answers such as 'it just happened' because they illuminate (rather than obscure) how the things that are closest in being are furthest away in analysis, and therefore the 'true' nature of the relation between human agency and everyday practice.

On the Nature of Being-in-the-World: Habitus, Dasein and the Body-Subject

Phenomenologists such as Heidegger (1962), Merleau-Ponty (1962, 1964) and Bourdieu (1977, 1990, 2000) set themselves against the notion that human beings can ever exist in any neutral sense, that is, apart from their being-in-the-world. Conversely the primary nature of being-in-the-world is contained in the 'habitus' (Bourdieu 1977) or 'Dasein' (Heidegger 1962) or 'body-subject' (Merleau-Ponty 1962) which, unlike the 'theoretical knowledge' contained in the social scientific view of the social world, consists of a 'practical sense' (cf. Bourdieu 2001) that emerges out of the everyday inhabitation of social space. This everyday inhabitation of social space produces *perceptions* and *expectations* that are products of – and oriented towards – objective positions occupied on the social and economic landscape and therefore partial to positions occupied rather than 'rounded'. Although the social and economic landscape has many sides (many of which can be seen from the panoramic view of the social scientist), then, Merleau-Ponty (1962) points out that these sides do not correspond to the experiences of the subject-on-the-landscape which perceives the landscape in terms of its past and immediate involvements in it rather than in terms of its 'geometrical truths' (Merleau-Ponty 1964: 14). And by encountering the social and economic landscape in terms of its past and immediate involvements (i.e. as a presence of the past in the present) the 'practical subject' sediments its being-in-the-world through a process of avoidance; that is, by only harbouring expectations of what is reasonable 'for the likes of us' and that are:

> ... durably inculcated by objective [socio-economic] conditions that engender aspirations and practices compatible with those objective requirements ... As an acquired system of generative schemes objectively adjusted to the particular conditions in which it is constituted, the habitus engenders all the thoughts, all the perceptions, and all the actions

---

1   Bourdieu also argues that scholarly practices that impute the intellectual relation to practice into the practical relation to practice always demand the type of 'satisfactory answer' that can only be prepared through an 'in advance' act of contemplation and, in doing so, serve to enforce the social relations of domination – of the theoretical reason of the dominant over the practical reason of the dominated.

consistent with those conditions, and non others ... [T]he habitus is an endless capacity to engender products – thoughts, perceptions, expressions, actions – whose limits are set by the historically and socially situated conditions of its production.

(Bourdieu 1977: 77 and 95)

Everyday human existence therefore involves a tacit understanding of what it is *to be* which becomes manifest in everyday practices on the social and economic landscape and a background structure of intelligibility that is oriented towards, and compatible with, the involvement of the body-subject in social space (Charlesworth 2000: 66). And given this correspondence between social positioning and intelligibility,[2] the social and economic landscape that envelops human beings appears as self-evident, rather than an object of knowledge and contemplation in which there would exist an awareness and recognition of the possibility that things could 'be otherwise' (Bourdieu 2000: 164). There is, then, an implicit collusion between social conditions and positioning that produces 'being' and the mental and perceptive structures that act to reinforce social conditions and positioning by simply accepting them as self-evident and inevitable (Bourdieu 2000: 145):

Owing to the quasi-perfect fit between the objective structures and the internalized structures which results from the logic of simple reproduction, the established cosmological and political order is perceived not as arbitrary, i.e. as one possible order among others, but as a self-evident and natural order which *goes without saying* and therefore goes unquestioned, [and so] the agents' aspirations have the same limits as the objective conditions of which they are the product. (Bourdieu 1977: 165-6)

However, being-in-the-world is not simply manifest in the form of *perception* and structure of *expectations* that inhabit the habitus, dasein and body-subject. It is also manifest in the way habitus, dasein and the body-subject develops a habituated orientation towards *acting* within the social and economic landscape so that:

... the most improbable practices are excluded, either totally without examination, as *unthinkable*, or at the cost of *double negation* which inclines agents to make a virtue of necessity, that is, to refuse what is anyway refused and to love the inevitable.

(Bourdieu 1977: 77)

The corollary of this is that the habitus 'belongs to', is 'possessed by' and 'attuned to' the demands of the social space it occupies to such an extent that, with an economy of effort, it is able to formulate practical responses that are appropriate to situations as they present themselves without having to undergo an express process of rational calculation, choice and statement of intention:

[The] schemes of perception, appreciation and action enable [the habitus] to perform acts ..., based on the identification and recognition of conditional, conventional stimuli

---

2   Indeed, it is this very *doxic* relation to the social world (or 'fields') we inhabit, which in our case is the scholastic field, that produces the *epistemic doxa* (cf. Bourdieu, 2000) of the scientific observer whose 'intellectualist disposition' leads them to leave unexamined the social conditions that produce an epistemological separation between their own intellectualist and reflexive orientation to the social world and 'practical reason' (Bourdieu, 2001).

to which they are predisposed to react; and without any explicit definition of ends or rational calculation of means [because 'it comes naturally' and 'just happens'] ... within the limits of the structural constraints of which they are the product and which define them ... The practical sense is what enables one to act as one 'should' ... without positing or executing a Kantian 'should', a *rule* of conduct ... The schemes of habitus, very generally applicable principles of vision and division which, being the product of the incorporation of the structures and tendencies of the world, are at least roughly adjusted to them, make it possible to adapt endlessly to partially modified contexts, ... in a practical operation of *quasi-bodily* anticipation of the immanent tendencies of the field.

(Bourdieu 2000: 138-9)

Habitus, Dasein and the body-subject are, then, socio-spatial products that provide human beings with a *doxic*[3] relation to their position in social space and therefore a dispositional orientation to social practice that 'operate[s] with and among artefacts [and stimuli] without reflecting on their nature ... [Artefacts and stimuli are] part of a world being managed, dealt with, navigated or simply lived in a day-to-day manner ... The question here is less *what is* the thing encountered, than *how is* this thing revealed' in the course of everyday practice (Thiele 1995: 48).

[I] take my place, through the medium of my body as the potential source of certain number of familiar actions, in my environment conceived of as a set of manipulanda and without, moreover, envisaging my body or my surrounding as objects in the Kantian sense, that is, ... as transparent entities, free from my attachment to a specific place or time ... There is my arm seen as sustaining familiar acts, my body as giving rise to determinate action having a [spatial] field or scope known to me in advance, there are my [familiar] surroundings as a collection of possible points upon which this bodily action may operate ... As far as bodily space is concerned, it is clear that there is a knowledge of place which is reducible to a sort of co-existence with that place ... *The whole operation [of the body] takes place in the domain of the phenomenal; ... It is never our objective body that we move but our phenomenal body, ...* since our body, as the potentiality of this or that part of the world, surges towards objects to be grasped and perceives them.

(Merleau-Ponty 1962: 120-21, *emphasis added*)

There are numerous examples of phenomenological research studies that have sought to challenge the 'mentalism' of social science. For my own purposes, it is useful to split these studies into two camps. Work in the first camp emphasises what I would call the *practical authority* of the body-subject, whereas work in the second camp builds on this by emphasising what can be usefully referred to as the *articulatory authority* of this practically oriented subject.

The Practical Authority of the Body-Subject

Merleau-Ponty's work on the phenomenology and primacy of perception (see especially, 1962, 1964) has informed numerous projects that have sought to emphasise the practical authority of the body-subject. Merleau-Ponty's starting

---

3   Bourdieu refers to the routine production of social action in this 'unknowing' way as 'doxa' (Bourdieu, 2000).

point reflects his concern to overcome the Cartesian problem of (mind over) the 'passive' body, in which the latter simply acts out the script that it is given by the higher authority of the former; the Cartesian mind is said to objectify the relation between the body and its landscape, thereby producing a stock of knowledge that informs the practical actions of the body-subject. For Merleau-Ponty, the mind does not objectify the relationship between the body and the landscapes that surround it. Therefore the mind does not map itself onto the body and it is not, therefore, the medium through which the practical actions of the body-subject can be understood. Conversely, Merleau-Ponty explicates body-in-space movement through a focus on how the human agency to navigate space becomes embodied within a 'corporeal or postural schema [that] gives us … the relation between our body and things, … our hold on them. A system of possible movements, or "motor projects" radiates from us to our environment' (Merleau-Ponty 1964: 5). This 'corporeal schema' – in which our previous experience of physical and social space produces a corporeal system of 'possible movements' – thus enables the body-subject to *unthinkingly* adjust to the demands that physical and social space places on it during its everyday activities so that:

> When I move about my house, I know without thinking about it that walking towards the bathroom means passing near the bedroom, that looking at the window means having the fireplace on my left, and in this small world each gesture, each perception is immediately located in relation to a great number of possible co-ordinates … The word 'sediment' [within the body means that] … this acquired knowledge is not an inert mass in the depths of our consciousness. My flat is for me, not a set of closely associated images. It remains a familiar domain around me only as long as I still have 'in my hands' or 'in my legs' the main distances and directions involved, and as long as from my body intentional threads run out towards it. (Merleau-Ponty 1962: 149-50)

Merleau-Ponty thus constructs a conception of the body-subject as an agent that actively appropriates (rather than an object that submits to the geometrical proportions of) physical space 'in the hands' and 'in the legs' in order to *enable* its navigation of places known to it through experience. A now famous example of this form of phenomenological analysis has been presented by David Seamon (1979: 161-2) who is critical of theories that emphasise the cognitive aspects of spatial movement practices because they are based on '*a priori* academic theorising' that inserts a false distance between the body-subject and environment-object and which fail to recognise 'that space is first of all grounded in the body. Through the body-subject the person knows where he is in relation to the familiar objects, places, and environments which in sum constitute his everyday geographical world.' Seamon exemplifies his argument with reference to data collected from his students who told him about how they had come to be able to 'automatically' motor themselves in home and urban space (through the gradual and experiential development of 'time-space' body routines) without having recourse to conscious or intellectual activity:

> When I was living at home and going to school, I couldn't drive to the University directly – I had to go around one way or the other. And I once remember becoming vividly aware of the fact that I always went there by one route and back the other – I'd practically

always do it. And the funny thing was that I didn't have to tell myself to go there the one way and back the other. Something in me would do it automatically – I really didn't have much choice in the matter. Of course, there would be some days when I would have to go somewhere besides school first, and so I would take a different route, but otherwise I would go and return the same streets each time.   (Quoted in Seamon 1979: 152)

I discuss the practical authority of the body-subject in more depth in Chapter 4, when I examine how and why crime and drugs were activities that, similarly, 'came naturally', 'just happened' to people living in deprived urban areas.

The Articulatory Authority of the Experiencing Subject

The epistemological doxa that underpins much social science that is the product of its being-from-distance leads to concomitant demands on subjects to articulate their experience in terms of their epistemic distance from their own practice. Questions are therefore formulated in terms that insert a distance between subject and object whereas a 'satisfactory' answer is judged in terms of the distance that the subject inserts between thoughts and practice. However, in doing so, the language of social research empties subjectivity of its involvements in the social world and therefore fails to capture the way in which speech emerges from the grip of its primacy of experience, that is, of its 'thrownness' into a social world so directly encountered. Phenomenologists such as Merleau-Ponty and Seamon have therefore shown that primary experience is manifest through the medium of the phenomenal body-subject which, as a primordial form of subjectivity, underlies the production of a more primitive language that collapses thought into practice and vice versa, i.e. Seamon's (1979) respondent talks in terms of 'not having to tell himself what to do'. For Merleau-Ponty (1962: 210), then, 'the categorical act is therefore not an ultimate fact, it builds itself up within a certain "attitude". It is on this attitude, moreover, that speech is based, so that there can be no question of making language rest of pure thought' (Merleau-Ponty 1962: 223). Thus:

> We must recognise first of all that thought, in the speaking subject, is not a representation, that is, that it does not expressly posit objects of relations .... I do not need to visualise the word in order to know and pronounce it. It is enough that I possess its articulatory and acoustic style as one of the modulations, one of the possible uses of my body. I reach back for the word as my hand reaches towards the part of my body which is being pricked; the word has a certain location in my linguistic world, and is part of my equipment .... Word and speech must [therefore] cease to be a way of designating things or thoughts, and become the presence of that thought in the phenomenal world.
>
> (Merleau-Ponty 1962: 209, 210 and 211)

In seeking an engagement between subjects and their practices, then, phenomenologists seek to understand the primordial relation between the actor and its life world by acceding articulatory authority to the mode of communication that expresses this primordial view but which is often overlooked as primitive in academic accounts that, as distant and neutralising, are insensitive to the primitive thought and its expression in language. In contrast to the articulatory authority that social science conventionally assigns to 'satisfactory' responses that are formulated at an epistemic distance from practice ('I did it *because* ...'), then, phenomenological acknowledgement of the primordial relation to being demands that articulatory authority be given to language that is constituted upon an inter-involvement of action, thought and speech and which results in a form of terminological expressiveness that is awkward in the way it emerges 'in the thick of it' but which reveals rather than conceals the practical 'point of view'. In a fascinating book, Charlesworth (2000) exemplifies how this happens when working class people are asked to articulate an opinion about Rotherham and respond that it is, simply, 'crap'. Rather than necessitating a probing question ('why do you say it is crap?'), Charlesworth eloquently argues that the challenge here is to understand the existential nature of the answer given:

> During interviews, I felt the pressure of having to push these people to take up an objectifying distance, to make explicit some of the things that they accept simply as 'there' and unalterable ... This was why questions like, 'How do you see Rotherham?' or 'How do you find Rotherham?' got one nowhere. The problem was that people simply didn't understand their lives in these ways: they lacked the instruments and, more importantly, they lacked these perceptual techniques because of the relation to their experience that the necessities of their lives mediated. (Charlesworth 2000: 142-3)

Therefore:

> When asked for an opinion of Rotherham this woman felt the one word, 'crap', uttered with a blank face, as though the question was one of an imbecile, in the tones of tolerant self-evidence and complete seriousness, was a satisfactory description of the place ... She reaches spontaneously for 'crap', the immediacy of her response shows that the response is not one that issues from a careful weighing of possible responses; she is not contemplating different aspects of her perception or experience, but feels 'crap' captures the experience of stultifying banality the town engenders ... It crystallises in a condensed meaning, a whole relation to the world, attitude to existence and being, and instantiates this in a sense that relates to the referential-whole of their lives ... Rotherham-crap is a direct expression of her experience ... [This] description takes the form of direct expression of experience that is primordially encountered. Instead of reports of a reflective, deliberative, aesthetic kind, one finds expressions that are closer to pain behaviour in form. (Charlesworth 2000: 114 and 119)

It is for this reason that Merleau-Ponty (1962: 178; also Merleau-Ponty 1964: 22) distinguishes between 'second order' expression and 'first order' or 'authentic' speech. The former is essentially 'speech about speech' and therefore a representative form of speech that 'sees itself' rather than the thoughts and feelings of a speaking subject with a certain style of being-in-the-world, which it actually conceals. The latter consists of the originating expressions that are formulated *for the first time* and which capture how the body-subject is enveloped by the social and economic landscape. These 'first order' articulations are therefore our primary meanings that 'feel themselves' rather than 'see themselves' and, as such, are prior to, and therefore arouse, the 'second order' thoughts that serve to conceal the primacy of experience. Capturing this 'authentic' form of speech as it is formulated unselfconsciously 'on the spot' ('Rotherham is crap') offers us a way of appreciating how perception and practice emanates from the density of lived experience. However, authentic speech is not only evident in unselfconscious and awkward terminology, such as 'crap', but also in the way speech operates in daily life: 'Our view of man will remain superficial so long as we fail to go back to that origin [of speech]' (Merleau-Ponty 1962: 214). Pearson's (2001) fascinating ethnography of recreational drug users in Inner London exemplifies how 'authentic' speech about drug use is best captured in these everyday terms (rather than through the mobilisation of 'why?' questions) when he quotes the following respondents:

> I'd had a right good go at it, trimmed it right back. Now I've got to bag all up all the rubbish haven't I? I hate that bit of the job, kept putting it off, putting it off. Anyway, last Sunday I thought, Fuck it. Jobs got to be done. Got in the garden with a can of beer, rolled a joint, and just got on with it.

> Are these people who work on the trains stupid or what? I was going up to Manchester, and I nipped out in the corridor for a puff. There I am puffing away, and along comes the ticket inspector. I thought 'Oh fucking hell, what's going to happen here?' I mean I had a ticket and all that, but .... He goes, 'Excuse me Sir, this is a non smoking compartment'. I goes, 'sorry mate, I thought you could smoke in the corridor, I'll put it out'. He didn't notice nothing. Just punched my ticket and walked off.

I discuss the articulatory authority of the experiencing subject again in Chapter 4 when I show that unselfconscious and so-called 'primitive responses' such as 'I don't know', 'it came naturally', 'it just happened' reveal more about the aetiology of crime and drug taking in deprived urban areas than the 'reasoned responses' that are usually sought by social researchers. I will therefore argue that such 'reasoned' responses conceal more than they reveal.

On Subject-Object Variability in the 'Natural Attitude'

The importance of phenomenology is that it highlights the epistemological contours of the academic relation to the field of practice and therefore the importance of assigning practical and articulatory authority to the body-subject, that is, the taken-for-granted manner in which it encounters the world that envelops it as a 'ready to hand' entity. However, although this provides us with an understanding of why the actions of the body-subject *tend* to correspond with those that are common in its life world (e.g. crime, drug-taking) and why the body-subject prefers to justify these actions in terms of its *engagement in* its practical life world (e.g. as 'it happened naturally') rather than in terms of its *engagement with* the academic life world (e.g. 'it happened because ...'), we have so far said little about the ability or tendency of the body-subject to take a critical (say, theoretical) 'point of view' of its life world as 'present at hand' rather than simply 'ready to hand'. This is significant because the relationship between drugs and crime is not simple or straightforward in the way that the 'official' political discourse suggests, that is, that drugs cause crime. Chapter 5 shows that there was variability in my interviewees' being-towards crime and drug use which varied over time. For example, although 'hard drugs' such as heroin were said to be 'everywhere' in the neighbourhoods my interviewees grew up in, and were occupying, they *initially* and *intentionally* avoided these drugs. Thiele (1995) argues that the challenge here is to acknowledge and understand that although the daily environment of human being is largely composed of what is 'ready to hand', the intentional detachment of something extant for intensive scrutiny (i.e. as 'present to hand') remains possible. Herein things come to be revealed as objects that permit focused observation, contemplation and interpretation.

Specifically, Heidegger argues that our 'average everyday' mode of being-in-the-world is inauthentic because *Dasein* becomes immersed in its practical concern with 'getting on with things' according to 'the way things are' (Heidegger 1962, 1978; see also Bourdieu 1977, 1990, 2000). In other words, the 'average everyday' mode of being for Dasein is inauthentic because it falls into, and becomes lost within, its 'they-self' which is a form of being that is complicit with the demands of its practical, everyday life world with-others (Heidegger 1962: 220; see also Heidegger 1978). And this absorption in its inauthentic they-self means that Dasein, in its default position, is unable to reach a genuine self-understanding or to find and grasp its own 'outmost possibilities':

> Being-with-one-another dissolves one's own Dasein completely into the kind of Being of 'the Others', in such a way, indeed, that the Others, as distinguishable and explicit, vanish more and more ... The Self of everyday Dasein is [therefore] the *they-self*, which we distinguish from *authentic Self* – that is, from the Self which has been taken hold of in its own way. As they-self, the particular Dasein has been dispersed into the 'they', and must first find itself. (Heidegger 1962: 164 and 167)

However, unlike the Dasein that is a product of the objective regularities that constitute the social and economic landscape it occupies – as ready to hand – and therefore permanently lost to its they-self, Heidegger argues that Dasein also has the potential to achieve authenticity (Heidegger 1962, 1978; see also Lucas 2002; Stewart 2002; Kisiel 2002). First, Dasein has a dual ontological status which is split between its lostness in its inauthentic they-self and its capacity for authentic selfhood, with the former repressing but not extinguishing the latter (Heidegger 1962, 1978). This means, of course, that Dasein can never *fully* identify with its location on the social and economic landscape and so is never fully domesticated or at-home in the location it inhabits. Second, this split ontological status of Dasein means that encounters with differentiated 'others' can disrupt its lostness because its (positive or negative) relation to these differentiated others can instantiate a mode of its possible self-relation and thus induce an anxious realisation of itself as an individual with an life to lead (Heidegger 1962, 1978). In other words, the differentiated 'other' constitutes a 'voice of conscience' that awakens Dasein by throwing it into an anxious confrontation with its own individuality (i.e. its lostness in its 'existential actuality') and its potentiality (i.e. its 'existential potentiality'). This necessitates an ethic of 'being towards care', which is the subject of Chapters 5, 6 and 7. These chapters discuss how disturbing encounters with various forms of 'other' (e.g. problematic, normalised) produced an individualised being-towards crime and drugs (e.g. '*I* don't want to end up like that heroin user'), which brings the variable complexity of my respondents' orientation to crime and drugs into focus.

Conclusion

This chapter has discussed the epistemological limitations of social theories of crime and drug use outlined in Chapter 2. The limitations of these established perspectives emanate from the epistemological relation that social scientists have to the social practices that they observe and seek to explain. This epistemological relation is based on their spatial and temporal distance from practice. In possessing spatial distance from the social and economic world that the subjects of their attention inhabit, social science tends to view the field of practice as a 'landscape' that can be read like a map. Researchers with different theoretical orientations take their own specific points of departure, and different routes, to explain how people arrive at destinations such as crime and drug use. In possessing temporal distance from practice, social science tends to assume that the subjects of their attention similarly objectify their own practices and that they are therefore capable of providing 'reasoned reasons' for what they do. The phenomenological ideas expounded in these chapters demonstrated the limitations of these approaches. Looking at the social and economic landscape from above, and demanding the same of research subjects, demonstrates an oversight to the notion that those landscapes constitute 'lived space' for those subjects who therefore see them from *within* rather than *above*. And seeking to understand the rationalities that govern practice from a distance, rather than those that emerge 'in the thick of things', demonstrates an oversight to the immediacy with which the body-subject engages in social practice. All of this adds up to a need to assign *practical* and *articulatory* authority to the body-subject. To illustrate this point, this chapter discussed examples in the work of others which provide an understanding of the immediacy of social practice ('I didn't even have to tell myself to go there') as well as the unselfconscious mode of communication that emerges from *within* rather than *above* the field of practice ('Rotherham is shit'). Finally, the chapter emphasised the importance of understanding how and when the body-subject deems it necessary to adopt a distant view of the social and economic landscape, and their practice. These ideas will inform Chapters 4-7 where I discuss my own data about the criminal involvements and drug use of a sample of people living in deprived urban areas.

Chapter 4

'Natural Attitudes' Towards Recreational Crime and Drugs

Introduction

In this chapter I develop a phenomenological understanding of 'recreational' crime and drug use, that is, what is often referred to as 'petty crime' and 'playful' use of 'soft drugs'. I start the chapter by returning to my discussion, in Chapter 3, of the academic and practical 'points of view'. This time I am concerned to unravel the epistemological and social consequences that result following the imposition of one (academic view) over the other (practical view). Following Bourdieu (1992), I refer to this as 'symbolic violence' because the imposition of the academic point of view involves the violation of a whole way of being, seeing and speaking 'practically'. First I discuss the social and personal consequences of my respondents' acquiescence to my invitations to them to reflect on the reasons for their actions. 'Looking back' with the 'benefit of hindsight' they would always describe their actions as 'stupid' even though this contradicted the non-reasoned reasons that they provided elsewhere when they were describing their practices, in their own terms, from within 'the thick of it'. Encouraging respondents to offer 'second order' representations of practice as 'stupid' therefore violated the 'first order' articulations of practice that they offered elsewhere which, of course, has epistemological consequences for social researchers. But it also has consequences for the subjects of research that have a tendency to adopt a subordinate position when invited into social science interviews and whom, as a consequence, offer a point of view on what they do that is incongruent with the 'average everyday' point of view that they carry with them.

Second, I discuss how the imposition of 'points of view' is not simply a matter of concern for the conduct of social science and therefore something that can be overcome with 'better' social research practice. Conversely, it is tied up with the relations of power and domination that prevail in the societies that social science is enmeshed in more generally. Following Bourdieu and Passeron (1977), then, I show that social inequalities are actually constituted via the imposition of arbitrary 'points of view' which serve as exclusionary mechanisms, especially when they are accepted by dominated groups as legitimate rather than arbitrary. I show this with reference to the education system that is constituted upon *bourgeois parlance* that dominated groups do not possess. As practitioners of *working class parlance* my respondents were ill-equipped to 'grasp' the bourgeois parlance necessary to succeed within the education system. However, their misrecognition of the 'natural legitimacy' (as opposed to arbitrary nature) of bourgeois parlance led them to internalise the consequences of their 'educational failures' which they talked about in terms of a 'personal deficit', for example, by referring to themselves as 'not very clever' or 'thick'. They never referred to their experiences in terms of exclusion or as a consequence of their domination by other social groups. When placed alongside the proximity to necessity that was a consequence of their residence in deprived urban areas, I show how these educational 'failures' reinforced their imminent relation to the future and thus quasi-bodily orientation to take-up opportunities as they presented themselves. Of import here was their constant exposure to the objective regularity of crime and drug use since this generated normative perceptions that were oriented to and complicit with those objective regularities, and therefore a doxic relation to these activities. This was particularly evident in the way my respondents talked about recreational crime and drug use as activities they engaged in because 'everyone was doing it', as well activities that 'just happened' as they were immersed 'in the thick of it' rather than prior contemplated.

Symbolic Violence of the Imposition of the Social Scientific Point of View

Chapter 3 discussed how practitioners of the different theoretical perspectives of crime and drug use outlined in Chapter 2 acknowledged their epistemological differences, but also how they thought their differences were solely a result of how they viewed happenings on the social and economic landscape. It also pointed out that there has been an epistemological silence regarding the key similarity that unites these various social theories of crime and drug use. This similarity is the social science 'point of view' that each of the perspectives shared which is manifest in the tendency to view the life world as a 'landscape' to be observed from above.

The consequences of the epistemological silence concerning this shared social scientific 'point of view' extend far beyond the tendency to represent social practices, such as crime and drug use, from a particular point of view. That is to say there is more at stake here than the mere production of competing 'points of view' that are the product of particular forms of being-in-the-world, where the priority given to one (the social science view) conceals the existence of the other (the practical view) thereby simply necessitating the revelation of that other point of view. Conversely, the successful domination of the *arbitrary* social science 'point of view' over 'other' points of view produces a misrecognition of the ontological status of that dominant view, which is that it constitutes *the* legitimate point of view rather than the imposition of a cultural arbitrary by an arbitrary power. Bourdieu and Passeron (1977: 4) refer to such perceptive domination as 'symbolic violence', which occurs when the practitioners of a point of view:

> ... manage to impose meanings and to impose them as legitimate by concealing the power relations which are the basis of its force, add[ing] its own specifically symbolic force to those power relations.

These relations of linguistic force and domination are at their most potent in interview situations where the interviewer and interviewee entirely accept the legitimacy of the social scientific point of view and therefore fail to question its ontological status even when it is apparent that the questions that are produced from that social science point of view are meaningless to the interviewee who is unable to formulate a 'satisfactory' response as a consequence (Allen 2005c). This might occur, for example, when an interviewee issues a response such as 'I do not know what you mean', yet the interviewer responds in kind by rephrasing the question, in order to accumulate a 'satisfactory' response from the social science point of view, rather than reflecting on the point of view from which the first question and answer were articulated, i.e. by seeking to understand the epistemological status of the first question and answer.

Even when researchers are aware of the arbitrary nature of the social scientific point of view, a key problem is that 'policy funders' of research misrecognise the arbitrary nature of the spatially and temporally distant view of the social and economic landscape that they share with social scientists. This 'epistemic doxa' of the policy funder results in their demand for social scientists that will accumulate a set of affirmative answers to a coherent (from the social scientific point of view) series of questions. In my own case, research funders were seeking affirmative answers to questions that invited interviewees to reflect (from the same spatial and temporal distance from social practice as the policy funder and social scientist) on 'how' and 'why' they were involved in crime and drug use. The linguistic violence contained in these demands was no more apparent than in the answers produced by the respondents who acquiesced to the invitation to reflect on their social practices from the distance demanded, even though it was apparent that the 'reasoned reasons' that they provided for their involvement in crime and drugs concealed the 'non-reasoned reasons' they gave at other points in the interview and which will be discussed later in the chapter. Respondents were uncritical of questions that imposed a spatial and temporal distance between them and their involvements in crime and drug use and, indeed, even welcomed the chance to 'look back' with the 'benefit of hindsight' and formulate 'reasoned reasons' for what they had done:

> Erm, with me, *looking back on it now, I can look back on it now* and say it was resentment against my father really. It was more of a rebellion against him and his authority than anything else ... It's a big issue with me dealing with my relationship towards my father ... Coz he used to say to me mam, he used to call me 'that son of yours'. He never used to call me by me name. He called the others Dave, John and Tracey, but he would just say 'that son of yours', 'where's that son of yours'? You know what I mean? He would never use me name, when he spoke to me he spoke to me directly, he never used to say Norman or ... So I always thought, why does he resent me, is it because of my [clubbed] foot?
>
> Norman

Dev similarly welcomed the 'opportunity' that was presented for him to 'look back' but his reference to the 'wondering whether' that this entailed implicitly suggests that his act of reflection constituted a 'second order' representation that did not correspond with the 'first order' representations that he and others gave elsewhere in their interviews:

> Err, I think I was just seeing how far I could push it, you know, before the authorities, before I got caught, *looking back*, before I got caught I think .... *I think* I blamed, I blamed a lot you know, when I was growing up the amount of times the police came to my house

for, err, for like the neighbours had phoned up the police because my dad was badly beating up my mum and then the police would come and my mam, my dad would say well it's a domestic so you can't get involved and that was the case then … And my mam used to say oh it's OK now, so you know, *I wonder if I was, yeah, rebelling against*, I could not understand why the police didn't intervene, you know, err, (pause), that's it really.   Dev

Had I neglected to ask questions designed to elicit 'first order' representations of crime and drug use (i.e. as they occurred 'in the thick of it') at other points in the interviews, my respondents' acquiescence to the social science point of view might, therefore, have *only* resulted in their production of 'second order' representations that linguistically violated the practices they were designed to elucidate.

This brings me to another key issue. Specifically, the second order discourses produced 'on reflection' by Norman and Dev exemplify a key commonality between each of the theoretical perspectives outlined in Chapter 2. This is the supposition of an epistemic distance between thought and practice which means that body-subject is assumed to objectify the marginal social positions that it occupies and, through this, arrives at an understanding of the 'constrained choices' that are open to it. The main implication here is that involvement in crime and drugs are not *entirely* the fault of the individuals concerned. However, herein lies the key issue. Although involvement in crime and drugs is presented as *not entirely* the fault of the individuals concerned, there is an implicit suggestion that crime and drug use is also *not entirely* the result of their occupation of marginal social positions and therefore partially a product of the 'choice reasoning' of the body-subject. For example, ecological theorists might argue that crime and drug use occur at the point when a fatalist point of view (e.g. 'I've nothing to lose so I may as well steal') about the social world is formulated, whereas post-modernist writers emphasise how crime and drug use tends to occur when the ethical point of view justifies it (e.g. 'Selling drugs is the only way to provide my daughter with the upbringing she deserves'). So some 'fault' is assigned to the individuals concerned, albeit implicitly, and the reason for this is that the social scientific point of view demands it but then seeks to 'cover it up' with references to 'constrained choices' that deflect our attention onto the social situation of the body-subject. Specifically, this is because the imposition of the social scientific point of view imbues the body-subject with a false spatial and temporal distance from its own practices which demands that it engages in 'reasoned reasoning'. This scholarly demand for 'reasoned reasoning' commits 'conceptual violence' on the practical and articulatory authority of the body-subject because it perforce necessitates that it objectifies its own 'deviant' acts 'with the benefit of reasoned hindsight' which means, of course, that it will acknowledge that those actions were constituted on deficient acts of constrained reasoning:

> [The social science point of view] leads him (*sic*) to cancel out the specificity of practical logic; either by assimilating it to scholastic knowledge but in an way that is fictitious and purely theoretical ('on paper' and without practical consequences), or by consigning it to radical otherness, to the existence and worthlessness of the 'barbarous' or the vulgar, which, as Kant's notion of 'barbarous taste' pertinently reminds us, is nothing other than the barbarian within.
> (Bourdieu 2000: 51)

When my respondents were encouraged to view their practices from the spatial and temporal distance of the social scientist, then, they provided answers that constructed their involvement in crime and drug use practices as the product of deficient reasoning, even though it was clear that they had not seen it that way *at the time* when they were involved in these activities. For example, when forced into an act of reflection, Bob described how the 'empty time' created by unemployment had resulted in his greater involvement with crime and drugs and that 'it looked stupid *now*':

Bob:	I just used to drink at night, before I'd go out and got drunk, so I'd just used to sit down and watch TV and have a drink, whatever. ... 'Till I lost me job, and I was there everyday 'cause all them lot never worked, they was all signing on and that's when it started.
CA:	Did you try ... you know when you lost the first job, did you try getting work after that?
Bob:	Yeah.
CA:	When you were in the hostel, yeah?
Bob:	Yeah, I'm still applying for jobs.
CA:	What happened?
Bob:	I went to two jobs and I didn't get either of them two, and then I started working for like, an agency, where you can just work what days you want, you know get employment from that agency, whether I felt like it or not.
CA:	Yeah, where were we? I've forgotten where we were (laughter).
Bob:	About hostels.
CA:	Yeah, yeah. So you didn't get the other jobs?
Bob:	Yeah, I started working for that agency, and it was just like ... just going in whenever I wanted, so all the other days I was just getting drunk, with all them lot, and going out with them lot, and going out with them lot, so, and I met Aidan after that ... Me and Aid, he just started doing stupid things, didn't bother working 'cause, yeah, we used to make more money doing that than what I did on that agency, so ... we was just going out, doing burg[lary] every night and stupid things.
CA:	Where about were you burgling then?
Bob:	Just up here [PLACE NAME], everywhere, just all round here, round my area and that.
CA:	And how often were you doing it?
Bob:	Every other night, and something. We always used to get the money and then go to Blackpool for a few days and then come back ... *It look's stupid now.*
CA:	Was there any reason why you got involved in burglary, rather than anything else?
Bob:	No, I just come out of the pub one night, and Aidan said, like 'come-on, we'll go and rob a shop' so I said 'right, whatever', drunk and just went and did it, and then, did it a couple of nights later, drunk again, and then, after that just thought it was so easy so I carried on doing it.

The implicit logic of the 'constrained choice' thesis is therefore as follows: Since a 'constrained choice' still constitutes a 'choice', it follows that there are other options and that, therefore, the objectification of the social and economic landscape by the body-subject that has become involved in crime and drugs (in this case Bob) has clearly resulted in the wrong option being chosen. Put another way, since normative standards of conduct provide an implicit benchmark for what constitutes a responsible choice (or act of human agency), and is the measure against which action can be judged, then a conscious rejection of those norms in favour of 'others' constitutes a deficient act of reasoning – even if that choice is deemed 'understandable' given the body-subject's occupation of a marginal social and economic position. The implication, then, is that the social scientific point of view constructs *conforming* and *deficient* acts of agency as differentially constituted (the latter is the product of a 'wrong' choice) and therefore crime and drug use as deficient acts of agency – even if protagonists of the range of theoretical perspectives discussed in Chapter 2 do not explicitly present it as such.

On the Practical Point of View

The notion that the body-subject adopts a spatial and temporal distance from its practice is based on a misrecognition of the arbitrariness of the academic form of being that, unacknowledged as such, results in the form of 'scholastic episemocentrism' that this book has shown to be ubiquitous in the field of crime and drugs research. For this reason, practitioners of the phenomenological point of view in philosophy, such as Martin Heidegger and Maurice Merleau-Ponty, and in sociology, such as Pierre Bourdieu, have argued that social scientists are no less strangers to their own practices than they are to the strange practices they observe, and that they therefore need to give:

> ... methodical consideration [to] the difference between the theoretical viewpoint and the practical viewpoint, which, ... is obligatory in the conduct of the most concrete operations of research in the social sciences – conducting an interview, describing a practice, drawing up a genealogy, *etc.* To perform the conversion of the gaze that is required for correct understanding of practice perceived in terms of its own logic, one has to take a theoretical viewpoint on the theoretical viewpoint and draw out all the theoretical and methodological consequences of the (in one sense too obvious) fact that vis-à-vis the situation and the behaviours that he observes, the scientist (ethnologist, sociologist, or historian) is not in the position of an active agent, involved in the action, invested in the game and its stakes.
> (Bourdieu 2000: 54)

It follows that there is a phenomenological necessity to adopt a critical stance vis-à-vis the social scientific point of view *of practice* (that provided the epistemic basis of the questions asked in the interview situations described above) in order to better understand the practical view of practice. Although Heidegger, Merleau-Ponty and Bourdieu are agreed on this point, however, they also have differences. For Bourdieu (1990), then, the implications of a sociological phenomenology extend beyond the need to ask better questions *about practice.* A sociological phenomenology also demands to know about the social conditions that mould the 'being-in-the-world' of the body-subject and, in doing so, makes possible some practices but not others, as he points out in a discussion of the limitations of philosophical phenomenology:

> The mode of knowledge that can be called 'phenomenological' sets out ... the primary relationship of familiarity with the familiar environment, and thereby bring to light the

truth of that experience which, however illusory it may appear from the 'objective' viewpoint, remains perfectly *qua* experience. But it cannot go beyond a description of what specifically characterizes 'lived' experience of the social world ... This is because it excludes the question of the conditions of possibility of this experience, namely the coincidence of the objective structures and the internalized structures which provides the illusion of immediate understanding, characteristic of the practical experience of the familiar universe, and which at the same time excludes from that experience any inquiry as to its own conditions of possibility. (Bourdieu 1990: 25-6)

We are moving here from questions of practice (manifest in the questions that are asked about practice) to questions of 'being' which, as we saw in Chapter 2, have been explored through the phenomenological concepts of habitus (Bourdieu), Dasein (Heidegger) and body-subject (Merleau-Ponty). From the sociological point of view, 'being' is a product of historical exposure to social conditions in the (privileged, marginal) social spaces occupied which are deposited, stored and incorporated into a way of being-in-the-world that provides the body-subject with practical and articulatory authority in the (privileged, marginal) social spaces that it occupies.

Now we have already seen that the social scientific point of view (or rather *epistemic doxa*) emerges from a form of being that is constituted upon a social and epistemological break from everyday practice, which is a consequence of the institutional privilege afforded to social scientists and that enables them to create spatial and temporal distance between themselves and everyday practice which is therefore viewed 'on the social and economic landscape'. The practical and articulatory authority that social scientists claim for themselves in the scientific field (and which is invested in them by respondents that are invited to participate in the social scientific field on terms dictated by the social scientist) therefore results in symbolic violence which is a version of the 'truth' that corresponds with the social science worldview rather than the practical worldview that we are now seeking to understand. Although we saw above that this *inappropriately* led some of my respondents to reflexively describe their 'deviant' practices as deficient acts of reasoning ('I was stupid'), the key question now concerns how the institutionalisation of this relation between the social scientist and respondent becomes inscribed in the everyday being of the respondent.

For Bourdieu, the problematic of 'being' is really an issue of power and domination in society more generally and this can be seen far and beyond the interview situation that I have analysed so far. Thus, Bourdieu has analysed social consequences of the imposition of arbitrary points of view, possessed by dominant social groups, in the fields of science (Bourdieu 1990, 2000), culture (Bourdieu 1984, 1993) language and discourse (Bourdieu 1992) education (Bourdieu and Passeron 1977) and so on. His work on education is of particular relevance to my concern to understand issues of power, domination and the 'being-in-the-world' of my respondents. For Bourdieu, parallels can be drawn between the authoritative relation that social science has to those that it invites to participate in science (because participants do not possess the conceptual instruments to adequately represent themselves within the scientific field) *and* the authoritative relation between pedagogic authority in the educational system (which is an instrument for the reproduction of legitimate culture as defined by the dominant classes that populate the educational system) and those that are subjected to pedagogic communication without having the conceptual instruments to comprehend it.

> There exist at the two extremities of the scale two well-defined modes of speech: *bourgeois parlance* and *common parlance* ... The bourgeois language can be handled only by those who, thanks to the school, have been able to convert their practical mastery, acquired by familiarization within the family group, into a second degree aptitude for the quasi-scholarly handling of language. Given that the informative efficiency of pedagogic communication is always a function of the receivers' linguistic competence (defined as their variably complete mastery of the code of [school] language) the unequal social-class distribution of *educationally profitable linguistic capital* constitutes one of the best hidden mediations through which the relationship ... between social origins and scholastic achievement is set up.   (Bourdieu and Passeron 1977: 115-16)

The key point here is that the social origins of my own respondents were in what are now termed deprived (formerly working class) urban areas; their parents had either been located in working class occupations or unemployed and there was little evidence of a history of educational success within their families. They commonly described negative experiences of school which suggested that the pedagogic form of communication that is a product and producer of *bourgeois parlance* (Bourdieu and Passeron 1977) committed linguistic violence on their *common parlance*. Furthermore, since my respondents did not recognise the arbitrary nature of the competence that is required to adequately receive pedagogic communication (and that the cultural legitimacy of those that master it is a product of their social domination rather than innate superiority), their 'failure' to grasp it inscribed itself on their being to such an extent that they talked about 'feeling incompetent'. This was manifest in the self-descriptions provided by respondents such as Grant. Grant's perception that the source of his educational difficulties were 'a personality thing' and that he was somebody that was 'not very clever' and whom 'lacked confidence' constituted a misrecognition of the arbitrary nature of the pedagogic power and domination that inscribed this 'social failure' on his being and thereby led him to produce these self-descriptions:

CA: How did you get involved in drinking everyday during the week?
Grant: I don't know, just, it was, it just freed the boredom up, I don't know, just boredom, lack of confidence, but I don't know, it's just no confidence, personality sort of thing, I think it was.
CA: Did school not help you with that?
Grant: No.
CA: For your confidence, No?
Grant: No, I just couldn't hack it, you know, I'm not very clever.
CA: What exactly was it about school that you didn't like?
Grant: I don't know, I used to like, you know, I liked the games and that, you know, games, and that, you know, I really liked the sporting side of it, but anything else, just wasn't interested.

The tendency for many criminologists to focus on whether or not offenders are in attendance at school, and therefore whether they have 'time on their hands' to commit crime (e.g. Cavadino 1994; Hagell and Newburn 1994; Horney *et al* 1995; MacKenzie and De Li 2002) is therefore somewhat misplaced. Some of my respondents were in attendance at school whereas others were not, yet both groups had become involved in crime and drug use. The key commonality between those that were in attendance at school, and those that were not (and that is often overlooked by a criminology that addresses educational issues yet remains untouched by some of the key works in the sociology of education) relates to the class biases built into the education system that, when mobilised through pedagogic form of communication, result in the marginalisation of young people from already marginal social groups (Bourdieu and Passeron 1977; Willis 1977; Charlesworth 2000). The deep sense of failure that inscribes itself within their already marginalised bodies effectively closes down education as a viable route to the future. When this sense of failure is placed alongside the fact that my respondents had grown up, and still lived in, some of the most deprived urban areas in Greater Manchester, the imminent proximity to necessity that this implied (which involved a concern with 'getting by' today and a concomitant rejection of the future orientation necessary to engage with an education system that demands a strategic approach to the accumulation of the qualifications and cultural assets on offer therein) resulted in a mode of being-towards-the-world that sought to grasp opportunities for satisfying necessity that were easily available to 'the likes of us'. Kal described the opportunities that were available to the likes of him as earning money 'some other way', which involved crime:

CA: How do you mean [crime is] 'a way of life'?
Kal: Don't know, it's like, other people like, don't do anything like, they're just good and all that, but I can't read or write proper, thing's like that, so, I don't really like entertaining getting jobs and things like that, I'd rather earn the money some other way.

For Kenny and David it involved working on markets, and 'robbing', rather than going to school when they were of school age:

Because I used to burgle I used to burgle people's houses and then just for getting someone's video and CD player I used get £70 each for them back in the 80s and instead of going to school I used to make £140 a day so that kind of saved me from going to school.   Kenny

Nothing they just half the time I didn't even go to school and when I was at school I didn't really like school so I didn't really go to school you see I used to always wag school always off school and now I wish I had just have got my head down. You just don't listen to people when you are young you do your own thing and I really wished I had stayed at school things like that ... I just didn't want to go to school I was working on the markets and getting a tenner a day on the markets and its lot of money when you are young so I used to wag school and go out robbing, depending on what time of year it was ... I used to go to school for gym and cookery or woodwork now and again that was it really and I didn't really go to school that's probably why I started getting in trouble and things like that.   David

The interesting aspect of what David says, above, is not simply the manner in which it reveals a form of being that is towards involvement in crime. It also concerns the manner in which he inserts a distance between his own subjectivity and the object of his concern, which is the educational system, and states that, on reflection, he 'wishes' that he had tried harder at school even though his direct encounters with the educational system *at the time* resulted in the necessary self-elimination of this option (cf. Bourdieu and Passeron 1977). Nevertheless, although these educational experiences left this mark on my respondents (whose internalisation of the cultural discrimination that marked them out as failures resulted in their misrecognition of their own 'stupidity' and therefore doxic complicity with their own being-towards-exclusion) they only made involvement in crime and drugs a *possibilty* rather than a *certainty*. Actual involvement in specific practices, such as crime and drug use, emerges out of primary and consistent experience of social spaces where these practices are endemic. This is because it generates perceptions and aspirations that are oriented to, and thus complicit with, the objective regularities that are inscribed into the structure of practical possibilities (e.g. crime and drug use) and non-possibilities (e.g. a career in higher education) in those social spaces. This was particularly evident in one of the ways in which my respondents sought to explain their involvement in crime and drug use, which was with reference to the objective regularity of what went on in the marginal social spaces that they occupied. Specifically, they referred to their involvement as something that was complicit with 'what everyone else was doing':

> Just watching them lot, doing their crime, and that just made me go and do it all day ... The lads I used to hang around with, they used to be all into things like robbing cars, and doing burglaries and all that, so I just got into them ... It's easy to get involved 'cause it's the company what you hang around with ... Yeah, but the way I got brought up, is, that I seen them all ... into drugs and that.					Kevin

> It's like, everybody were doing it, so ... it's like a common thing, you know, I suppose, everyone did it, everybody, that I knew did it ... It's just a normal thing to do then, when you're a kid isn't it ... I don't know [why we] ... were doing it.					Grant

> Everyone else was doing it [cocaine], all me mates were doing it ... So I just go with them, do what they do, and just go with them.					Norman

The discourses produced by Kevin, Grant and Norman are not only indicative of the doxic complicity that existed between my respondents and the social spaces they occupied. They are also indicative of the 'practical authority' of the body-subject whose form of 'being-towards' what went on in those spaces (crime, drug use) resulted in a dispositional orientation towards those practices which would 'just happen' as and when the opportunity arose 'in the thick' of social life. This was most apparent when my respondents communicated with me through 'first order' language:

CA:		If you can start by how you got involved in crime, how did you come to get involved in crime?
Spencer:	It's just doing things with me brother, and going out ... It just happened like, come across something and pinched it, and then just, whatever ... Petty little things like CDs and tapes to get some money.
CA:		How did you start doing that, though, what was going on?
Spencer:	Just boredness ... It's just like... it's not something you plan, you're gonna go out and do, it's just, you're out there and you think, you come at the shop and

do it, you don't think you offend anyone, really, you just … take it, and that's it really …

CA: Yeah. Being bored?

Spencer: Maybe watch the telly, but I just said, when you go outside, and there's nothing to do, and then you have a wander somewhere, and you come across something you can pinch and you take it. Just really the same thing, we'd just hang about until you get bored, and then … maybe think of somewhere to go, but you're not really thinking about pinching something, you're just thinking about going there, and then you get there, and you see an opportunity, and you think 'Well I'm bored, I may as well just go and do it'.

And:

If we seen somebody with a phone, and somebody would *just* take the phone off them. If we seen like a nice car or something, we take the car, if we see a, just a little car parked anywhere, you know could go and just rob it as well, anything what comes into our head what we do, what we do, we just do it.

Kevin

And:

CA: Tell us how you first got involved in crime, then.

Kal: It's just like when you're young and messing about and that, and then you just get in trouble and that, and then when you get older, I don't know, like you do things for money and that, and like, when you've got no money, don't know, really.

CA: What was the first time you got involved in anything, how did it happen?

Kal: Erm … Think it was round here, we was all messing about or something, and I smashed a window over the road there, with a crow bar, and that's how it all started off, from smashing windows, to going pinching cars … for no reason, and things like that. I don't know, it just all leads to a different thing.

CA: Do you know why you did it, like?

Kal: I don't know. It's just things that happen.

Kenny and Mike provided a similar description of the 'practical authority' of the body-subject and its ability to perform a practical operation that was a product of quasi-bodily orientation to opportunities for crime that presented themselves 'in the thick of it', this time by referring to crime as something that happened 'on the spur of the moment':

Most of the time it was spur of the moment.

Kenny

It's just a spur of the moment thing, well it was with me. I didn't go out and say 'oh I'll go out and rob this car' or go out and it's just there and it just happens and that's how it used to be like … It just happened when you were out it was just the spur of the moment you didn't really plan it or 'owt like that. The only thing we used to plan was when we used to go and knock the buffet trains when we were young and break into them at night time but that was the only thing we used to plan like, nothing else … So it's just the spur of the moment thing like when you go out like when you are out with the lads and things like that when you are younger and you go out on the beer and then some trouble starts somewhere then you just all get in there and have a little fight its just what you used to do

when you were younger and things like that you are always fighting amongst yourselves
and just I don't know really it just keeps you on your toes and so.   Mike

And as activities that were 'opportunistic':

> On my estate, a lot of the kids we were, you know, we were all that much alike, but yeah,
> I mean the lads I knocked with, they were doing it, and yeah everyone was at it ... It was
> just, I don't know, it's just opportunist, you know, you go looking for any, you come
> across it really, you know what I mean?   John

The latter quotation, from John, is particularly interesting because it illustrates a
common tendency among the respondents, which was an inability to provide
'reasoned reasons' ('I don't know') for their action. This is significant because it
highlights how a social scientific demand for my respondents to provide 'reasoned
reasons' for their involvement in crime and drug use only encountered epistemic
silence (articulated here as 'I don't know' or 'it just happened') because, as each of the
respondents quoted above show, the authors of these practices were unable to provide
such reasoned reasoning. This moves us, then, from a concern with the 'practical
authority' of the body-subject, that seeks to understand practice 'as it happens', to a
concern with the 'articulatory authority' of that same body-subject (rather than social
science) which reveals why 'the work of articulating that experience [is] so difficult
and ... why dominated people are so often reduced to silence in the face of [social
science] discourse' (Charlesworth 2000: 121).

> Our view of man will remain superficial so long as we fail to go back to that origin [of
> speech], so long as we fail to find, beneath the chatter of words, the primordial silence, and
> as long as we do not describe the action which breaks this silence.
>
> (Merleau-Ponty 1962: 214)

The notion that John cannot produce an 'articulate' answer to 'why' questions about
his involvement in crime and drugs suggests that there is collusion between the urban
social conditions that produce perception and expectation and the mental structures of
perception and expectation that reinforce those social conditions by unquestioningly
accepting their apparent inevitablism (doxa), which becomes manifest in the inability
to articulate a 'reasonable' explanation for practice. Given this correspondence between
the objective structure of urban social space and the mental structure of perception, the
social world appears as self-evident (i.e. beyond exploration and therefore explanation)
rather than an object of knowledge whereas perception becomes 'possessed by' and
'attuned to' the social space it occupies to such an extent that its involvement in that
space takes place without reference to 'reasoned reasons'. And since 'thrownness' into
that social space is the primary condition of involvement in the world, the often crude
and unselfconscious form of language that is used to articulate the imminent form of
'being-towards' that space (that is indicative of imminent proximity to necessity and
therefore a relation to the world that is based on a lack of epistemic distance) is different
to the form of language that is possible for the social scientist and others that are able to
stand at a distance from necessity, rather than in proximity to it, and for whom the use
of language is attached to the struggle for distinction and cultural domination:

It is in the relation to language that one finds the principle underlying the most visible differences between bourgeois language and working class language. What has often been described as the tendency of bourgeois language to abstraction, formalism, intellectualism and euphemistic moderation should be seen primarily as the expression of a socially constituted disposition towards language .... The distinguished distance, prudent ease and contrived naturalness which are the foundations of every code of society manners, are opposed to the expressiveness or expressionism of working class language; which manifests itself in the tendency ... to shun the bombast of fine words and the turgidity of grand emotions, through banter, rudeness and ribaldry. (Bourdieu and Passeron 1977: 116)

This unselfconsciously crude form of language was present in the descriptions that my respondents often provided in their answers to questions about the places they had lived in. Like Charlesworth's (2000) working class respondents that described Rotherham as 'shit' as if the self-evidence of this perception, from the marginal position of a working class respondent, meant that no further explanation was required, my own respondents similarly referred to the places that they had inhabited as 'shit' without further elaborating their answer in response to 'probing' questions. Indeed, the crude and uncompromising nature of such answers were given in order to describe the utter horror and pain of exclusion in the places they had inhabited and did not even pretend to constitute a valid view that could be taken as a point of departure for a discussion about the relative merits of the places they had lived in.

Matthew: I don't know anyone else that's been in like care homes and that. People who I lived in a care home with, it weren't like a gaol, it was like a normal house, like, but I've been in children's homes, you know like proper children's homes and that, we just used to go out and just fuck about all day.
CA: What are they like as places to live?
Matthew: Shit.
CA: Yeah. Why?
Matthew: It's just horrible, it's just shit.

When it came to offering a linguistic description of involvement in crime and drug use, then, my respondents made similar recourse to an uncompromising form of language that simply presented it 'as it was' rather than sought to provide an answer that could provide the starting point for a discussion of the possible reasons for involvement in crime and drugs. The manner in which the central mode of explanation for crime and drug use was articulated in terms such as 'I just did it', 'we just did it' (which is tantamount to saying 'it was simple as that, no reason, there is nothing more to be said') was therefore prevalent in the transcripts, as indicated in the quotations above as well as those below which exemplify this tendency:

I'd just go out and do it.   Adam

Well didn't know I were gonna get into the crime, until we just started hanging round together, and we just got into it. 'Cause like we had nothing else to do, so we just done it.
                                                                                       Kevin

[We] just used to go in [PLACE NAME], I don't know, just did it, you know ... I don't know how I got involved with it.   Matthew

The other 'first order' description of involvement in crime and drugs that possessed 'articulatory authority' contained references to a 'natural inclination' towards these activities which, of course, is another way of expressing the doxic relation that existed between my respondents and the endemic nature of what went on (crime, drug use) in the social spaces they inhabited, as well as their consequent refusal to respond to social scientists demands for 'reasoned reasons'. My respondents described their involvements in crime and drug use as 'a natural progression' or 'a natural choice' for 'the likes of us':

> Err, I won't say peer pressure because I don't believe in that. I don't believe that people are gang led and all that ... I think it was just a *natural choice* ... [It was] not like one did it and we all followed kind of thing, ... [where someone would say] 'go on, it's your turn', and all that. [There was] none of that, none of that peer pressure. I don't believe in that. It was just something we got into. So a lot of older people who we seen, the older lads, they were doing things so it was just a *natural progression* that we followed them up, if you know what I mean. So basically that's how I got into it ... You went through a rite of passage, if you could say it in that term, you know what I mean? ... I just felt it's the norm. That everybody got in trouble, you know what I mean? ... [It was] like a rite of passage because, like I said before, you seen the older lads doing things when you were younger and when you got to their age, you did them. You know what I mean, so you generally just progressed up the ladder.
>
> Norman

> It's a *natural progression*. Everybody's doing it so whatever graft you are doing, what you are doing, how you're making money, everybody is grafting. It's just you are making money.
>
> Oliver

When respondents were probed, with a view to encouraging them to provide a 'second order' rationalisation of their involvement in crime and drug use, a common refrain (exemplified in many of the quotations above as well as below) was that they 'didn't really know' because these activities 'came naturally' to them and 'just happened':

> Kevin: [I] didn't know I were gonna get into the crime, ... we just got into it. 'Cause like we had nothing else to do, so we just done it ... Yeah, it just come naturally.
> CA: ...'cause you said before that you didn't think about it, it just sort of happened?
> Kevin: Yeah.

Insofar as my respondents were able to provide 'reasoned reasons' for their involvement in crime and drug use, then, this was by recourse to a 'naturalistic' discourse that served to dis-identify the author of crime and drug use with the acts that they were involved in. For example, Judith sought to displace the authorship of her mother's criminal activities onto the 'disease' of kleptomania:

> It's just that me mum was a kleptomaniac, you know what I mean? Like she stole a motorbike one time but I don't know, it might of from what I've seen, like cause we only like live with her a few times in the year and that and so, so it's like when you come home from school you was wondering whether you was going to stay at the place tonight, or whether you was like moved off, shipped out to like me mother or something.   Judith

Conclusion

This chapter has sought to develop a phenomenological understanding of 'recreational' crime and drug use. Specifically it has shown that the 'symbolic violence' that is a consequence of the imposition of the academic point of view involves the violation of a whole way of being, seeing and speaking 'there-practically'. 'Looking back' with the 'benefit of hindsight', then, my respondents would always acquiesce to invitations to describe their actions from an objectifying distance and, when they did, referred to them as 'stupid' even though this contradicted the non-reasoned reasons that they provided when they were describing their practices, in their own terms, from within 'the thick of it'. Encouraging respondents to offer 'second order' representations of practice as 'stupid' therefore linguistically violated the 'first order' articulations of practice that they offered elsewhere.

I also discussed how social inequalities are constituted via the imposition of arbitrary 'points of view' in society more generally and which serve as exclusionary mechanisms, especially when they are accepted by dominated groups as legitimate rather than arbitrary. With further reference to my own data, then, I discussed how my respondents were ill-equipped to 'grasp' the bourgeois parlance necessary to succeed within the education system as well as how their misrecognition of the 'natural legitimacy' (as opposed to arbitrary nature) of bourgeois parlance led them to internalise the consequences of their 'educational failures' which they talked about in terms of a 'personal deficit'. For example, my respondents would commonly refer to themselves as 'not very clever' or 'thick' even though they demonstrated high levels of intelligence in a variety of ways, for example by providing me with their own critique of capitalism. Despite this, however, they never referred to their own experiences in terms of exclusion or as a consequence of their domination by other social groups, indicating their practical (if not rhetorical) complicity in their own domination and exclusion. When placed alongside their proximity to economic necessity, these educational failures reinforced their imminent relation to the future and thus quasi-bodily orientation to take up opportunities as they presented themselves. Of import here was their constant exposure to the objective regularity of crime and drug use since this generated normative perceptions that were oriented to and complicit with those objective regularities, and therefore a doxic relation to these activities. This was most noticeable in the way my respondents talked about recreational crime and drug use as something they did because it was 'what everyone doing' as well as things that 'just happened' and that they therefore described as they occurred 'in the thick of it' rather than as activities that had been prior contemplated.

Chapter 5 builds on the phenomenological understanding of crime and drug use that I have sought to commence in this chapter. It does this by examining why my respondents had a doxic relation to 'recreational' drug use but why this did not *initially* translate into an equal preference for drugs such as heroin and crack cocaine. It also examines how and why my respondents subsequently engaged in serious drug use (e.g. heroin, crack) despite their initial desire to desist from such involvements.

Chapter 5

Becoming a Problematic Drug User

Introduction

Although previous chapters have argued that language ('fucking shit') and practice ('drugs came naturally', 'we just took them') emerge *from within* a form of being that is immersed in its imminent and doxic relation to the objective regularities that constitute its social world ('everyone was doing it'), the subjective relation to the world is *not simply* governed by the mundane brutality of the everyday experience of economic dispossession and constant exposure to the consequences of urban deprivation. Drawing influence from the work of Martin Heidegger, this chapter argues that the relation to the world that I have referred to as 'imminent' or 'immersed' is only sustained through what I will now refer to as 'confirming encounters', that is, social encounters *with similar others* that reinforce the self-evidence of a doxic relation to the world that 'just happens' to produce a language and practice of recreational crime and drug use. This is why Heidegger refers to the 'average everyday' mode of being as 'they-self' (which possesses a 'worldliness' that comes from its 'being-with-others') as opposed to 'myself'. The evidence of this average everyday mode of being, of course, is present in the speech forms employed by respondents which described recreational crime and drug use through the public language of 'we', for example, by expressing themselves in terms such as 'everybody was doing it'.

However, this is only part of the story. Specifically, the form of they-being that Heidegger (1962) refers to as a 'dictatorship of others' can be undermined by what he refers to as a 'call of care' (i.e. to find 'myself') which, for my respondents, was initiated by what I will be referring to as 'disturbing encounters'. The important thing to note here is that 'encounters' can only be disturbing if they have an existential basis, that is, a *specific* 'appeal' or 'meaning' to a form of being-in-the-world that is a consequence of *direct relevance* to the life being lived in that world. The first part of the chapter shows that encounters are experienced as disturbing when they project *problematic others* onto a *potential self*, that is, they provide a picture of what one could potentially become. Thus, recreational drug users with a doxic relation to drug use ('we just do it, everybody does it') frequently describe how they were disturbed by encounters with heroin users in their 'circle' ('they were dirty, scum'). Such disturbing encounters transformed their imminent relation to the world (and therefore 'worldliness') into a problematic that, as such, became a focus of thematic attention. This induced an individualised relation to the world and, in turn, ethic of being-towards-care which I show to be expressed in a much more private language of 'I', 'me', *etc.* ('I said to myself that I would never be like that').

However, 'disturbing encounters' occur in existentially different situations. Although one disturbing encounter might produce desistance from problematic drug use, another disturbing encounter might project individuals towards problematic drug use. This is exactly what happened to respondents in my sample, specifically, when *normalised others* were projected onto a *problematic self*, that is, when a normative picture of what one should be highlights the 'abnormality' of what one is. Leder's (1990) phenomenological concept of dys-appearance informs my analysis at this point. Leder argues that our mundane experience of ordinary everyday life, which we tend to take for granted, is characterised by the *disappearance* of the body-subject. However, this disappearance can be ruptured by encounters that disturb our taken-for-granted attitude towards the body-subject. This is what happened to respondents that underwent a realisation that they had suffered from sexual abuse in the course of discursive encounters with normalised others. For these respondents the once-taken-for-granted body now 'appear[ed] as a thematic focus of attention, but precisely in a dys-state' (Leder 1990: 84). As a socially and emotionally painful state of awareness of not 'matching up' to normalised others, dys-appearance resulted in a dys-state of being-towards-care ('I need something to block out *my* problem') which was different to the state of being-towards-care that produced an initial resistance towards heroin ('I am better than them with *their* heroin problems'). The nature of this difference is manifest in the way the body-subject, in this dys-state of care, had a disposition to grasp what was 'there for it' to 'numb the pain' which was the heroin that was 'everywhere' in the urban spaces they occupied. However, since *care* was still an issue for the body-subject in its dys-state of being-towards-care, it only engaged in moderate levels of heroin use via comparatively safe consumption practices such as 'chasing the dragon'.

Disturbing encounters were not, however, the only route into problematic drug use. I also discuss how this occurred following 'disturbing episodes', most notably experiences of bereavement. The final part of the chapter develops a phenomenological interpretation of insights from the sociology of death and dying literature in order to understand more about the specific 'disturbing episode' of bereavement. I argue that the sequestration of death (which has become hidden behind the walls of hospitals, mortuaries and so on) has enabled us to deny our mortality on an everyday level and thereby maintain a sense of meaningfulness. However, the sequestration of death means that experiences of bereavement are even more traumatic when they come, which momentarily undermines the sense of meaning and purpose that we establish on an everyday level. Readers that have experienced bereavement will be familiar with the consequent feeling that life and its projects (careerism, money) suddenly appear all too trivial. The recreational drug users describe similar feelings in the final part of the chapter. Although disturbing encounters with heroin users were an existential 'call' that initiated their 'being-towards-care', their pursuit of care was parasitic on their personal sense of meaningfulness which was evident in the way they made constant reference to 'I', 'me', *etc*. Conversely, the sense of meaninglessness that was engendered by bereavement was evident in the way they stared to refer to not caring about themselves, anyone or anything. This leads me to suggest that bereavement initiates a 'being-against-care' that, in contrast to the dys-appearing group, resulted in their immediate descent into serious heroin use 'big time'.

'Being-Towards-Care' and the Revulsion of Smack Heads

For Heidegger, our 'average everyday' mode of being-in-the-world is 'fallen' and immersed in a practical concern with 'getting on with things' (Heidegger, 1962, 1978) and, in doing so, human-*being* can be seen as a process of 'becoming' that occurs as Dasein constantly discloses itself-in-the-world in the course of getting on with its routine and mundane everyday activity. For example, the average-everyday tendency of Dasein to 'just do' things that 'everyone else is doing' reveals its 'they-self' and the social world as ready-to-hand, i.e. something that is 'there-for-me' and self-evident. In other words, the complicity of Dasein with-others and the social world that it inhabits (that results in its 'worldliness') reveals its 'existential actuality', that is, of what we are, who 'the likes of us' are and 'what the likes of us do'. Chapter 4 thus showed that involvements in recreational crime and drug use were 'natural inclinations' to my respondents, who approached these activities as 'ready-to-hand' and could only explain this involvement with recourse to their 'they-self', i.e. 'everybody was doing it'. And given its doxic complicity with-others and the social world, we have also already seen that Dasein is frequently unable to articulate its existential actuality in terms other than 'I just am' and 'we just do' which means that, in its default position, Dasein is unable to reach a genuine self-understanding or to find and grasp its *own* 'outmost possibilities'. In other words, lacking any conception of being other than what it is with-others (i.e. its actuality in the here and now), Dasein conflates its existential actuality with its existential potentiality in a way that blinds its ability to see its potential as anything more than it currently is with-others:

> Being-with-one-another dissolves one's own Dasein completely into the kind of Being of 'the Others', in such a way, indeed, that the Others, as distinguishable and explicit, vanish more and more.   (Heidegger 1962: 164)

Nevertheless, a key ontological claim in Heidegger is that *Dasein* also has the potential to achieve a more authentic state of individuality, in which individuality is understood as a mode of being-towards the world that is based on a critical distance rather than immanent complicity (Heidegger 1962, 1978; see also Lucas 2002; Stewart 2002; Kisiel 2002). It seems, then, that the 'everyday' mode of being-they, which was manifest in recreational crime and drug use, does not constitute a totalitarian form of being since the inclinations of 'they-self' can be treated with reticence. For Heidegger, this is because the self-revealing nature of *Dasein* means that it necessarily has a dual ontological status which is split between its *lostness* in its inauthentic they-self and its *capacity* for authentic selfhood, with the former repressing but not extinguishing the latter (Heidegger 1962, 1978). The question is, how is the capacity for authentic individuality realised?

The first point that needs to be made is that the average-everyday relation to the world that is immersed and imminent (and which results in lostness in they-self in which Dasein is ordinarily buried) can only be sustained through what I now refer to as 'confirming encounters', that is, social encounters *with similar others* that reinforce the self-evidence of an already doxic relation to the world that 'just happens' to produce a language and practice of recreational crime and drug use. For example, we saw in Chapter 4 how social encounters that happened on an average everyday *confirmed* the sense of they-self that had already been established:

> On my estate a lot of the kids were, you know, we were all that much alike … I mean the lads I knocked with they were doing it, and yeah everyone was at it.   John

> It's like a common thing, you know, I suppose, everyone did it, everybody that I knew did it … It's just a normal thing to do then when you're a kid isn't it.   Grant

The second point concerns how Dasein is liberated from its average-everyday mode of they-being that results in drug use 'just happening' because 'everyone was doing it'. This brings us to a key purpose of universal moral appeals (such as the government campaign to 'Just say NO to heroin') which issue a universal 'call to care' to individuals that are potential heroin users. Now Heidegger argues that such 'universal' appeals to 'care' are likely to fall on 'deaf ears' because they will appear as preaching from 'on high'. One need only refer to a typical response to the universal moral calls that the political establishment periodically issue (e.g. 'Drink and Drive' and 'Stop Smoking' campaigns), which tends to be that killing pedestrians and cancer is 'what happens to other people'. The universal moral call therefore tends to be ignored. For Heidegger, then, the effective call *must* have an existential basis which is to say that that it must be able to make a direct 'appeal' (and possess intimate meaning) that will be 'heard' and resonate with a particular form of being-in-the-world by revealing *its specific* projection-towards the subject of the call.

> Hearing the appeal correctly is thus tantamount to having an understanding of oneself in one's ownmost potentiality-for-being, that is, to projecting oneself upon one's *ownmost* authentic potentiality for becoming …. In understanding the call, Dasein is *in thrall to its ownmost possibility of existence.*   (Heidegger 1962: 333-4)

For my respondents, this happened as a consequence of what I refer to as 'disturbing encounters' that projected *problematic significant others* (heroin users 'in my circle' that 'look like scum') onto a projected self ('this could easily happen to me'). Disturbing encounters with *problematic significant others* thus produce a 'voice of conscience' that awakens Dasein by throwing it into an anxious confrontation with its being-with-others (i.e. its lostness in its 'existential actuality') and its own individual potentiality (i.e. its 'existential potentiality') which is revealed as more than it currently is. That is to say, encounters with problematic others reveal a disjuncture between existential actuality and existential potentiality which, in this case, is the *negative* potential to become a heroin user. Heidegger argues that realisation of 'existential potentiality' necessitates an ethic of 'being-towards-care' that places demands on Dasein to take a distancing relation to its they-self and its being-with-others in order to avoid such negative potential (or, alternatively, to realise a positive potential). Heidegger refers to the nature of this 'new' relation between Dasein and the social world as 'present-at-hand', that is, a relation to be modified rather than something to be treated as self-evident.

Most of my respondents made reference to how 'disturbing encounters' with people that shared their urban social space revealed the tragic consequences of heroin use and induced a realisation of their own potential, as a recreational drug user, as more than it currently was, i.e. problematic. That is to say disturbing encounters with the tragic consequences of heroin use meant that most respondents adopted a relation of intentional detachment from it (as a present-at-hand entity) and therefore avoided using it even though it was said to be 'everywhere' in the urban spaces that my respondents grew up in, and were occupying. In contrast to the *public persona* of they-self which respondents used to 'confirm' the unproblematic nature of their recreational drug use (e.g. '*everybody* was doing it around here'), they now talked about how their disturbing encounters with heroin users (with whom they shared urban social space) had induced an *individualised* sense of anxiety and thus 'being-towards-care'. So, whereas interviewees used a *public voice* to explain their doxic relation to their recreational use of drugs (i.e. '*everybody* does it around here'), they were now using a *private voice* (care) to explain their resistance to heroin which was considered to be a threat to their own lives-to-be-lived. For example, respondents such as Graham talked about avoiding heroin because of 'what it does' to people that shared his social space:

CA:	Had you ever been offered heroin before?
Graham:	I'd not been offered it but I'd been in company of people on it.
CA:	But you'd never thought you wanted any before?
Graham:	No, I were anti-drugs really.
CA:	Was there any reason why you were anti-drugs up until that point?
Graham:	'Cos I'd seen what it did to people. I'd seen what a state they got in.

Benoit *et al* (2003) suggests that such a resistance to heroin is most apparent in the 1990s cohort of drug users because this cohort had the benefit of seeing 'adults close to them struggle with addiction to heroin and crack cocaine in the 1970s and 1980s and learned a major lesson: to avoid using drugs ... As a result of these negative experiences, crack and heroin have been heavily stigmatised' by this generation (Benoit *et al* 2003: 511). Surveys have shown, then, that members of the 1990s cohort of recreational drug users refer to experiences of observing adult heroin users as setting a standard of 'what not to do' resulting in a generation, born after 1970, that despised heroin injectors and 'crack heads' (Benoit 2003: 521: Parker *et al* 1998). The crucial point here, then, is that disturbing encounters with heroin users (rather than moral appeals of a more universal nature) result in a revulsion of heroin because they possess an existential significance to recreational drug users who are clearly anxious about the negative potential for their projected selves to become just like these problematic significant others that share their urban social space. Stanno, Kenny and Oliver, who fall into this category, thus described heroin users as 'scum' because they were 'dirty', 'scruffy', 'diseased' and 'responsible for everything' that was 'bad':

I wouldn't even talk to a heroin addict; I'd just tell them to piss off if they come near me, even if they were selling stuff dirt cheap, I just thought they were scum ... The people I used to hang about with were never into class A drugs, it was just like cannabis and having a drink. I wouldn't even talk to a heroin addict, I'd just tell them to piss off if they come near me in the pub or on the street ... I just thought they were scum.   Stanno

Because of what comes with them all the crime the scruffiness the dirtiness the diseases and the underhandedness the way that they will come into your house making you believe that they are OK and the next thing they have gone off with your missus purse or your social book or your kiddies money or you know what I mean.   Kenny

I didn't want to know just dirty smack heads. They kill people. They burgle. They are responsible for everything.   Oliver

Yet, despite thinking of heroin users as 'scum', interviewees such as Graham, Stanno, Kenny and Oliver also described how it had *not* been hard for them to eventually become heroin users themselves:

I didn't want to know just dirty smack heads ... And then I became one of them. *It's not hard to get from one to the other, not hard at all.*   Oliver

Becoming a Problematic Drug User

The common place revulsion of 'smack heads' amongst my respondents meant that only *one* respondent described his use of heroin as a 'natural inclination' and therefore as 'ready-to-hand' just like cannabis, shoplifting and so on. Significantly this was one of the older respondents that went 'straight into' using the drug when it appeared on the urban scene in the early 1980s because he had no experience of the dangers it presented. (This contrasted him from *later cohorts* who talked about how their first-hand disturbing encounters with the tragic consequences of heroin use rescued them from *complete lostness* in their 'natural inclinations' towards drug use, thereby resulting in a modified 'natural attitude' that was based on a revulsion of heroin.) For those in the *original cohort* of heroin users from the 1980s such as Frank, then, heroin use was 'fashionable' in the 'areas they were living in at the time' and so 'came naturally' in the same way that recreational drug use was said to 'come naturally' in Chapter 4:

Frank:	Back then, 20 odd years ago, it wasn't a case of, back then, it was like fashionable to use drugs back then. You weren't sidelined back then. You weren't slagged off back then if you used drugs. The explosion of it really took off in the 80s.
CA:	What drugs were you using at the time?
Frank:	Heroin. Speed at first, but more or less straight onto heroin ... Because that was the drug of choice back then. Like I say, when I were 15 when I tried it a few times, when I was 15, 16, it wasn't heavy. I was [living] in a different area at the time. It was like 'have a bit of this, it'll pep you up'. There didn't seem to be anything devious about it. It seemed to be helping me when I was flagging at parties and whatnot.
CA:	How old were you?
Frank:	Let's see, I was 15. 38 now [in 2002]. It was 23 years ago, around 1980 ... We'd never heard of HIV and hepatitis then. Never even heard of it. I tell you the most disturbing thing. We used to have all different size pins for needles and what have you and some lads had lost their veins and some lads found it easier to have smaller needles fitted. We just used to go and take it, all sorts. There could have been up to 6, 7, 8 people on one needle.

The only other 'smooth' route into heroin involved a handful of respondents that had started to use heroin 'by accident' and 'without realising what it was'.

> I used to hate heroin and heroin addicts I used to really hate them and detest them and I used to smoke cannabis all day and all night and one day this girl come around to the flat and she had something on some foil and she said do you want a couple of lines of this so me, not knowing quite what it was, I said 'yeah' so I had some and I was sliding off the settee so what had taken me all day and all night to reach a certain state of euphoria and I had got to that stage within minutes rather than it taking all day so that was the change for me.
>
> Kenny

And:

> CA: So how did you, when you first took heroin how did that come about then?
> Angela: I met my boyfriend, he didn't tell me he was a heroin addict at first, he was just like, him and his friend were saying, oh we are going to score ... He didn't tell me he was addicted at first, and he kept saying, oh buy this, buy this with your money, you know what I mean? ... I didn't realise he was addicted at first, because I didn't know what it was like, you know, being addicted to heroin ... I didn't realise what it [the drug he was taking] was.

'Disturbing Encounters' and 'Disturbing Episodes' as Routes into Problematic Drug Use

Since 'smack heads' were universally regarded as 'scum' by the majority of respondents that exhibited an *initial* and *intentional* resistance towards heroin, the routes into heroin for most respondents were much more complex and protracted. Their heroin use did not simply 'just happen' (either 'in the early 1980s' or 'by accident'). Conversely, it was initiated by 'disturbing encounters' or 'disturbing episodes' that either compromised *or* destroyed the ethic of 'being-towards-care' that had produced their initial resistance towards heroin. Disturbing encounters involving sexual abuse left my respondents with dys-appearing bodies that were a source of social pain and suffering they wanted to 'block out'. Their primary need to 'block out' these painful memories compromised the primacy of the ethic of being-towards-care which resulted in moderate levels of heroin use to 'numb the pain'. I refer to this as a dys-state of care. My respondents' disturbing episodes of bereavement resulted in their momentarily trivialising their own lives-to-be-led. The resulting sense of personal meaninglessness instantiated a complete *breakdown* in the ethic of being-towards-care which was exemplified in the way they referred to 'not caring about anything or anyone' and therefore 'getting into heroin big time'. I refer to this as a state of being-against-care.

Disturbing Encounters and Dys-appearance: Sexual Abuse and Heroin

We have seen that they-self is sustained by 'confirming encounters' that reinforce its complicity with its 'average everyday' social location. Since they-self is constituted upon a ready-to-hand relation to 'oneself' and its being-with-others, its own being is not a thematic focus of attention, i.e. as present-at-hand. That is to say, they-self ascribes more or less the same existential value to itself as it does to the others that it is with (Heidegger 1962). Conversely, the ethic of being-towards-care is parasitic on (and only possible as a consequence of) the value that individuals ascribe to their authentic self vis-à-vis others. The realisation of such value arises out of 'disturbing encounters' with *problematic significant others* that have an existential 'relevance' to they-self because they provide a negative projection of its existential potentiality (i.e. this is what I could be, e.g. a heroin user) out of its current existential actuality (i.e. this is what I am, e.g. a recreational drug user). As we have seen, this perforce necessitates the taking up of a modified relation to they-self and its being-with-others (as present-at-hand rather than ready-to-hand) as well as a need to make investments in the avoidance of its negative potential-for-being, for example, through the production of discourses that stigmatised heroin within their peer group as well as avoidance of direct contact with heroin users. That is to say, the ethos of being-towards-care necessitates that the authentic self becomes the subject of (and subject to) a thematic focus of attention that distinguishes it from its being-with-others. It is simply a matter of avoiding 'ever *becoming* like that'. However, disturbing encounters that project *problematic* others onto self (e.g. 'I could be like that heroin user if I don't watch it') were simply one manifestation that induced an individualised relation to being-in-the-world that, in the case outlined above, resulted in my respondents' initial resistance to drugs such as heroin. Disturbing encounters also occurred within existentially different situations, specifically, when *normalised others* were projected onto a spoiled self. The social pain or realisation that one possessed a spoiled identity resulted in a descent into problematic drug use. Leder's (1990) phenomenological concept of dys-appearance can helpfully illustrate this point.

Leder (1990) argues that our mundane experience of ordinary everyday life, which we tend to take for granted, is characterised by the *disappearance* of the body-subject. The disappearance of the body-subject happens when, for example, we are not ordinarily aware of the social characteristics of our comportment or when, on an everyday level, we do not even regard our comportment as socialised at all. In Heidegger's (1962) terms, the body-subject is something that we do not need to pay attention to because it is 'ready-to-hand', that is, 'fit for purpose'. The disappearance of the body-subject is however ruptured by encounters that disturb our taken-for-granted attitude towards it by creating a sense of:

> ... bodily discomfort, of being left out in the cold: all of which makes the body present, makes it 'dys-appear'. The information that animates the world is dominated by ... a specific hegemonic form of carnality, which excludes as it constructs ... Exclusion is everywhere and *each time it is experienced*, it is experienced in the form of carnal self-recognition.   (Patterson and Hughes 1999: 604; *my emphasis*)

Skeggs (1997, 2005) has shown how this occurs when the generalised manner of our comportment is 'out of place' in an unfamiliar situation. For example, she talks about how her respondents' felt that their working class posture become apparent to them (that is, 'dys-appeared') on encountering middle class social spaces where they were required to make their bodies 'perform' in a way that was consistent with the hegemonic form of middle class carnality. Specifically, working class women told Skeggs how they felt uncomfortable when they were required to participate in a social function for senior managers of the company in which their husbands had recently been promoted. For Patterson and Hughes (1999) 'dys-appearance' is also a consequence of encounters with the hegemonic form of the 'perfect body' that is embodied in *normalised* others and which produce:

> ... a vivid, but unwanted consciousness of [the spoiled] body. Here the body undergoes a mode of 'dys-appearance' which is not biological, but social. For example, in the context of [a spoiled body] ... one's body 'dys-appears' – is made present as a thematic focus of attention. When one is confronted by [their spoiled body] ... one is simultaneously confronted by oneself ... When one encounters [their spoiled body] ... one's body 'dys-appears' ... it is stunned into its own recognition by its presence-as-alien-being-in-the-world.
>
> (Patterson and Hughes 1999: 603)

This might be as a result of social responses to an acquired disfigurement (Hawkesworth 2001) or, in the case of many of my respondents, experiences of sexual abuse when the dys-state of awareness of not 'matching up' to *normalised others* means that the spoiled ('disfigured', abused) body becomes a negative focus of thematic attention and therefore a source of social pain and suffering. Since dys-appearance makes the spoiled body a thematic focus of *negative* attention, and instantiates an individualised relation to the body-subject, a key question concerns how this alien body-subject manages its social pain and suffering.

Now in the same way that universal appeals to 'care' ('Just say NO to heroin') fall on *deaf ears* if they do not have existential 'relevance' to the being-in-the-world of the body-subject, the body-subject is also *blind* to the universal range of 'calls' to care (e.g. availability of counselling and other services whose purpose is to address the pain of abuse) that have no existential appeal, meaning or relevance to it. Confronted by social pain and suffering, the alien body-subject only has a disposition to see and grasp what is 'there for it' which, in the case of my respondents, are the drugs that 'just happen' to 'be there' for it. It follows that this *dys-state* of being-towards-care ('I need something to block out *my* problem') is different to the state of being-towards-care that produced an initial resistance towards heroin ('I am better than them with *their* heroin problems') because the perforce necessity to manage the social pain of dys-appearance opens the door to *moderate* levels of problematic drug use (e.g. glue sniffing, small doses of heroin, *etc.*) that enable it to 'numb the pain'. Hence, 'dys-care'. Respondents that had realised their experiences of sexual abuse in conversations with normalised others thus talked about how the dys-appearance of their abused bodies had resulted in their making *some* (i.e. relatively moderate rather than reckless) use of 'hard' drugs to 'block out' and 'to forget' experiences of sexual abuse. Joanne thus continued to avoid heroin but started to engage in glue-sniffing for these very reasons:

> I was only twelve I didn't mention that before, and it was just something 'cause when I was younger I got sexually abused by a part of the family so *I just used to sniff to, just get*

off my face and just try and forget what happened ... [I first realised I had been sexually abused when] I was speaking to my friend, 'cause it was my brother that sexually abused me, and I was speaking to my friend, ... talking about what was right and wrong about sex and things like that, and her mum overheard us, so she sent me to social services, and I got examined and all that, and found out that I had been sexually abused ... *That's when I started sniffing, to block it out, just to like, get off, just get off my face, that's all I ever wanted to do, get off my face, and not think about it.*   Joanne

Lee described himself as a 'late developer' because he only began to take heroin to 'control his feelings' and 'kill his emotions' when he had to confront and confess his past experiences of sexual abuse to normalised legal others:

I had to go through all the trials of the kids' home staff and that's what gave me the breakdown ... From '95 to '97. In '97 I had a total breakdown and me taking heroin wasn't to get addicted but I did know one thing, *it killed all my emotions* ... [At] 25, I was a late developer. It's not the sort of development you want is it, in your life? ... I couldn't handle the pressure, ... all the pressure of the court case ... *I used smack to try and control me feelings.*   Lee

And although Roy described how he became involved in heroin 'by accident' when seeking to assist a friend 'come off' heroin, he later admitted that it occurred as a result of the consequent re-emergence of his childhood experiences of sexual abuse in his consciousness which he just wanted to 'blank out':

Roy: Me flat was getting decorated, so I stayed in some feller's flat. And his niece was on heroin and crack cocaine, and liked her and I wanted to help her get off it, so I moved in, staying there, [and] I ended getting on it myself, getting on heroin and crack cocaine.

CA: How did that come about then ... when you were trying to help her get off it, why were you trying to help her get off it?

Roy: ... She's got two kids and I know her mum and that, I just wanted to help her, but then when I tried to help her, you know, she said to me to 'try it' and I tried it and just got hooked on it.

CA: Yeah. And what was it about that situation that made you want to help her. I mean had you seen other people being on smack or anything like that before?

Roy: Yeah, I'd seen it on the telly and what's it's name, and her mum used to look after me, see, she's a lot older than me, she's thirty two, and I was only sixteen when I got with her ... And her mum used to look after me and she's got two kids, and I just wanted to help her get off it, 'cause of, you know, the kids, I just wanted to help her, but as I say, I just ended getting on it myself.

CA: How come you were so concerned about [her kids] then?

Roy: 'Cause I'd seen what it was doing to her kids and that, 'cause her mum would help me when, you know, me dad used to abuse me and that, I just wanted to help her ...

CA: Was your concern partly to do with the fact that you'd been abused then?

Roy: Yeah. And 'cause, you know, [the kids] wouldn't get fed [because] all the money would get spent on smack. It's just sad.

CA: So, your concern was partly because of what you'd experienced?

Roy: Yeah ... [Like I said, I had been] sexually abused as well, by me dad ...

CA: Was that anything to do with the fact that, you know, when you were offered the heroin, that you tried it.

Roy: Yeah, to *blank everything out*, that's what I said it was, *to blank everything out* 'cause when I had it, you know, [I was] just oblivious to everything, so, *I wasn't thinking about all the things that had happened to me*, so, it just kept happening.

Death, Being-Against-Care and Heroin

Disturbing encounters with normalised others resulted in the dys-appearance of the abused body, which was a source of social pain and suffering that my respondents sought to 'block out' by their moderate use of drugs such as heroin. This dys-state of being-towards-care (in which care remains an issue, but is compromised) contrasts with existentially 'disturbing episodes', such as bereavement, which produced a very different mode of being-towards drugs such as heroin. Specifically, sociological research has shown that modern experiences of death produce a sense of existential meaninglessness (and therefore what I call a mode of 'being-against-care') that, for my respondents, resulted in an *excessive* use of heroin and crack cocaine. So how does this happen?

The tendency for modern societies to take the management of death away from the family and communities (Adams 1993) so that it can be 'hidden' within the walls of hospitals, mortuaries and so on (Prior 1987, 1989) has resulted in a sequestration of death from public space that is said to have begun in the 1860s (Prior 1989; see also Aries 1974). Seventy five per cent of people now die in hospitals and other institutions (Walter 1994:153) reflecting spatial contours of the 'isolation of death in general' (Prior 1987: 358), for example, with dead bodies now 'laid out' in funeral parlours rather than at home (Adams 1993). This has led Elias (1985: 85) to note how 'never before have people died as noiselessly and hygienically as today in these [modern] societies, and never in social conditions so much fostering solitude'. For Giddens (1991) and Mellor (1993) an 'unintended consequence' of sequestration (Giddens 1991: 167) is that it ensures 'the threat of personal meaninglessness [presented by our own mortality] is *ordinarily* held at bay' thereby enabling individuals to concentrate on the meaningfulness and significance – and thus overlook the triviality – of the life being lived (Giddens 1991: 202; also Willmott 2000). Thus, modern individuals are enabled to assign meaning and significance to their everyday life-to-be-lived, and therefore being-towards-care and pursuit of existential potentiality, because the exclusion of death from public space *ordinarily* represses the threat of personal meaninglessness (Giddens 1991; Mellor 1993; Willmott 2000). Indeed we have already seen that my respondents' avoidance of heroin use was personally meaningful in the sense that it was considered to be a threat to their own lives-to-be-lived that were therefore deemed significant and valuable *at that point in time*. Thus, they talked about avoidance in terms that highlighted the meaning and significance of lives-to-be-lived, for example, by referring to 'what it did to people'.

However, the sequestration of death also maximises the existential significance of actual *personal encounters* with death which, it follows, can *momentarily* render 'absurd and futile, the projects and institutions that [ordinarily] endow lives with meaning' (Willmott 2000: 650). Thus personal encounters with death (e.g. of a 'loved one') can lead modern individuals to *momentarily* trivialise their own life-to-be-lived which they *ordinarily* invest with significance and meaning (Hockey 1990). By bringing into focus the potential triviality and meaninglessness of the everyday life-to-be-led, then, the sequestration of death can fundamentally undermine the modern individuals mode of 'being-towards-care' which, in this instance, leads to a breakdown in Dasein's resistance towards its they-being, that is, as projected towards heroin. Following bereavement, respondents thus talked about how they had experienced a loss of meaning and significance to their lives which had meant that they 'no longer cared about *themselves*' and, indeed, 'no longer cared about *anything*' and which resulted in their involvement in the heroin use that was 'everywhere' in the urban spaces that they occupied. In effect, they were describing a new mode of being-against-care:

> I started taking heroin when I was about I think about 21 because at the time *I was just at a low point I didn't really care* ... A lot of things happened at the same time I had split up with my girlfriend and I had lost my job and ... my father died, everything had just you know gone down the drain.   Brian

Furthermore, since a typical death in modern societies is no longer that of a child, and because most people now die when they are elderly and retired, the loss of a child is now far more traumatic than the loss of any other relative (Goody 1959; Blaumer 1966; Walter 1994). This was exemplified in the even more dramatic and impassioned speech employed by Carolyn, below, who repeatedly talked about how she did not care about her own life-to-be-lived, other lives-to-be-lived or 'anything else', to the extent that she 'ended up in a complete mess':

> My brother died a cot death and that, so I tried to deal with that, but I couldn't, so I just used the heroin to run away from everything, I couldn't deal with it ... I used to dwell on it [the cot death] a lot, and then I just thought 'bugger it, I don't think about it as much when I was using the heroin', so I just carried on ... Just to feel secure I suppose, when you're on like, a high, *you don't care about anything, you don't care about how your family feel, or nothing. You don't even care about yourself, eventually, you just end up in a mess, not eating, you lose a lot of weight, and then you just end up worse and worse.*   Carolyn

Indeed, the commonality between bereavements that involved a child and those that involved the loss of someone that was 'dead close' was the tendency for bereaved individuals to allow their loss of self-significance to lead them into especially serious levels of heroin use. For example, Joanne and Margaret described 'going totally off the rails ... getting bang heavily into crack' and having 'really bad binges' as a result of the loss of their children:

> I ended up getting pregnant by the lad, that I was with and er ... he ended up beating me up, I ended up losing it ... [I was] Just going on seventeen, and I ended up getting depressed, ended up cutting my wrists open ... 'cause I ended up losing twins and it did my head in so I ended up going proper off the rails ... *So I just ended up taking more drugs ... I started going wild and I went off the rails totally ... And it was just; I ended up taking, getting bang heavily into crack ... [and] injecting heroin.*   Joanne

And:

> I had a bad experience last year, I had a little baby, and she died, five weeks old, so I went on a mad one after that, really bad binge ... Oh! God, [it lasted] for about three months ... If that's not enough to turn anyone to drugs, I don't know what is.   Margaret

Significantly, then, bereaved individuals talked about how this complete loss of 'being-towards-care' (both to oneself and 'everything') resulted in their *complete* falleness into their they-self (being-against-care) which became manifest in their *total* susceptibility to the heroin use that was endemic in the urban spaces that they occupied. Bereaved interviewees thus talked about how they purposely went 'into self-destruct mode' or 'off the rails' and thus went 'straight for heroin, big time' or 'on a mad one, a really bad heroin binge'. For example, Oliver described how he went into 'self destruct mode' after losing his mother with whom he was 'dead close':

> When I was eighteen me Mum had just died, my Dad has always been in and out of jail all his life so it was easy for me to step into that criminal fraternity as it were and like I say my Mum died so *I was going to self destruct sort of thing so it was whatever drug that [worked]* ... Me Dad had never been on the scene so me and me Mum we were dead close. It's a long story. She committed suicide while I was there and me head went a bit funny so I [went into] ... *self destruct mode* ... Until I was eighteen until me Mum died I wasn't involved in any criminal activities apart from smoking cannabis ... [When she died] I was doing the normal criminal things. I was taking a lot of amphetamines after she just died. I started loads of wiz. Staying out all night. Stealing cars. Anything really. Anything and everything and then I got into heroin ... *I went straight for it big time*. Either way I have not looked back since and now I am on 75mg a day methadone and I have got a habit.
> Oliver

Indeed, respondents that were desisting from heroin use at the time of the research identified the death of family members as the 'one thing' that could turn them back to heroin use.

> CA: You've got a motivation to stay off it [heroin] at the moment. What would undermine that motivation do you think?
> Anthony: Me family get wiped out. My family get wiped out and I've got nothing, I've not got another care in the world then, I'd just ... [silence].
> CA: Is that what keeps you going?
> Anthony: Yeah.
> CA: Who's your family?
> Anthony: Me aunty and me cousin. Her daughters. They're close family. I don't really. Don't get me wrong, I love me mum to bits but I don't have a mother and son, really, proper mother and son bond. We're always arguing and stuff all the time. I don't need none of that.

The problematic drug use practices of bereaved individuals therefore differed markedly from those that had experienced sexual abuse. The 'dys-appearance' of respondents that had experienced sexual abuse meant that they were preoccupied with 'managing pain' rather than with the fundamental existential issues of 'human being' that personal encounters with death raised. They talked about their dys-state of 'being-towards-care' (i.e. needing to 'block out the pain') rather than being plunged into a mode of 'being-against-care' (i.e. 'no longer caring about *anything*'). Since 'being' remained an issue for them (and given that coping with 'spoiled' being was their main issue of concern) they only talked about their *partial* falleness in their they-self and thus *moderate* use of 'hard' drugs to help them to 'block out' *specific experiences* rather than drugs that would result in their self-destruction. Thus, as we saw earlier, Joanne and others talked about how they sought to 'block out' their experiences of sexual abuse by engaging in practices, such as glue sniffing, that were less widespread in their neighbourhoods and comparatively safer than heroin use:

> I was only twelve I didn't mention that before, and it was just something 'cause when I was younger I got sexually abused by a part of the family so I just used to sniff to, just get of my face and just *try and forget what happened* ... [I first realised I had been sexually abused when] I was speaking to my friend, 'cause it was my brother that sexually abused me, and I was speaking to my friend, ... talking about what was right and wrong about sex and things like that, and her mum overheard us, so she sent me to social services, and I got examined and all that, and found out that I had been sexually abused .... That's when *I started sniffing, to block it out, just to like, get off, just get off my face, that's all I ever wanted to do, get off my face, and not think about it.*   Joanne

Joanne only subsequently began to use heroin and crack cocaine in response to an experience of bereavement at the age of seventeen when she 'went off the rails' and which also resulted in her suicide attempt:

> I ended up getting pregnant by the lad, that I was with and er... he ended up beating me up, I ended up losing it ... [I was] Just going on seventeen, and I ended up getting depressed, ended up cutting my wrists open ... 'cause I ended up losing twins and it did my head in so I ended up going proper off the rails ... *So I just ended up taking more drugs ... I started going wild and I went off the rails totally ... And it was just, I ended up taking, getting bang heavily into crack ... [and] injecting heroin.*   Joanne

Conclusion

This chapter has taken forward the analysis presented in previous chapters by drawing on the phenomenology of Martin Heidegger to examine the nature of 'being' more fully. This was necessary because my respondents' comportment towards crime and drugs was multi-faceted and complex. That is, my respondents were not in slavery to a totalitarian habitus that produced singular and uncomplicated dispositions towards crime and drugs. Conversely, the 'natural inclinations' of habitus or Dasein, that is, the 'existential actuality' of they-self is 'revealed' to it in the course of 'disturbing encounters' with problematic others in the context of its 'average everyday' practice with-others. These encounters instantiate distance between Dasein and its practice and, through this, a realisation of the potential projection of Dasein towards these problematic others and therefore as 'lost' in its they-self. It follows that the authentic being of Dasein was revealed through its 'private voice' which denoted what it objectified as significant to 'I' rather than how it was 'lost' to 'they'. This was illustrated in the way my respondents always talked about their 'disturbing encounters' with heroin addicts by using a 'private voice' that denoted how 'I' or 'me' was 'shocked' into desistance. Yet the same respondents later came to develop 'serious' drug problems which resulted in their involvement in more serious forms of acquisitive crime.

The latter part of the chapter discussed the relationship between two modified forms of being (dys-care and against-care) and problematic drug use. The dys-appearance of the spoiled (e.g. abused) body-subject in encounters with normalised others made the self a focus of thematic attention but in a very negative way, for example, by highlighting its social pain and suffering. Although being-towards-care was still an issue, this was described as a dys-state of care. The primary and overwhelming need was to be able to cope with this social pain and suffering by grasping what was 'there for them'. This was exemplified in the way survivors of abuse referred to their 'moderate' heroin use as a way of 'blocking out feelings'. An entirely different mode being-against-care was induced by experiences of bereavement which momentarily led my respondents to trivialise their life-to-be-led. The momentary sense of personal meaninglessness that instantiated the complete breakdown in their ethic of being-towards-care was exemplified in the way bereaved respondents referred to their heroin use as a consequence of their suddenly 'not caring about anything or anyone'. Having identified these two (dys-care, against-care) modes of being-towards problematic drug use, Chapter 6 will explore their criminological consequences. Key considerations will be the manner in which the different modes of 'being' induced by experiences of bereavement and sexual abuse translated into the nature and extent of the propensity for involvement in crime.

Chapter 6

Criminological Consequences of 'Becoming' a Problematic Drug User

Introduction

Previous chapters have argued that specific acts such as recreational crime and drug use (Chapter 4) and problematic drug use (Chapter 5) are best understood, in phenomenological terms, as consequences of a socially constituted mode of 'being-towards'. This chapter takes forward the idea by examining the criminal consequences (that is to say, types of criminal involvements) of the different modes of being-towards problematic drug use that I identified in the last chapter. These were the modes of being-towards problematic drug use prompted by the experiences of sexual abuse ('dys-care') and bereavement (being-against-care). The first part examines the *immediate* criminological consequences that followed-on from *becoming* a problematic drug user within these two different modes of being-towards. The second part of the chapter examines the *longer term* criminological consequences that follow from *being* a problematic drug user (that is, as the extremities of drug habits change over time and according to circumstances), also within these two different modes of being-towards.

First, the being-against-care to which my bereaved respondents made reference translated into a particular way of *becoming* a serious drug user. They went for drugs such as heroin 'big time' and therefore took copious amounts of such drugs whilst also engaging in the more dangerous practice of injection. The first part of the chapter discusses how this also necessitated an immediate change in the *level* of their criminal involvements. This group described their involvement in acquisitive crime as 'prolific'. Although it did not result in a change in the *nature* of their criminal involvements (which remained focused on shoplifting) it opened up the possibility that their criminal involvements would become more serious. Although they were mainly shoplifters, then, they talked about street robbery, which brought the threat of violence, as 'an option' that was 'on the agenda'. The chapter then goes on to discuss how and why the dys-appearing group were quite different to the against-care group. For dys-appearing respondents, becoming a serious drug user meant using drugs such as heroin, but in moderation and via the comparatively safer practice of 'chasing the dragon'. This was reflected in the immediate criminal consequences that followed-on from their becoming a serious drug user. They were able to moderate their involvement in crime, and some even described themselves as 'giro junkies', that is, users that were able to restrict their drug use within existing income limits thereby avoiding increased involvement in crime.

The second part of the chapter discusses the problems that this dys-appearing group encountered as a consequence of their 'being' a serious drug user over the longer term. This is because the nature and extent of their serious drug use changed, increasing in some cases to habits that cost £400 per day. At this point they described how their *a priori* revulsion of physical harm was a consequence of what I have referred to as their dys-state of being-towards-care in which 'care' remain an issue, albeit compromised. Since violent acquisitive crime (e.g. street robbery) was not an option for them, they described how they 'planned' their involvement in acquisitive crime. This enabled them to identify a way of securing the required income without resorting to forms of violent crime that they sought to avoid. By and large they were thus able to 'stick with' involvement in the same forms of crime that they had always been involved in, that is, shoplifting. Involvement in violent acquisitive crimes, such as street robbery, was a one-off occurrence that came about 'in desperation' when their plans had failed to deliver the income that they required to sustain their drug habit on a given day.

Immediate Criminal Consequences of *Becoming* a Problematic Drug User

The criminal consequences of *becoming* a problematic drug user were contingent on my respondents' forms of being-towards problematic drug use. By this I mean the *immediate* impact that problematic drug use had on the criminal activities of my bereaved respondents, that had developed a being-against-care, was different to the impact it had on abused respondents that suffered 'dys-appearance' but for whom 'care' was still an issue, albeit in a dys-state. Chapter 5 showed that the former group were united by their tendency to talk about their descent into hard drugs as a consequence of their loss of care for 'themselves, everyone and everything'. They progressed into drugs such as heroin and crack 'big time' and talked about having 'mad binges' during which they 'could easy go through £400 a day' (Norman). Norman described how this resulted in a tendency to 'go robbing constantly' in order to obtain funds to procure the prolific amounts of heroin that they were consuming *from the beginning*:

Norman:	I haven't been to school for years, know what I mean, I was in college for a few months, then our kid died, you know me brother died, yeah me brother died then, that's when I went out robbing with me mates and that, know what I mean, I left college completely.
CA:	How old was your baby brother?
Norman:	Eleven weeks old.
CA:	How old were you then?
Norman:	About fifteen, nearly sixteen or something.
CA:	And how did that, kind of impact on you, 'cause you talked about your mum getting battered like, but how did that death impact on you?
Norman:	Yeah, it was hard at the time, I went and talked to me mum, and then after me brother told me our kid's died, I thought he was messing around, and then he wasn't. Know what I mean. And I just went off in me head, and since I went I off in me head, know what I mean.

CA: Did you get worse at that point, in terms of what you were getting up to, when your kid brother died?

Norman: I was doing all kinds of madness, I was out all day, from eight in the morning, robbing, constantly robbing.

Although this need to be 'constantly robbing' actually involved increased levels of shoplifting, it demanded that other possibilities were considered. For example respondents such as Norman also talked about how they now felt it necessary to 'do some proper jobs' that might involve violence (in his case, petrol station robberies) in order to feed his 'problematic' drug use:

> I said [to my partner] 'I'll start doing some proper jobs, get some proper money'. But I've robbed. I've spent as little as £30 a day on it and I've spent as much as £800 a day on it. I got two grand out of [BANK NAME] once ... I got not guilty on that and I got it about four o'clock on a Wednesday afternoon, I woke up Friday morning and not a penny and I never left the house and it all went on crack ... I dig it, I inject it, but if I had a £100 now and I left here I'd buy £90 worth of crack and £10 worth of heroin.   Norman

Conversely respondents that had experienced 'dys-appearance', and for whom being-towards-care was still an issue, tended to take protracted routes into problematic drug use (e.g. heroin via glue sniffing), and used only moderate amounts of hard drugs in a relatively safe way (e.g. by 'chasing the dragon' rather than injecting). Their entry into hard drug use, then, did not perforce necessitate 'robbing constantly' in order to obtain the funds to procure the substances they required. Conversely, this comparatively moderate group of problematic drug users were able to control their drug use within limits, which meant that they were also able to moderate their involvement in crime *from the start*. For example, Todd described how he primarily depended on alcohol to 'numb the pain' of sexual abuse, how heroin was a 'bonus' for him, and how he could 'take-or-leave' heroin depending on whether he had the funds to pay for it:

> But like I say ... I'd drink and I'd be happy [during the week]. The drugs would be a bonus ... Friday, Saturday, Sunday I'd make up for it then, and I was using it, I was spending, £100, £100, and I was buying like 10 bags in the 2 days but depending, if I had any money left Sunday, which I very rarely did, I would have bought an average of about £100 on heroin, £50 on drink, cigs and that, but it never got, with me it never got to the stage where I was, every day I was going out and having 2 and 3 bags a day, it never got to that ... I could take it or leave it.   Todd

This tendency of dys-appearing respondents to moderate their use of heroin, and therefore involvement in crime, sheds some new light on some of the work of Pearson (1987); Pearson also found that heroin use with little or no crime was possible, especially if the user was willing to restrain their use within affordable limits but, unlike here, he did not identify which heroin users this applied to. It also resonates with the similarly limited work of Hammersley *et al* (1989) whose study of heroin users in the late 1980s similarly found that 'some respondents ... spoke ... of low status "giro junkies", meaning people who only took moderate amounts of heroin at the weekend ... Such people are controlled users' (Hammersley *et al*

1989: 1041). A recent study in the USA by Desimone *et al* (2001) also found that 'as long as withdrawal pain does not immediately jump to an unbearable level whenever consumption falls, users can … lengthen the time between doses [rather than commit crime]. Indeed users report regular periods of abstinence arising from an inability to afford purchases' (Desimone 2001: 630). This was certainly the case with Angela who described how, prior to obtaining a methadone script, she would 'struggle through' the 'tossing and turning' of heroin withdrawal until she next had the money to buy heroin or, alternatively, how she would use the money that she did have to buy some methadone so that she did not have to engage in crime to obtain heroin:

CA: How much were you on when you were addicted?

Angela: It depends on my money, when I get paid I'll go out and score, so I'd probably have it for about two or three days and then just keep to my methadone then.

CA: Before you got methadone and you were addicted to heroin did you get in any trouble then?

Angela: No, I use to just struggle until I got [my giro] paid again, or try and go out and buy some methadone … There's quite a few people that I knew that sold methadone then, before I was on prescription …. I've always had people that would like give it, you know, give it to me when they saw that I was ill, you know, so … [Otherwise] I'd just lay there tossing and turning, I've been there for a couple of days without money or methadone.

Longer Term Criminological Consequences of *Being* a Problematic Drug User

The link between drugs and violence tends to be defined in terms of the capacity of the former to lead to the latter, either due to the pharmacological properties of drugs *or* in the course of acquisitive crime that has been committed to obtain funds to support a habit. Some research studies have reported that the incidence of violent crimes – as measured by convictions – increases amongst heroin users (Gordon 1973; Patch 1972). However, other studies have found that 'the weight of evidence suggests that the probability of violent behaviour is not substantially increased by heroin' (Greenberg and Adler 1974: 245), and that violent crimes are *rarely* committed by heroin addicts because of the calming effects of opiates (Chein *et al* 1964; Dai 1970). The research literature also makes claims that crack cocaine and cocaine are associated with violent crime. For example, Grogger and Willis (2000) used various sources of data, including FBI reported crime rates from 27 metropolitan areas (taking account of the year in which crack arrived in each area) and emergency room admissions data collected by the National Institute on Drug Abuse (NIDA), and found that 'the arrival of crack had a sizeable and significant positive effects … [it] *caused* murder rates to rise by 4.4% per 100,000 population' (Grogger and Willis 2000: 523, *my italics*). They summarise their article by stating that:

… the arrival of crack cocaine led crime to rise substantially in the late 1980's and early 1990's. The most prevalent form of violence – aggravated assault – rose significantly.

(Grogger and Willis 2000: 528)

Other studies have, however, questioned the notion that crack cocaine and cocaine are associated with violent crime. For example, research by Best *et al* (2001) found that crack users were involved in significantly higher levels of acquisitive crime than non-crack users but that, like heroin users, their involvement in crime was largely restricted to non-violent crimes such as shoplifting and handling stolen goods. Desimone (2001) has also provided a critique of the thesis that the 'crack epidemic' causes violent crime. He cites the studies of Johnson *et al* (1995), who interviewed 724 crack users in Manhattan during 1988-1989, and found that most respondents that reported violence whilst using crack were already violent before initiating crack use. For Johnson *et al* (1995), then, an adequate explanation of violence cannot be found in drug use and so should be sought elsewhere. That said, one way of understanding violence might lie in the work of Dunlap *et al* (2002) who have argued that constant exposure to the objective reality of violence in the 'total institution' of the inner city results in the normalisation of violence, which is often the reason for its perpetration (see Chapter 2). This appeared to be the case for some of my respondents, such as Rick, who described how their constant exposure to the normal regularity of domestic violence had taught them about the need to 'look after' themselves:

CA:	What kind of influence, do you think, seeing the violence then, and seeing your mum getting battered, had on you?
Rick:	Starting to care about nothing apart from myself, and that kind of thing.
CA:	Because of seeing your mum getting battered?
Rick:	Yeah. Look after myself, ... so I thought I'd do it myself, know what I mean ... Me mum getting battered more that was the hardest thing to watch.

Nevertheless, the 'socialisation' perspective provides a limited explanation of violent crime. This is because it fails to appreciate that many drug users possess a form of being-towards that reviles violence yet, somehow, still commit acquisitive crimes that are violent in nature. I am making specific reference here to my dys-appearing group of respondents.

Dys-Care and the Revulsion of Violence

We have already seen that 'dys-appearance' produced by experiences of sexual abuse results in a dys-state of being-towards-care that results in moderate levels of hard drug use. These respondents were able to manage their drug habits without recourse to excessive levels of acquisitive crime, i.e. by remaining a 'recreational criminal' rather than 'career criminal'. However, although these respondents could describe the various ways in which they managed their use of heroin and therefore desisted from involvement in significantly higher levels of acquisitive crime (i.e. they were 'giro junkies') almost all of these respondents had also found themselves 'in deep' with drugs such as heroin at some point in their 'drugs careers'. At various points in time, then, their habits had, at their worst, cost them between £40 and £150 a day (which, incidentally, contrasted with bereaved respondents whom mentioned regular habits costing up to £400 per day):

It got up to maybe half a gram a day. At the time it was about £40 [a day].   Lee

Between two of us, him and me, you know like, [we were spending] about a hundred pound a day between us both, so, I suppose, something like that.   Grant

I'd have to say [my habit was costing me] about a hundred and fifty, and upwards you know what I mean ... A day, Yeah it was like getting total.   Judith

The tendency for drug use to escalate at various points in time was said to necessitate deeper levels of involvement in acquisitive crime. However, in contrast to bereaved respondents like Norman who talked about 'starting to do some proper jobs' (he specifically mentioned petrol station robberies), survivors of sexual abuse such as Mike described their needs in the less dramatic terms of simply 'having to do *more* crime':

I don't think I would have done so many things [acquisitive criminal acts] what I have done if I hadn't been drinking or taking drugs I don't think I would have done.   Mike

The tendency to become more involved in crime, as problematic drug use escalates, raises a key issue. This concerns *exactly* how *and with what consequences for others* dys-appearing respondents were able to acquire the necessary funds to sustain their escalating habits. Now a key claim made by the political establishment has long been that problematic drug use is responsible for violent acquisitive crimes such as most street robbery. Yet, this claim appears to be based on little or no evidence and, furthermore, misunderstands the criminal orientations (being-towards-crime) of the large number of drug users that have suffered from dys-appearance as a result of sexual abuse or some other form of disturbing encounter with normalised others. An understanding of the dys-appearance of the (abused) body-subject is critical because this is what made the 'spoiled self' a thematic focus of negative attention (to 'numb the pain' of the social suffering of alienation) which was attended to by recourse to what was 'there' which, as we have seen was heroin. The dys-appearance of the body-subject in its encounters with normalised others (i.e. as a result of a realisation of its experiences of sexual or other forms abuse) meant that it was particularly sensitive to issues of harm which were a thematic focus of attention. This translated into a mode of being 'against street robbery' because it often resulted in physical harm to others. Although they were selected for interview because they had been involved in a violent street crime, then, the vast majority had been reluctant to undertake street crime and, consequently, had only been involved in street crime as a 'one-off' that occurred at a low point in their lives. For example, Joanne said she 'wouldn't wish street crime on her worst enemy' (even though she had been involved in a street crime) because she had been physically and sexually abused by her own brother:

Yeah, because my brother used to beat me up ... You know, it's not the kind of life I'd wish anyone to have, I really wish that no sexual abuse had ever gone on, to anyone, 'cause I wouldn't wish it on my worst enemy, never mind anyone else, and being beat up, I know what it's like and I know how you feel after you've been beat up, so that's one of the reasons why I didn't like ... I wouldn't do street robberies, but I was involved in one, 'cause I was with the wrong person.   Joanne

Dev similarly talked about how he had made 'choices' about the crimes he was prepared to undertake, and that street crime was not one of them because of his own experience of violence:

> No, I wouldn't take something off the street, no, because, err, we are all human beings and nobody likes to be hurt, and, err, no matter, you know ... I've made choices, and, err, I'm not into harm, you know, physical violence I don't like, because having had it myself, I've had physical violence against me.   Dev

When they had become involved in street robbery, then, they had been reluctant to use violence:

> There were two other guys with me. All I did was take the wallet out his back pocket. I wouldn't punch or kick him. That's just me you know, but no I don't like street crime because I have had it done to me. I mean I have had knives put down me throat and I have had my jaw broken. No, there's no way. I couldn't put anyone through that.   Nigel

> This is not to say that no violence occurred. Violence did occur, but as a last resort, for example, when the victim displayed resistance.   Roy

These claims about involvement in street robbery were common amongst the dys-appearing respondents that had been sexually abused and did not simply constitute rhetorical denials that they would ever do such a thing. There are two reasons for surmising this. First, Greater Manchester Police statistics at the time of the study showed that 6 per cent of offenders accounted for 60 per cent of street crime. This suggests that, inversely, the vast majority of street crime offenders accounted for a relatively small number of street crimes and are only likely, therefore, to engage in street crime on a broadly 'one-off' basis for reasons already described. Second, research has shown that self-reports of drug use and involvement in criminal activity are reliable and valid indicators because, when checked, they tend to account with official records (White *et al* 2002; Nurco 1985). Thus, interviewees that claimed to have only ever engaged in violent acquisitive crimes as a one-off were quite prepared to describe incidents where they had willingly and deliberately committed acts of violence that, critically, were a consequence of their own dys-state of being-towards-care and therefore targeted towards *specific others* rather than because they had a disposition towards violence. For example, Lee, who was a victim of sexual abuse and therefore repulsed by the idea of committing harm against *generalised others*, also talked openly about how, on a number of occasions, he had 'kicked the fuck out of' paedophiles:

> Oh yeah, because I don't believe in abusing people. Pretty passionate about it ... I'm going to tell you a story now, right? ... I was seeing this girl, local girl, had a little sister. I was seeing Rachel for about eighteen months, which was when her sister was ten and a half up to about twelve. And she was like a little sister to me; do you know what I mean? We was getting really close, I'd go down and see ... had a key to the fucking house, do you know what I mean? Sort of relationship. Anyway, there's a knock on me door. I'd been split up from Rachel for about six months and she's stood there, the little 'un. She's in tears so I bring her in and apparently a local doorman, one of the local pubs, had given her amphetamine and acid and sexually assaulted her, do you know what I mean? ... So

off I went that night … Anyway, found myself in this guy's house that night. Smashed me way in. Kicked fuck out of him … Mashed him … really fucking went ballistic on him. Police turned up, his wife was upset about him. Police turned up, he's on the floor, blood everywhere. What I'd been doing is I'd been pulling his cupboards off the wall, smashing them on his head. I broke his legs; he had his arm twisted… Smashed up, do you know what I mean? … He left, he left … got smashed up badly … his face was that badly scarred he scares children. Children … scared of him instantly coz he's so badly scarred. Not such a bad thing is it, if he scares children? So that's it basically.   Lee

On becoming problematic drug users, then, most of the dys-appearing respondents that had experienced some form of abuse simply continued to commit the types of non-violent acquisitive crimes that they had always been involved in, such as shoplifting, but now more regularly. For Angela, this meant 'all day, everyday':

I've known people to go out and be at it all day until they come back with, erm, I don't know how much it is, like a 16th of heroin, or an eighth of heroin I don't know how, I've never bought that much, that amount, I don't know how much that is, but they do go out shoplifting all day and wait until they've got like a large amount of money and then go out and buy a large amount of heroin.   Angela

The ones I know, the smack heads and things are just like shoplifters and things like that. They only do it every so often until they get really bad.   Mike

This corresponds with the findings of a plethora of previous studies which have found that all types of drug abusers are more likely to commit property crimes, such as shoplifting, and are less likely to commit crimes against persons (Nurco *et al* 1985; McBride and McCoy 1982; Inciardi and Chambers 1972) and that crimes against the person therefore appear to be committed by social groups other than narcotics users. That said, the tendency for problematic drug use to result in higher levels of involvement in crime was not inevitable for respondents that had experienced abuse. For example, survivors of sexual abuse such as Joanne chose not to exacerbate their involvement in crime but, instead, decided to beg to feed her habit, not least because it was profitable as well as 'harmless':

I was used to still taking drugs everyday, going out begging, selling Big Issues, you name it I did it, well, I weren't actually a Big Issue vendor. I just used to get Big Issue's off people to use to beg with … You can make a lot of money … I used to go out on a Saturday night, say about eight or nine o'clock, by about ten or eleven, I'd have fifty, sixty quid in me pocket … Different people give you different amounts. I've had ten-pound drops. I've had twenty-pound drops.   Joanne

Brian described how he would pawn his brother's equipment, rather than committing crime during periods when he had been unable to maintain his consumption within limits:

It weren't a problem at first because I was getting it for free because I was minding it for person who was selling it at the end of the night then after that I just started pawning things in sometimes they didn't belong to me like my brother's equipment and things.   Brian

And Judith opted to obtain more money to procure crack cocaine by 'sponging from other people' as well as continuing to operate as a sex worker; she simply obtained enough 'punters' each day to pay for her daily habit..

Judith:	I'd [often] go and sponge off somebody else that's smoking.
CA:	So was the burglary just a one off then?
Judith:	Yeah! Yeah! Cause I did it like to get like to get some more smoke.
CA:	Right, right. How come that was a one off then?
Judith:	It wasn't my sort of crime, I've always liked credit cards, I was like pushed into that [burglary] so to speak, so, I mean like really I prefer to do this [sex working] because I don't think like that it's hurting anybody you know what I mean? What I'm doing.

Street Crime is What Happens When You Are Busy Making Other Plans

Although dys-appearing survivors of abuse reported higher levels of involvement in crime to support their escalating habits at various points in time, they were only prepared to undertake certain crimes (mainly shoplifting) and not others (mainly street robbery) and had therefore sought to avoid involvement in violent acquisitive crimes such as street robberies. Yet they had each been selected for interview on the grounds that they had been involved in violent acquisitive crimes such as street robberies; albeit it became apparent during the fieldwork (and subsequent statistical checks) that these involvements in street robbery were broadly 'one-off'. This raises the question of exactly how violent acquisitive crimes such as street robbery came to occur and with what consequences for the protagonists of those robberies.

Although the dominant political discourse presents problematic drug users as 'chaotic' (due to their alleged inability to control their desire for drugs) and their consequent involvement in violent acquisitive crimes such as street robbery as 'irrational', this is based on some fundamental misunderstandings. This becomes clear when we compare their approach to undertaking 'recreational crime' with the approach they took to acquisitive crime, whose purpose was to secure funds to procure drugs such as heroin. Specifically, Chapter 4 showed that recreational crime was, first, not a consequence of recreational drug use and, second, tended to occur 'in the thick of it'. That is to say, recreational drug users had a socially constituted ready-to-hand comportment towards petty crimes which were therefore described as acts that were 'just' performed when opportunities presented themselves. However, when the same people (that had also endured experiences of sexual abuse) became 'problematic' drug users, they objectified their involvements in crime as 'present-at-hand'. Since their involvement in crime was now serious, and partially driven by their need for drugs, they needed to take a stance about how they would obtain funds and, in doing so, rejected acquisitive crimes that might involve violence as a legitimate means of securing the necessary finance. Far from being 'irrational', then, they objectified their involvement in crime from the distance of someone that was present-at-hand to the entity being objectified. This meant that they had to formulate a strategy to obtain the funds to support their drug habit on a given day in ways that were acceptable to themselves, since this would ensure that their involvement in acquisitive crime was compatible with their being-towards-crime rather than dictated by their immediate need for drugs. In order to avoid the 'rattle', then, these respondents were ordinarily organised so that they were able to 'stick to' involvement in crimes that they deemed acceptable, in order to obtain funds to procure their drugs, and thus avoid placing themselves in a situation where they would need to undertake an unacceptable crime, such as street robbery, out of their desperation for drugs. Thus Les talked about how the heroin addicts he knew tended to be 'organised':

> You have got to be organised to be a heroin addict. You have got to know where [to go] … You don't get a lot of people going out really [as] an opportunist. Being on heroin he would know what things they are going to do.   Les

Street crime was thus described as something that happened when the main plan (e.g. shoplifting) had gone awry. For example Oliver (who latterly developed a revulsion of street robbery as a result of the death he had apparently caused during its execution, but whom had earlier described street robbery as something that was always 'definitely in mind') now described street robbery as an option that was only 'at the back of your mind' if the main plan failed to produce the necessary pecuniary rewards:

> … it was just something that happened the second time like you say it was in the back of me mind, it was a plan C, plan D, whatever.   Oliver

All of these respondents had made recourse to the 'Plan C' and 'Plan D' that was 'in the back of their minds' at some point. There were two key reasons for this. First, the interviewees in this study talked about how the opportunity to implement 'Plan A' (i.e. shoplifting) was being eroded 'these days' because retail outlets were becoming more effective at targeting shoplifters:

> You go into shops and you know straight away that you are being watched and you can't do nothing …. And these days they've got radios through to every shop, so you go from one shop like by the time you get to the second one they've got your description. Stanno

Second, when interviewees had 'been out all day' seeking shoplifting opportunities, but without success, they described how 'the rattle' that would begin to set in undermined their ability to make choices about the types of crime they were prepared to become involved in, and thus how they had had to revert to 'Plan C' or 'Plan D':

> I remember I had been out all day trying to get a graft the general way, the supermarket, anything I could [and] it just wasn't happening [so] five hours later I was nearly crawling back home and saw somebody drawing some money out of a hole in the wall and I grabbed his wallet.   Oliver

Whilst shoplifting was largely a planned activity, then, most of the interviewees described their involvement in street crime as the product of desperation that required them to 'suppress' their normal rules of thumb in the service of opportunism:

> Because that's the kind of person I am now, … maybe it's my own [rules]. I have got my rules and it's just you suppress them in order to get what you want.   Oliver

Nevertheless, despite 'rattling' due to the absence of shoplifting opportunities, respondents such as Stanno described how they sought out specific opportunities involving certain types of victims (such as students) but avoided opportunities that would involve other types of victim, such as older and disabled people, even though it would have been easier for them to commit a street robbery against older or disabled people in their weakened state:

> I didn't do it [street crime] like on a regular basis, it was just, what's the word, it was just desperation at the time if I couldn't get money from shoplifting ... then I'd go and mug someone ... I've never robbed like old age pensioners or people with disabilities, it's like students.   Stanno

The point being made by the respondents above, then, was that problematic drug users that had experienced one or other form of physical (usually sexual) abuse tended to make choices about the types of crime that they were prepared to be involved in, and formulated plans so that they were able 'stick to' these crimes and thus avoid involvement in others, mainly street crime. Involvement in street crime occurred when these choices disappeared.

Conclusion

This chapter has examined the criminal consequences of problematic drug use. I have already discussed how the mode of being-against-care that my bereaved respondents exhibited meant that they went for drugs such as heroin 'big time' and therefore took copious amounts of such drugs whilst also engaging in the more dangerous practice of injection. The first part of this chapter followed up on this by examining how becoming a 'big time' drug user necessitated an immediate change in the level of their criminal involvements. Their involvement in acquisitive crime, notably shoplifting, was 'prolific' whereas they talked about violent acquisitive crimes such as street robbery as 'options'. The mode of 'dys-appearance', which involved a high degree of social suffering, was quite different. This mode of becoming a serious drug user meant that drugs such as heroin were used but in moderation. This was reflected in the immediate criminal consequences that followed. Dys-appearing respondents were able to moderate their involvement in crime, and some even described themselves as 'giro junkies' that restricted their drug use within existing income limits thereby avoiding increased involvement in crime. Thus progression into serious drug use did not automatically result in higher levels of involvement in crime *or* the committal of more serious crimes, such as street robbery.

However, the second part of the chapter examined the problems that this group encountered as a consequence of 'being' problematic drug users over the longer term, when the daily cost of their drug use increased to up to £150 per day. Nevertheless their *a priori* revulsion of violence (which was a consequence of how experiences of sexual abuse made physical harm a thematic focus of attention) meant that street robbery was not an option for them under any circumstances. Conversely, they described how they 'planned' their involvement in acquisitive crime because this enabled them to identify ways of securing their required level of income without resorting to the violent forms of acquisitive crime they sought to avoid. By and large they were thus able to 'stick with' involvement in the same forms of crime that they had always been involved in, that is, shoplifting. Involvement in street robbery was a one-off occurrence that came about 'in desperation' when their plans had failed to deliver the income that they required to sustain their drug habit on a given day. I take this analysis forward in Chapter 7 which shows how different forms of being-towards drugs and crime are also associated with specific comportments to drug treatment. This is important because an understanding of being-towards treatment enables me to identify those for whom (and the circumstances in which) treatment is likely to be effective and ineffective.

Chapter 7

Confrontations with the 'Soiled Self'

Introduction

The 'dys-appearance' induced by experiences of abuse and the being-against-care that resulted from experiences of bereavement produce specific forms of comportment towards problematic drug use (Chapter 5). Both forms of being-towards problematic drug use can also be associated with particular levels and types of criminality (Chapter 6). This chapter is concerned to understand *whether* and *how* these different forms of comportment towards problematic drug use, and their particular criminal consequences, are also associated with specific forms of being-towards treatment and therefore specific routes *out* of drug use.

Now earlier chapters have shown that respondents in a dys-state of being-towards-care (as a consequence of their experiences of abuse) reviled acquisitive crime that involved violations of the body. This resulted in their production of a discourse that was manifestly and unambiguously against violent crime. The exception to this appeared to be isolated incidents of violence that were *targeted*, for example, at the perpetrators of the type of abuse that they had themselves suffered. Yet all of these respondents had also been involved in drug related violent acquisitive crimes such as street robberies that, broadly speaking, were 'one-off'. The first part of this chapter shows how their realisation of 'what they had done', which represented the antithesis of their being-towards-crime, stunned them into what I call 'psychological low points'. It also shows that this 'shock' reinforced their imminent relation to necessity (which we saw earlier to be a penchant for 'dealing with things' in the 'here and now' and converse absence of a future orientation stretching across time) and thereby produced a felt necessity to access *immediate* treatment to tackle their drug use 'now'. Their current and immediate feeling was, after all, that they simply could not allow such a thing to happen to them again. These respondents were presented with a problem when they realised that detoxification treatments were not immediately available to them. I discuss the impacts that this had on their desire for desistance.

There was little sense that involvement in violent acquisitive crimes such as street robbery would present a similar challenge to the comportment of being-against-care that resulted from experiences of bereavement. This is because the mode of being-against-care produced a tendency to 'not care about anything or anyone' thereby resulting in prolific crime where street robbery was always 'an option'. The route out of problematic drug use taken by this latter group was therefore different to the route taken by those that reached 'psychological low points'. The second part of the chapter discusses how this latter group sought to tackle their serious drug use when they reached what I term 'physiological low points'. Physiological low points occurred when their bodies could 'take no more drugs' thereby requiring immediate desistance. Since detoxification services were not immediately available to drug service users, respondents that were at physiological low points would formulate alternative desistance strategies. A common strategy involved the deliberate committal of crime to receive a 'jail break' since respondents were better able to rattle in prison where they were also able to access treatment services such as detoxification. I discuss the impact that the 'jail breaks' route to desistance had for my respondents' longer term drug use, as well as the impact that it had on their future criminal career trajectories.

Psychological Low Points

Experiences of sexual abuse produced 'dys-appearing bodies' that were once taken-for-granted but now a thematic focus of *negative* attention that needed to be 'blocked out' by drugs such as heroin. The moderate use of these drugs was indicative of the manner in which dys-appearance undermined the primacy of (but did not destroy) the ethos of being-towards-*care* which was still an issue for survivors of sexual abuse that were preoccupied with coming to terms with the violation of their own bodies. However, since care was still an issue for the dys-appearing body, and since normative standards of care were established in relation to normalised others that had not been violated ('I did not realise it was wrong until I talked to X about it'), the violation of bodies became a thematic focus of attention which manifested itself in revulsion of street robbery as a means of generating an income to support drug use ('I would not want to inflict what I have experienced on someone else'). Involvement in street robbery thus tended to be the product of a perceived lack of choice and was a one-off event that had been undertaken with reluctance. Street robberies were described by dys-appearing (abused) respondents as a 'bad point' in their lives and how the realisation of this had made them cry:

> I'm out on the shops with the knife, she's like that 'Don't hurt me, don't hurt me' I said 'I don't want to hurt you' I said 'all I want is the money' I say to her 'open the till' and she said 'No 'cause your going to hurt me' so I said to her 'Look' I threw the knife on the floor I said 'just open the till' she opened the till and I started shaking, and when I got out of the shop I started crying 'cause I felt bad for what I'd done, but, I needed the money, and that was the only way I could get it ... They upset me, but the armed robberies more, because I had the knife and all that, you know, the people, getting upset and that ... When you're doing the armed robberies, you're there with them, while you're waiting to get the money, you know, you're seeing how they're reacting.   Roy

Joanne similarly described how street robbery was a particularly 'low point' that made her realise that she needed to 'sort her head out':

> It's not like I'm a thief, and I'll thieve off anyone. I won't do that. I'd thieve from shops, and that's the only place I'd thieve from. Manchester got a bit too much, you know, all the police mainly and things like that. So when I got arrested, and I got done for this robbery, street robbery, I was like, you know it was like, it was a bad time, it was time for me to sort me head out ... I felt guilty, knowing that the drugs had made me do something like

that. When I look back, it was just … You know, I couldn't understand how I turned out like that, I don't know why, … but, I felt terrible after it, you know … It just proves what the drugs can do to you.   Joanne

Carolyn similarly talked about how she hated the way in which her body was violated during the course of her job as a 'sex worker'. Her own experiences of corporeal violation meant that she 'could not believe' how much she had 'lowered herself' when she committed a street robbery on one of her 'punters' to avoid 'having to do my job':

> I've shoplifted, which is still something wrong to do, but, to have pounced on someone, and demand money off them, is not a nice thing is it? And that's just not me, and I couldn't believe it'd gone that far … I started in prostitution, that's what started it off, got worse and worse into it, and because I didn't want to do it, I just ended up robbing the guy, it was the night I just thought I'd had enough, I don't want to do this, and I thought it would be easier to rob him than do anything with him, it's just … I don't know, I couldn't believe I'd even done, lowered myself to do something so daft, *that's why I just wanted the prison in the end.*   Carolyn

Psychological Low Points and the Imminent Nature of Need

Although members of the dys-appearing group described how involvement in street robbery made them realise that it was now 'time to sort me head out', this was easier said than done. This was largely because the nature of the help they were seeking from drug services was not readily available. Specifically drug services employ 'care planning' as a key tool. This is based on the notion that drug users are assessed at the point of entry whereupon a 'plan' is formulated to assist them to address their drug use. The critical point to note about 'care planning' is that it is future oriented and requires drug users to be 'stabilised' on methadone before seeking 'appropriate' ways to eliminate drug use from their lifestyles. Although detoxification services are available, then, drug users are often told that they must first stabilise their drug use and sustain contact with the drug service. Drug services often consider detoxification when this has been achieved, which can take up to 12 months of regular contact with the service (Kearney and Allen 2005). The future oriented nature of care planning, then, requires drug workers to view the lives of drug users from the same spatial and temporal distance that academic researchers have conventionally viewed drug use. That is to say, drug workers are required to understand a drug user's present situation in relation to a desired future that can be 'aimed for' and 'worked towards'. Furthermore, they are required to encourage drug users to see themselves, and their own situation, from a similar spatial and temporal distance and therefore to objectify their own needs.

The problem here is that these drug users have spent their entire lives at an imminent proximity to necessity, which can be seen in the immediacy of their comportment to the future. Everything about their comportment towards recreational drug use and crime (which occurred 'in the thick of it') suggested this to be the case. The same is true of the way they grasped drugs such as heroin that were treated as ready-to-hand during disturbing encounters and episodes ('I was offered it and took it because I just needed to block the feelings out'), rather than by objectifying the universally available means of coming to terms with their existentially disturbing experiences (e.g. counselling services). My respondents' lives, then, might best be described as 'living in the here and now' where what is *here* and what is *now* is all that really matters.[1] The sense of 'horror' that was induced by involvement in street robbery simply reinforced this imminent relation to necessity which, in this case, was to eliminate drugs from their lifestyle 'here and now', before they did it again:

> I went to CDT for some help and they put me on a three month waiting list. Three months! And I said, 'How am I supposed to wait for 3 months?' I said 'anything could happen. I could have died'. But they said three months 'cause there were that many people. But looking back now I can understand it because there is a lot of people who need help out there but at the time I was like 'what about me', kind of thing, thinking that they weren't helping me.
>   Alan

There is something interesting about the 'second order' discourse that Alan produced in the quotation above, that is, when he 'looked back' on his experiences of drug treatment. However, this 'second order' discourse is less than useful to us because it does not provide us with an accurate description of his relation to drug treatment in the immediate urgency of the circumstances in which it was sought (which is a point I have made elsewhere in this book in other drug-using contexts). This comes through in his 'first order' discourse, which is the part of the quotation that refers to how he felt 'at the time' and 'as it was happening' ('Three months! How am I supposed to wait for three months?'). This first order discourse suggests that drug users at 'psychological low points' approach drug services to gain immediate access to detoxification, rather than for a methadone script which is what they were offered and which they thought had been introduced for purposes of social control (i.e. to reduce crime) rather than to assist them realise their immediate desire to become 'drug-free':

> When I first came here, right, … I said to him I don't really want methadone, can you help, and this is the problem because with the government, what it is if someone realises they've got, erm, they've got a problem, yeah, with the heroin, a lot of them what they want to do, once they realise they've got a problem, they want to, they want to get off it, but they don't want to start using the methadone, but what the government are doing is you have the methadone, that's it, keep quiet, keep the crime down and that's it, but it's wrong because when I came here to get me into a detox unit in a couple of weeks, now it's

---

1   Lalander (2003) has previously referred to drug users tendency to live in the 'here and now' as a lifestyle choice made by members of a subculture. For Lalander, then, the 'buzz' of living in the 'here and now' is a lifestyle choice that distinguishes the subculture from mainstream society, which demands a future planning orientation, e.g. to engage in education for the purposes of accumulating qualifications, to defer some forms of consumption until an income level has been achieved that will justify it, *etc*. I completely disagree with Lalander. My respondents' tendency to live in the 'here and now' was not a lifestyle choice. Such choices were simply not open to my respondents. Conversely, my respondents' imminent comportment to the future was a product of dispositions that were socially structured and that made an imminent relation to the future their only option.

impossible because they haven't got the resources, haven't got the money to do it so, erm, I ended up getting on the methadone and once you are on that methadone that's it, that's it, it's like 5 times harder to get off than heroin ... Oh yeah, you can be on it, you can be battling for months off it, but that was, I mean I did, I know a lot of people who've been in the situation where they've gone to someone and they've asked for help [getting into detox] and they've not got it just for the simple fact that there's no money to do this sort of thing ... I was scared of like coming off the methadone, withdrawing off the methadone ... The methadone, ... that's the biggest problem ... I mean, all right, it might cut crime down and that ... [but] it's just a trap isn't it, once you are trapped with that methadone, that's it, you've nowhere to go then, your life is on hold then, you are just on hold, life is on hold until you get off it, but that's it, so that's it ... That's what I'm saying. If they could change something like that, get someone in [to detox] straight away, they should have like a 24 hour emergency place where someone, you know, ... they can get them in straight away, get them sorted, give them one chance if they fuck it up that's down to them. Todd

Indeed methadone was devalued simply because it 'put off' desistance from drugs which was what my respondents felt they required 'here and now':

I think it [methadone] puts off the inevitable, err, coming off drugs, err, I think they should have, there should be something, something different than methadone, because methadone, ... more often than not it's stronger than any street heroin ... So if you want to come off heroin, if you want to be normal like normal people are, working people with cars outside their house and all this, it's like 7 times harder to get off methadone than it is to get off heroin ... I don't know what the answer is, but I tell you, I know for a fact it's, it's 7 or 8 times stronger than street heroin. Dev

Unable to elicit the immediate help they felt they needed from drug services, at 'psychological low points', these drug users appeared to develop a sense of fatalism. Unless their drug use could be immediately eliminated 'here and now' (whilst they were consumed by their own self-loathing following involvement in violent acquisitive crime) respondents felt that they could not plan and work towards a future without drug use. This bred a sense of hopelessness in users such as Todd who began to feel 'sod it, what's the point of being squeaky clean when nobody will help me':

When you are getting no help off no one, you are phoning up everyone, you are trying to get help, and they say 'well, come back next month at a certain time'. Next month! And when you are getting no help, getting any help off any one that's when it gets you down, that's when you think 'sod the lot of them'. Then I'm going to go out and, that's the problem ... One thing leads to another and that's it, you are getting into so much trouble, you think 'oh sod it'. I'm not saying it's just that. It's not just that ... I was thinking well what's the point, what's the point. Todd

The sense of hopelessness and dejection that lack of access to treatment bred in respondents such as Nigel had much more serious consequences. He attempted suicide:

I was really on my own and I felt it. I actually slashed my wrists four times ... I did that one first [points to wrist] and then I did that one [points to other wrist] ... I was just sat next to telephone box where someone could phone up for me and if they did, they did, and if they didn't, they didn't. That's the way; I just looked at it that way. I said in my mind I am going one way [to either live] or other [to die] because that's what was happening, erm, and someone did phone up.   Nigel

Although a sense of hopelessness was a consequence of the immediacy of need that resulted in demands for detoxification 'here and now or never', there was no necessary relationship between a lack of immediate access to detoxification and the emergence of this sense of hopelessness and fatalism. This sense of hopelessness and fatalism only set in when my respondents *defined* their immediate need to totally desist from drug use 'now'. However, the anxious confrontation with self that involvement in street robbery had produced (and which resulted in this imminent need to 'do something now' to address problematic drug use) was interpreted in other ways by other respondents. These other respondents defined their immediate needs in terms of a need to ensure that they 'never again' became involved in street robberies or other crimes that violated the bodies of generalised others. This group wanted immediate help *but* of whatever form that would ensure that they could control their drug use and thus involvement in crime which, of course, presents a direct contrast with the 'fatalistic' group that rejected methadone and whom were in a downward spiral. Although immediate lack of detoxification was a problem for the fatalistic group that wanted it 'here and now or never', this other group of respondents used methadone as a way of managing their drug use and therefore involvement in crime. For example Angela described how methadone 'took a lot of weight off her shoulders' since she knew she would not be ill ('rattling') which is what had prompted her involvement in a street robbery:

> [Using methadone] meant I didn't have to suffer, err, worrying about the next day or, you know, when money ran out, you know, it's just there, it takes a lot of weight off, you know, weight off your shoulders … Knowing that, you know, you are not going to be ill the next day and, you know, you've got something there.   Angela

Dev similarly talked about using methadone as a 'stop gap' rather than as a replacement for heroin which enabled him to manage his involvement in crime when he did not have the money to buy heroin:

> Heroin, no, if I get, if I get a bag I'll take it, err, it's not that, I know it's wrong, but I think, in my opinion I don't think a lot people on methadone are stabilised on methadone, I think, err, most people on methadone take heroin and use methadone as a stop gap when they can't, when they haven't got the money to buy heroin they will take the methadone.
> Dev

Psychological Low Points and Phenomenology of Social Bonds

The existential crises that emerged from involvements in violent acquisitive crime such as street robberies were not simply addressed via recourse to drug services, although that was the main route that *everyone* described as their first port of call. It also prompted some respondents to turn to their family for help. Now Fishbein and

Perez (2000) have previously focused on the socialising effects of social bonds with parents, peers and societal institutions and argue that the extent to which individuals bond to pro-social family and peers acts as protective factors against crime and drug abuse and therefore necessitates programmes that strengthen social bonds (see Chapter 2).

The argument of Fishbein and Perez (2000) contains elements of accuracy; relationships are important factors in desistance from crime (see Allen 2001, 2003b; Allen and Barkley 2002). However, the material and argument presented in this book would also suggest that it contains a significant level of misunderstanding (even if we went along with their spurious assumption that these bonds would be 'pristine' as opposed to the 'spoiled' social bonds that most of my respondents had with significant others, such as abusive parents). This misunderstanding occurs because they assume that pro-social bonds *always* have the potential to be a positive influence, yet these pro-social social bonds had not proved influential upon my respondents at all *until this critical point in time*. What we need, then, is to develop a phenomenological understanding of the existential significance of social bonds which explains why they work for respondents in some (but not other) modes of being-towards drugs and crime, and some (but not other) points in their drug careers.

Now we have already seen that lostness in they-self (which is a product of the social relations of domination as well as a doxic relation towards the objective regularities that are constitutive of social space) is a result of the 'confirming encounters' with-others that happen on an 'average everyday'. Chapter 4 showed how this resulted in 'natural attitudes' towards recreational crime and drugs. The idea that 'role models' can have any positive effect in such 'average everyday' situations is an ontological fallacy. This is because the simplistic idea that 'you can be like me rather than the likes of yourselves' has little existential relevance or meaning to they-self which has a doxic relation to the social space it occupies. Indeed, even if 'role models' were in a position to encourage the take up of new possibilities in the 'legitimate opportunity structure' (e.g. the sudden availability of 'good jobs' as a result of an economic development initiative) Bourdieu points out that a 'hysteresis effect' would be at work, which is the disjunction between these new opportunities and the dispositions of the they-self to grasp them ('they are not for the likes of us') thus leading to 'missed opportunities'. The hope that role models can provoke a 'positive' reaction from they-self in its 'average everydayness' is therefore highly questionable because they present it with *universal* ideas about 'what its life could be like' that hold no existential relevance to its being-in-the-world or life-being-led. Social interactions with role models are therefore better thought of as 'uneventful encounters' because, quite simply, they do not register as existentially significant at all.

That is not to say that Fishbein and Perez are entirely wrong and that social bonds can never have positive effects. It is simply a matter of 'good timing'. We have already seen that the capacity for authentic selfhood results from 'disturbing encounters' with 'problematic others' that disrupt the 'falleness' in they-self that is established on an 'average everyday'. They do this by acting as a 'voice of conscience' that awakens Dasein by inducing a mode of its possible self-relation and anxious realisation of itself with a life to lead (Heidegger 1962, 1978). That is, they throw Dasein into an anxious confrontation with its they-self as well as its being-with-others (i.e. its lostness in its 'existential actuality') and its potentiality-towards itself and others (i.e. its 'existential potentiality'). Now the key difference between 'disturbing encounters' and 'uneventful encounters' is that the latter occur with 'outsiders' that we could never be which means that they have no existential relevance. The former, on the other hand, occur with those whom we already are or, given time, will become without evasive action, i.e. they provide 'relevant' images of they-self and its existential actuality as well as existential potentiality. This became clear in Chapter 5 where my respondents talked about how 'disturbing encounters' with heroin users resulted in their revulsion of heroin addicts and desistance. Involvement in violent acquisitive crime was similar because it provided an image of what Dasein *had* become, which was existentially troubling because of its prior revulsion of this image. This perforce necessitated action to desist from the problematic drug use that had resulted in their involvement in street robbery and therefore 'opened up' the possibility that relationships with significant others (role models that had always been prepared to offer help) would be drawn on to assist Dasein in its now desperate state. This was when Mike:

> ... started to see family life and things that I like lived with my family when I was younger, me family loved me and all that. I am surprised me Mam is still alive, all the crap I gave her when I was young. Police had her going every night, me, I was wild when I was young and I just calmed down.   Mike

It was at her lowest psychological point (following involvement in a street robbery) that Joanne renewed her relationship with her mother who provided her with a home and her emotional support to help her desist from heroin and from whom she eventually won back respect:

> Joanne: I've got respect of my mum again. Mum did see me when I was on the drugs, and she didn't like me, didn't like it. I was, I'd shrivelled down to five stone ... And it was like death warmed up. Everyone called me death warmed up, 'cause I looked horrible, but other than that I did it for myself, I come off them for myself, I wanted off.
>
> CA: How important do you think those things [house, family] are to helping you stay off smack?
>
> Joanne: It's a big difference, a very big difference ... When you're homeless and you're sleeping rough you look dirty, something like that. I kept myself clean as much as possible. You know having somewhere to be warm, get your head in a proper bed, instead of sleeping on, like a blanket on pavement, cold and shivering, and being rattling in a morning, 'cause when you're rattling, it's just like you've got no energy, you don't want to do anything, you just feel like collapsing and just dropping, and you don't want to do anything, and you're just constantly being sick, and you know, I couldn't say, I couldn't say anything that is good about taking drugs, 'cause there's nothing good about taking drugs, and I wouldn't wish me worst enemy on them. I'd rather just stay away. ... I've got respect of my family again, and that's all I wanted, respect. I wanted off the drugs, I've done it, and I'll never go back, I'll never go back. Being down and out like, plus people when you're out there, and you're homeless, people treat you like you're scum of the earth.

Physiological Low Points

The extent to which the bereaved respondents had 'gone for' drugs such as heroin 'big time' meant that they were more likely, than the dys-appearing group, to encounter such depths as 'physiological low points'. Physiological low points occurred when the problematic use of drugs such as heroin and crack cocaine had taken place to such an extent that, quite simply, their bodies could not take any more. (If the criminal consequences of serious drug use did not 'catch up with them' then the pharmacological effects of drug use tended to catch up with them instead.) The issue here is that 'psychological low points' invited a choice: although users felt an imminent impulsion to address their problematic drug use, and ideally sought immediate detoxification, they also had the option of managing their drug use by either using methadone or seeking help from family. Conversely, respondents that hit 'physiological low points' had no choice but to desist because their bodies 'could not take any more drugs' and thus 'needed a break'.

CA: Have there been any other times when you thought you had to get off [heroin]?

Adam: There were a lot of things where I thought 'fuck, I've got to get off this now', yeah, 'cos I used to wake up in the morning feeling like I was dying and I didn't want to feel like that anymore. I needed the heroin to like get by.

And:

I was looking so rough and, you know, I had one foot in the grave basically and I didn't like what I was doing, I didn't like the daily routine of what I was doing, getting up in the morning, rough as a dog, going out thieving, because [at the times of the day when] you're not using drugs, the rest of the day you're just spending, pinching, thieving, scoring. And it's a horrible way to live your life and you're just living your full day thieving, scoring, smoking the drugs, back out again, thieving, scoring, smoking the drugs, back out again, that's all I were doing all day.　　　　　　　　　　　　　　　　　　Steve

Offenders with bodies that were 'desperate' to desist from using drugs such as heroin and crack cocaine (and in the absence of interventions that could assist them to do so) exhibited a willingness to commit crimes with the deliberate intention of being caught. The purpose of this was to receive a prison sentence which would enable them to access the detoxification treatment that was said to be more readily available in prison *or* at least enable them to suffer the 'rattle'.

Adam: Usually when I'm really bad and I'm on about 5, 6 bags a day and you know I'll be doing anything for a bag. I'd think to myself 'I could do with a bit of jail now' ... I've had the chance when the police have been coming to me house, I've seen them coming, I've had the chance to get off, do a runner, but I've thought 'no, it'll get me away for a bit, give me a break' (laughs).

CA: So you let yourself get caught?

Adam: Yeah, I didn't run, sometimes you just think 'fuck it'.

CA: How many times did you do that then, allowed yourself to get caught?

Adam: Twice.

CA: And you got sentences both times?

Adam: Yeah.
CA: And when you were inside, were you able to come off it?
Adam: Yeah.
CA: So how did you come off it?
Adam: Erm, it's pretty easy really 'cos inside, I know you can get it (heroin) just as easy as out here but me mind wasn't always on it when I was in there so when there was times that I couldn't get no money to get it (heroin) I'd just turn my mind off it and I wouldn't think about it. But if I had some bad news or something I would have to think of a way to get some.

The gravity of the crime that was committed for the purpose of receiving a 'jail break' was contingent on the length of the 'break' that the body required. For example Joanne was prepared to commit a serious crime because she felt that her body needed at least 12 months in prison.

> I needed a long sentence to get my head round coming off the drugs, I needed more than three months in prison to come, to get off, 'cause even when, like you go into jail for three months ... three months isn't long enough to get you off the drugs. You've to be in there for at least twelve months, twelve months' jail sentence, so your body clock's back to normal. It takes about twelve months for that to happen.   Joanne

So crime was not always committed for the purpose of procuring drugs. Respondents at physiological low points regarded the committal of crime as a means of 'achieving' a prison sentence since this provided a 'jail break' that enabled them to desist from involvement in drug misuse and crime. Furthermore, having gone through 'the rattle' during their 'jail break', some respondents were also hoping that they would be better able to manage their drug use and involvement in crime upon release. However, this was often wishful thinking for respondents such as Carolyn who talks about how easy it was to go from a 'celebratory wrap' on release and then 'back to square one':

> I was with, erm, my ex-partner, and I'd get out, and he was drug addicted, so he was still using, so I carry on and celebrate being released and that, and then one thing led to another, and I'd end up just shoplifting again a few days later to support me habit again. Within a week, I was back to square one.   Carolyn

Using prison as a way of providing the body with a 'break' therefore propelled respondents that encountered physiological low points into an entirely different dynamic than those that encountered psychological low points. We have already seen that the psychological nature of the latter route resulted in a return to kinship networks for help to fundamentally address drug problems. The desire to provide the body with a 'jail break' was, however, entirely different. Although prison sentences provided the body with a break, they had longer term consequences for respondents that were also hoping to reduce their level of drug use, when they came out, to more manageable levels. Since the family relationships of this group remained fractured (not least because this group were not ready to mend kinship relationships that had broken up as a consequence of their involvements in problematic drug use and crime) they were unable to return to the 'family home' on release from prison. Since a return home was 'not an option', many problematic drug users had 'no option' but to seek shelter with former associates that were users. This hastened their return to crime, such as shoplifting, in order to generate money to procure drugs that could then be used as 'rent':

> I know a lot of people who were drug addicts that would put me up but would only put me up if I took drugs round. So I'd go round with a couple of rocks and a couple of bags and say 'listen, I've got a couple of things here, can you put me up tonight?' They'd say 'yeah course you can coz you've got drugs'. If you went round with nothing then they'd say 'no'. But because they're drug addicts and you wave the drugs underneath their nose they'll say yeah as long as you keep supplying. So you've got to go out shoplifting.   Norman

Conclusion

Forms of being-towards problematic drug use and crime are associated with forms of being-towards treatment and, therefore, the specific routes that drug users take to address their problematic substance use. The 'dys-appearance' induced by experiences of abuse produced an *a priori* revulsion of crimes that involved violations of the body. When these respondents became involved in one-off street robberies, then, the realisation of 'what they had done' produced 'psychological low points' that necessitated *immediate* treatment to tackle their drug use. The immediacy of these respondents' relation to their need to address substance use meant that they would demand detoxification. Their demands, in this respect, were not unreasonable. They simply reflected the imminent relation that *all* of my respondents had to their needs, given their general proximity to necessity as well as the existential crisis caused by their involvement in street robbery which had prompted them to regard 'dramatic action' as necessary. Given this imminent relation to the need to desist from substance use, the absence of immediate access to detoxification resulted in two outcomes. Respondents that defined their imminent needs in terms of their problematic *drug use* became fatalistic about their situation, given the lack of immediate access to detoxification services. Some of these respondents returned to their previous levels of involvement in crime whereas others had even attempted suicide. These were phenomenological consequences of their inability to access the service that their being-towards drugs treatment demanded at that point in time. Conversely, respondents that problematised their involvement in crime (the 'symptom') over their drug use (the 'cause') were more likely to use methadone as a way to manage their involvement in crime and were successful in doing so. Generally speaking, then, methadone led to a partial desistance from involvement in crime, particularly when it was used as a 'stop gap'; albeit Margaret did claim to have desisted from crime during the 2½ years of her methadone treatment.

On the other hand, the being-against-care that resulted from experiences of bereavement produced specific forms of comportment towards serious drug use and towards the criminal consequences of serious drug use. Since this group did not share the *a priori* revulsion of violent acquisitive crimes possessed by the other group, involvement in street robbery did not fundamentally challenge the comportment of being-against-care (i.e. the tendency to 'not care about anything or anyone' thereby enabling street robbery to be 'an option') that resulted from experiences of bereavement; although there were some instances of *post ante* reflections on involvements in these types of crime that subsequently led to its revulsion. Given the absence of a psychological disposition that would have problematised street robbery, the nature of drug use by this group was prolific and largely unmediated by involvement in crime which meant that they tended to address their problematic drug use at the 'physiological low points' that they were much more likely to encounter, i.e. when their bodies could take no more. Since their bodies were now demanding a 'complete break' from drugs for a time limited period (and given the lack of immediate access to detoxification services that would have enabled them to achieve this) they purposely committed crimes that were punishable with prison sentences. However the tendency to take a 'prison route' out of drugs resulted in them being enmeshed in another dynamic that was a consequence of their homelessness on release from prison and lack of kinship support.

Chapter 8

Conclusions

This book has presented an account of the form of being that emerges out of close proximity to economic necessity (urban poverty, dispossession and so on) and that results in crime and drug use. The purpose of doing this has been to highlight the epistemological blindness of holistic and scholarly accounts of problematic drug use. My argument has been that the limits of the holistic point of view derive from its purported ability to 'see everything, know everything and do anything'. This is because it hastily and unjustifiably locates the responsibility for welfare failures at the door of welfare recipients, thereby 'necessitating' coercive welfare measures (Crawford 1999; Allen 2003). I have also argued that the limits of the scholarly point of view derive from its innate tendency to view the social and economic world as a landscape. The scholarly doxa that impulsively objectifies the social and economic landscape from a spatial and temporal distance results in a form of research questioning that assumes (and therefore asks) that respondents do the same thing when, this book has shown that this is not how they relate to the social and economic landscape.

There is a key difference between these holistic and scholarly perspectives that demand 'reasoned reasons' (Question: But when you said 'it just happened, what do you mean by that'? Answer: 'I suppose it was stupid') and a phenomenological approach that seeks to understand 'first order' forms of articulation that often have no justification other than a confirmatory statement of what has been done (Statement: 'It just happened'). Scholarly demands for 'reasoned reasons' perforce necessitate a satisfactory 'confession' (Foucault 1979) that encouraged my respondents to assume culpability for the 'stupidity' that defined actions that were now located 'in their past'. The disjuncture between the respondents' present perception ('I was stupid') and the historical activity to which they refer (drug use) was based on the imputation of the spatial and temporal distance of the scholarly relation to practice into the agents' relation to their practice, thereby assigning a level of reflexivity (which is that of the scientific observer) to respondents that are the object of social scientific observation.

The problem with this imposition of reflexivity in an interview situation is that it provides respondents with the time and space to 'look back' and decide that they were 'stupid'; time and space that was simply not available to them 'in the thick of it'. However, it is this lack of recognition of the different conditions in which an interview is undertaken and those in which everyday practice takes place (which results in the supposition that reflexivity exhibited in the former situation can be easily transferred to the latter situation) that subsequently justifies the imposition of 'reasonable expectations' on those objects of observation *in their everyday life* – whether implicitly or explicitly. After all, the respondents have now confessed that they are entirely culpable for their actions and that they can 'learn' from this.

The fact that this confession is 'false' in the sense that it has been extracted under the duress of a research interview (whose form and content is misrecognised by respondents as legitimate) is simply overlooked.

The consequences of this are all too apparent in the 'holistic' approach to welfare policy and practice. Specifically, the fact that drugs issues have now been brought onto the 'holistic' regeneration agenda (Home Office 2002) and that a range of 'social' needs are now supposed to be addressed by 'holistic' drug treatment regimes (Audit Commission 2002; National Treatment Agency 2002a, b; Home Office 2004) is universally regarded as a good thing (Allen 2003a). However, my purpose here is not to reflect on the purported advantages of discrete policy initiatives that have taken a 'holistic turn' (e.g. regeneration initiatives, drug treatment programmes), not least because this is why they tend to be judged in such uncritical ways and talked about in such gushing terms. After all, who could possibly argue with a holistic approach when previous failures to address the range of problems that are commonly faced by drug users, such as homelessness, are well known? Conversely, I have argued elsewhere (Allen 2003a) that discrete welfare policies and practices that are holistic in nature can only be properly understood when it is accepted that they are situated within a broader apparatus of holistic welfare policies – not all of which are so holistic or generous of spirit. The key is to understand the nature of the inter-relation between discrete welfare policies and practice within this overall apparatus of welfare provision, which contains both holistic and less than holistic elements. Such an exercise brings the 'bottom line' into focus which is that the individuals' failure to respond appropriately to the opportunities provided by 'holistic' welfare policies and practices (e.g. regeneration and drug treatment programmes) demands measures that are more coercive. This is necessary, of course, because drug users are clearly culpable for their own failure to respond to the opportunities supposedly provided by a holistic welfare system that can 'see everything, know everything and do anything'. In other words, it demands a clamp down. This was happening in two distinct ways in my case study site.

First, drug using offenders were being automatically 'fast tracked' (i.e. coerced) into treatment. The assumptions being made here were not only that 'drugs cause crime' and therefore demand treatment. They are also that the offender (who knows s/he has been 'stupid') is culpable for this situation. Since these offenders know they could have done otherwise, but simply lacked the will, it follows that the rational policy and practice response is to coerce the individual into changing behaviour that they know to be wrong. The problem here, of course, is that coerced treatment does not work and there is a volume of evidence that suggests this to be the case. This book has shown that the reason for the ineffectiveness of treatment programmes (which is overlooked by the holistic and scholarly views of drug use) is that it fails to engage with the form of being that produces a specific comportment towards drugs. Put simply, forcing treatment onto people that have a 'natural attitude' towards drug use will not work. They simply do not have the dispositions to want to grasp it, or to comprehend why it should be grasped. It simply makes no sense to them and is an irrelevance that is being forced on them by others. This came though most clearly in Chapter 7 amongst respondents who talked about methadone programmes as a form of social control.

The second form of clamping down on drug related offending in my case study site was occurring through the imposition of prison sentences with drug treatment orders. This book has shown the perversities that this authoritarian programme creates. Drug treatments are forced onto prisoners at points where they are simply not receptive to them. This is not only unethical (because it is a result of the holistic imperative towards coercion rather than understanding offending behaviour) but also a waste of money. The converse of this is that my respondents talked about the absence of (what they deemed to be) relevant treatment options on encountering psychological and physiological low points. One solution to this conundrum was to commit an offence that was serious enough to warrant a custodial sentence, in order to access drug treatment. This was not simply an occurrence that my respondents relayed to me in the context of their own lives. They also referred to the regularity with which they were aware it happened in general. In other words, the notion that some drug users commit crime in order to receive a prison sentence, and therefore drug treatment, was 'common knowledge'.

Offenders that are able to attract a custodial sentence, and thereby access treatment, are also required or encouraged to undertake associated rehabilitation programmes such as 'Addressing Substance Related Offending' (ASRO). Having examined drugs and crime initiatives such as ASRO, it seems to me that their problem is that they, too, are based on the same holistic and scholarly fallacies that this book has discussed, i.e. they are based on the assumption that my respondents could, in future, make 'reasoned' decisions about involvement in crime and drugs that were taken at a spatial and temporal distance from these practices. For example, an ASRO programme (that I was involved in as a social scientific observer) sought to 'divert' offenders from further involvement in crime by improving their 'thinking skills'. Such programmes were underpinned by the idea that offenders *can* make 'rational choices' about the activities that they are prepared to become involved in, according to the costs of involvement in those activities. It is simply a matter of 'teaching' them how to do it. Yet course participants such as Adam commonly referred to how the pedagogic reasoning that was taught in the classroom seldom transfers into the 'real world' where the dispositions of the habitus orient its response to social situations as they present themselves to the habitus 'in the thick of it':

Adam:	Like [on the course we talked about] what would you do if certain things happened, you know, that kind of thing, like 'think first'. You are supposed to do all them kind of things really, but.
CA:	Has that been any good for you?
Adam:	I've done them all each time I've been to jail and each time I've just gone out and done the same kind of things.

The problem with the measures described above, then, is that they are based on holistic and scholarly demands that emerge from a lack of recognition of the social and institutional privileges that allow policy makers and scholars to view and objectify the social and economic world as a landscape, i.e. an object of contemplation. Adam's response to the above question simply reiterates what other respondents have said throughout this book. Specifically the logic of everyday practice is that it is seldom objectified from a spatial and temporal distance in advance of the performance of any given act (i.e. by examining the social and economic scene 'in the round' and asking the question 'shall I do it this way, or that way?'). Everyday practice occurs 'in the thick of it' and therefore needs to be understood as such, even though this is seldom the case given the epistemological silence that surrounds the fact that the scholarly view is exactly that, a point of view that is both limited and limiting.

The book has tried to express this other (practical) point of view which emerges from a form of being in the world that scholarly researchers have too often overlooked, silenced or epistemologically abused. (The most dramatic example of this can be seen in the way my respondents referred to their own 'stupidity' when they were subjected to the scholarly point of view which they misrecognised as *the* legitimate point of view on the social and economic world.) My analysis of the form of being that emerges out of a life lived in close proximity to economic necessity in deprived urban areas has been based on an analysis of the manner in which practice emerges in dispositional relation to the immediacy with which the objective regularities, that are characteristic of the social spaces occupied by my respondents, present themselves. The doxic relation that habitus, in its 'average-everydayness', has to the social space it occupies therefore results in 'recreational' forms of criminal activity and drug use that could not be 'justified' via recourse to 'reasoned reasons'. As socially structured dispositions (that were a product of constant exposure to the consequences of urban deprivation) they 'came naturally' and 'just happened'. They were 'what you do'.

A phenomenological approach is sensitive to this harmony between the habitus and the necessities inscribed in social space that it occupies. A phenomenological approach is also acutely sensitive to why articulations of 'non-reasoned reasons' for practical actions, that are entirely compatible with the necessities that present themselves in the marginal social spaces being occupied, are indicative of an enduring form of being, that is, a form of being that is deeply inscribed and marked by its inhabitation of marginal social spaces. This is an ontological issue which demands the understanding of different forms of being before imposing social expectations.

The marginal social spaces that my respondents occupied were those 'traditional working class areas' of Greater Manchester that, over the course of the last few decades, have since become known as 'deprived urban areas'. The social consequences of this urban marginalisation and deprivation have been the growth of crime and drug use to endemic levels. Over the course of a few decades, then, one can witness how working class dispositions once suited to the industrial complex (Charlesworth 2000) have been replaced by dispositions that are a consequence of the economic and social dispossession suffered by subsequent generations of working class people, e.g. the emergence of a 'natural attitude' to crime and drugs. With two exceptions, my respondents were all below 40 years of age (the majority between 20 and 40 years of age) at the time of the interviews and therefore part of these subsequent generations that had left school in the post-industrial Britain of the mid-1970s, 1980s and 1990s. This book has shown that the elements of this generation that occupy deprived urban areas commonly exhibit a form of being that is not simply 'out of touch' with the post-industrial complex that they are now expected to engage with by *New Labour's* 'welfare to work' policies. Their dispositions are actually hostile to the demands of the new post-industrial complex; given that they are oriented towards the illegitimate opportunity structure which, for so long, has provided them with the only real choices that they have ever known. Given this situation it is important to remember that these hostile dispositions are not simply a product of their marginalisation by changes in the capitalist mode of production, but also of government policies and a middle class educational system that too often makes working class people feel utterly worthless (Charlesworth 2000).

Given the deeply inscribed and enduring nature of my respondents' dispositions, which were most dramatically exhibited in the first order speech forms that they employed ('I don't know, you just do'; 'I'm stupid') there is little point in holistic welfare policies that provide a range of opportunities but then demand an 'appropriate' form of responsiveness to those opportunities. This is because my respondents simply do not have the dispositions to be able to formulate an 'appropriate' response to such opportunities. There is even less point in coercive measures (e.g. enforced drug treatment when it is not wanted) that force forms of behaviour onto people that have failed to respond to prior opportunities to 'change their ways'. Such coercive measures fail to understand the necessity for a harmony between the principles that govern treatment programmes and the form of being that is engaged with that programme. For example Chapter 7 showed that drug treatments were considered to be a poor excuse for social control when they were not wanted *but* that the same treatments did work when my respondents were 'ready' for them. This was when they were at psychological or physiological low points (or their like), in which case their form of being was against drugs and therefore broadly compatible with the ethos of treatment programmes.

Other supporting evidence for this proposition about the need for a level of compatibility between 'being' and treatment (which is overlooked by holistic and scholarly points of view) is evident in studies that have shown methadone prescribing to be associated with immediate reductions in crime but that, crucially, retention in methadone treatment has only a *slight* effect on crime reduction in the longer term (Rothbard *et al* 1999). Since crime and drug use is an expression of a form of being, then, short-term coercive measures may work in a way that longer term retention in treatment does not. In the same way that we find a level of harmony between the dispositions of the habitus and the social space that it occupies, and which results in a 'natural' comportment to the practical necessities that are inscribed into that space, a similar level of harmony needs to exist between the habitus and treatment programmes if their effectiveness is to be enduring. It is largely for this reason that researchers such as Greenberg and Adler (1974: 259) have argued that 'it is necessary for programme administrators to have detailed knowledge of the characteristics of the population their programme is serving'.

Although Greenberg and Adler are arguably on the right lines here, this book has shown that programme administrators do not simply require details about the socio-economic characteristics of drug-using populations. They require an understanding of forms of being towards and against treatment, and the points in time when forms of being towards treatment are compatible with the ethos of treatment programmes. Rather than seeking to coerce individuals out of drug use, the solution to individuals' drugs problems in 'normal' circumstances (i.e. when they have a natural attitude *towards* drugs) might simply be to keep them alive until they are 'ready' to engage with treatment programmes (i.e. when they have a being-towards-treatment). After all, it is debatable whether such urgent and coercive measures are required to tackle drug problems when, this book has shown, there is no such thing as a straightforward link between drugs and (violent) crime. Indeed Chapter 6 showed that the onset of drug use often has little effect on involvement in crime and that, when it does, there is little evidence that it results in violent crime. Of course such a suggestion goes against everything that the holistic and scholarly points of view – that problematise drug use – preach. But it is *one* logical conclusion of a phenomenological form of analysis that is sensitive to the form of being that results in orientations towards and against drugs and drugs treatment at different points in time.

In a nutshell, then, my argument is that if economic restructuring results in the withdrawal of opportunities from working class people, and social policies exacerbate their marginalisation over the course of decades, they become fucked up. One does not have to look hard for evidence of the numerous attacks that Conservative and New Labour governments have waged against marginalised groups such as single parents and drug users over the last couple of decades (Jacobs *et al* 2003). Of course it does not always suit policy makers to marginalise fucked up populations, and to fuck up marginalised populations. Indeed it *now* suits policy makers to develop an apparently more liberal focus (through the development of the so-called 'social inclusion' and 'holistic welfare' agendas) on the same 'fucked up' people that they have previously sought to marginalise. And fuck up. They are unashamed about the reasons for doing this, which are because 'fucked up' people are regarded as a threat to the so-called 'respectable' social groups that have extracted benefits from the economic restructuring of the last few decades. Of course, the representation of these 'holistic' initiatives as somehow 'liberal' and 'inclusive' is highly contentious given that they are situated within a welfare policy apparatus that presents 'opportunity' at one end and coercion at the other, for those that are apparently too stupid to respond to the aforementioned opportunities. My argument would be that if it takes decades for economic restructuring (aided and abetted by both Labour and Conservative governments) to fuck people up and turn them into drug users, then it will take decades to undo the damage that has been done. That said, perhaps it would be best to keep drug users alive until that damage has been undone (and they are ready for treatment) rather than to exacerbate it further by forcing them into treatment. A phenomenological analysis suggests that this is the very *least* that should be done for people that have suffered from the consequences of social and economic dispossession and marginalisation for their entire lives.

Bibliography

Adams, S. 1993. 'A gendered history of the social management of death and dying in Foleshill, Coventry, during the inter-war years', in Clark, D. (ed.) *The Sociology of Death*. London, Blackwell, pp. 149-68.

Adler, P. 1985 [1993]. *Wheeling and Dealing: An Ethnography of an Upper Level Drug Dealing and Smuggling Community.* 2nd Edition. New York, Columbia University Press.

Advisory Council on the Misuse of Drugs. 1998. *Drug Misuse and the Environment.* London, Home Office.

Agar, M. 1973. *Ripping and Running: A Formal Ethnography of Heroin Addicts.* New York: Seminar Press.

Ahmed, A.G., Salib, E. and Ruben, S. 1999. 'Psychiatric disorders in first degree relatives of patients with opiate dependence', *Science and the Law*, 39(3), pp. 219-27.

Aldridge, J., Parker, H. and Measham, F. 1999. *Drug Trying and Drug Use Across Adolescence: A Longitudinal Study of Young People's Drug Taking in Two Regions of Northern England.* London, Home Office/Drugs Prevention Advisory Service.

Allen, C. 2000. 'On the "physiological dope" problematic housing and illness research: Towards a critical realism of home and health', *Housing, Theory and Society*, 17(2), pp. 49-67.

Allen, C. 2001. *'With a Little Help from My Friend': The Nature and Effectiveness of a Tenancy Support Service for Ex-Offenders*. Manchester, National Probation Service.

Allen, C. 2003a. 'Desperately seeking fusion: On joined-up thinking, holistic practice and the *new* economy of welfare professional power', *The British Journal of Sociology*, 54(2), pp. 287-304.

Allen, C. 2003b. 'On the logic of *new* welfare practice: an ethnographic case study of the "new welfare intermediaries"', *Sociological Research Online*, 8(1), http://www.socresonline.org.uk/8/1/allen.html.

Allen, C. 2004. 'Bourdieu's habitus, social class and the spatial worlds of visual impaired children', *Urban Studies*, 41(3), pp. 487-506.

Allen, C. 2005a. 'The links between heroin, crack cocaine and crime: Where does street crime fit in?' *British Journal of Criminology*, 45(3), pp. 355-72.

Allen, C. 2005b. 'On the social relations of contract research production: Power, positionality and epistemology in housing and urban research', *Housing Studies*, 20(6), pp. 989-1007.

Allen, C. 2005c. 'On the epistemological limits of the "'area effects" debate: Towards a phenomenology of urban deprivation', *Housing, Theory and Society*, 22(4), pp. 196-212.

Allen, C. 2006. 'Minding its own business? The social organisation of entrepreneurial scholarship @ enterprising-university.co.uk', paper presented to ESRC seminar on *The Social Relations of Contract Research Production*, Kings College London, 27 April.

Allen, C. and Barkley, D. 2002. 'Housing for offenders: The role of understanding relationships in "Supporting People"', *Probation Journal*, 49(4), pp. 267-76.

Allen, C. and Kearney, J. 2005. *Two and a Half Cheers for Salford Drug Service.* Salford, Salford City Council.

Allen Collinson, J. 2004. 'Occupational identity on the edge: Social science contract researchers in higher education', *Sociology*, 38(2), pp. 313-29.

Anderson, T.L. 1993. 'Types of identity change in drug using and recovery careers', *Social Focus*, 26(2), pp. 133-45.

Anderson, T.L. 1998. 'Drug identity change processes, race, and gender. I. Explanations of drug misuse and a new identity-based model', *Substance Use and Misuse*, 33(11), pp. 2263-79.

Anglin, D.M. and Perrochet, B. 1988. 'Drug use and crime: A historical review of research conducted by the UCLA drug abuse research centre', *Substance Use and Misuse*, 33, pp. 1871-914.

Anslinger, H.J. and Thomkins, W.F. 1953. *The Traffic in Narcotics.* New York: Funk and Wagnalls.

Apospori, E.A., Vega, W.A., Zimmerman, R.S., Warheit, G.J. and Gil, A.G. 1995. 'A longitudinal study of the conditional effects of deviant behaviour on drug use among three racial/ethnic groups of adolescents', in Kaplan, H.B. (ed.) *Drugs, Crime, and Other Deviant Adaptations: Longitudinal Studies (Longitudinal Research in the Social and Behaviour Sciences: An Interdisciplinary Series).* New York, Plenum, pp. 211-39.

Aries, P. 1974. *Western Attitudes towards Death: From the Middle Ages to the Present.* Baltimore, John Hopkins Press.

Atkinson, P., Coffey, A., Delamont, S., Lofland, J. and Lofland, L. 2001. *Handbook of Ethnography.* London, Sage.

Audit Commission 2002. *Changing Habits: the commissioning and management of community drug treatment services for adults*, London, Audit Commission Publications.

Ball, J. and Ross, A. 1991. *The Effectiveness of Methadone Maintenance Treatment.* New York, Springer.

Ball, J.C., Rosen, L., Flueck, J.A. and Nurco, D.N. 1981. 'The criminality of heroin addicts: When addicted and when off opiates', in Inicardi, J.A. (ed.) *The Drugs-Crime Connection.* Beverly Hills CA, Sage, pp. 39-65.

Barton, A. 1999. 'Breaking the crime/drugs cycle: The birth of a new approach?', *The Howard Journal of Criminal Justice*, 38(2), pp. 144-57.

Bauman, K.E. and Ennett, S.T. 1996. 'On the importance of peer influence for adolescent drug use: Commonly neglected considerations', *Addiction*, 91(2), pp. 185-98.

Bauman, Z. 1987. *Legislators and Interpreters: On Modernity, Post-modernity and Intellectuals.* Cambridge, Polity.

Bauman, Z. 1991. *Modernity and Ambivalence.* Cambridge, Polity.

Baumer, E., Lauristen, J.L., Rosenfeld, R. and Wright, R. 1999. 'The influence of crack cocaine on crime rates: A cross city longitudinal analysis', *Journal of Research in Crime and Delinquency*, 35(3), pp. 316-40.

Bean, P. 2002. *Drugs and Crime*. Cullompton, Willan.

Bean, P.T. and Wilkinson, C.K. 1988. 'Drug taking, crime and the illicit supply system', *British Journal of Addiction*, 83, pp. 533-9.

Beaumont, J., Loopmans, M. and Uitermark, J. 2005. 'Politicization of research and the relevance of geography: Some experiences and reflections for an ongoing debate', *Area*, 37(2), pp. 118.

Bennett, T. and Wright, R. 1986. 'The impact of prescribing on the crimes of opioid users', *British Journal of Addiction*, 81, pp. 265-73.

Benoit, E., Randolph, D., Dunlap, E. and Johnson, B. 2003. 'Code switching and inverse imitation among marijuana-using crack sellers', *British Journal of Criminology*, 43, pp. 506-25.

Benson, B.L. and Rasmussen, D. 1991. 'The relationship between illicit drug enforcement policy and property crimes', *Contemporary Policy Issues*, 9, pp. 106-15.

Benson, B.L., Kim, I., Rasmussen, D. and Zuelke, T.W. 1992. 'Is property crime caused by drug use or drug enforcement policy?', *Applied Economics*, 24, pp. 679-92.

Berger, P.L. and Luckmann, T. 1967. *The Social Construction of Reality*. London, Penguin.

Bernburg, J.G. 2002. 'Anomie, social change and crime', *British Journal of Criminology*, 42, pp. 729-42.

Best, D., Sidwell, C., Gossop, M., Harris, J. and Strang, J. 2001. 'Crime and expenditure among polydrug misusers seeking treatment: The connection between prescribed methadone and crack use and criminal involvement', *British Journal of Criminology*, 41, pp. 119-26.

Blauner, R. 1966. 'Death and social structure', *Psychiatry*, 29, pp. 378-94.

Bourdieu, P. 1977. *Outline of a Theory of Practice*. Cambridge, Cambridge University Press.

Bourdieu, P. 1984. *Distinction: A Social Critique of the Judgement of Taste*. London, Routledge.

Bourdieu, P. 1990. *The Logic of Practice*. Cambridge, Polity.

Bourdieu, P. 1992. *Language and Symbolic Power*. Cambridge, Polity.

Bourdieu, P. 1993. *The Field of Cultural Production*. Cambridge, Polity.

Bourdieu, P. 2000. *Pascallian Meditations*. Stanford CA, Stansford University Press.

Bourdieu, P. 2001. *Practical Reason*. Cambridge, Polity.

Bourdieu, P. and Passeron, J.-C. 1977. *Reproduction in Education, Society and Culture: 2nd Edition*. London, Sage.

Bronfenbrenner, U. 1979. *The Ecology of Human Development*. Cambridge MA, Harvard University Press.

Cavadino, M. 1994. 'Persistent young offenders', *Journal of Child Law*, 6(1), pp. 2-6.

Charlesworth, S. 2000. *A Phenomenology of Working Class Experience*. Cambridge, Cambridge University Press.

Chein, I. and Rosenfeld, E. 1957. 'Juvenile narcotics use', *Journal of Law and Contemporary Problems*, 22, pp. 52-68.

Chein, I., Gerard, D.L., Lee, R.S. and Rosenfeld, E. 1964. *The Road to H*. New York: Basic Books.

Clapham, D. 1997. 'The social construction of housing management research', *Urban Studies*, 34(5-6), pp. 761-74.

Coffey, A. 1999. *The Ethnographic Self*. London, Sage.

Collins, J.J., Hubbard, R.L. and Rachal, J.V. 1985. 'Expensive drug use and illegal income: A test of explanatory hypotheses', *Criminology*, 23, pp. 743-63.

Cooley, C.H. 1902. *Human Nature and Social Order*. New York, Scribner.

Crawford, A. 1999. *The Local Governance of Crime: Appeals to Community and Partnerships*. Oxford, Oxford University Press.

Crow, G. 2002. 'Community studies: Fifty years of theorization', *Sociological Research Online*, 7(3), www.socresonline.org.uk/7/3/crow.html.

Cuskey, W., Ispen, J. and Premkumar, T. 1973. 'An Inquiry into the Nature of Changes in Behaviour Among Drug Users in Treatment', in National Commission on Marijuana and Drug Abuse, *Drug Use in America*. Washington DC: US Government Printing Office, pp. 198-357.

Dai, B. 1970. *Opium Addiction in Chicago (2ⁿᵈ Ed)*. Montclair, New Jersey: Patterson and Smith.

Deegan, M.J. 2001. 'The Chicago School of Ethnography', in Atkinson, P., Coffey, A., Delamont, S., Lofland, J. and Lofland, L. (eds) *Handbook of Ethnography*. London, Sage, pp. 10-25.

Defleur, L.B., Ball, J.C., Snarr, R.W. 1969. 'The long term correlates of opiate abuse', *Social Problems*, 17, pp. 225-34.

Delanty, G. 2001. *Challenging Knowledge: The University in the Knowledge Society*. Buckingham, Open University Press.

Desimone, J. 2001. 'The effect of cocaine prices on crime', *Economic Inquiry*, 39(4), pp. 627-43.

Dole, V.P., Nyswander, M.E. and Warner, A. 1968. 'Successful treatment of 750 criminal addicts', *Journal of the American Medical Association*, 218(10), pp. 1536-41.

Donohew, L., Clayton, R.R., Skinner, W.F. and Colon, S. 1999. 'Peer networks and sensation seeking: Some implications for primary socialisation theory', *Substance Use and Misuse*, 34: 1013-23.

Duff, C. 2004. 'Drug use as a "practice of the self": Is there any place for an "ethics of moderation" in contemporary drug policy?', *International Journal of Drug Policy*, 15, pp. 385-93.

Duff, C. 2005. 'Party drugs and party people: Examining the "normalisation" of recreational drug use in Melbourne, Australia', *International Journal of Drug Policy*, 16, pp. 161-70.

Dunlap, E., Golub, A., Johnson, B. and Wesley, D. 2002. 'Intergenerational transmission of conduct norms for drugs, sexual exploitation and violence: A case study', *British Journal of Criminology*, 42(1), pp. 1-20.

Edmunson, W.F., Davies, J.E., Acker, J.D. and Myer, B. 1972. 'Patterns of drug abuse epidemiology in prisoners', *Industrial Medicine and Surgery*, 41(1), pp. 15-19.

Elias, N. 1966 'Problems of involvement and detachment', *British Journal of Sociology*, 7(3), pp. 226-52.

Elias, N. 1985. *The Loneliness of the Dying*. London, Continuum.

Ennett, S. and Bauman, K.E. 1994. ,The contribution of influence and selection to adolescent peer group homogeneity: The case of adolescent cigarette smoking', *Journal of Personality and Social Psychology*, 67, pp. 653-63.

Estrada, F. 2001. 'Juvenile violence as a social problem', *British Journal of Criminology*, 41, pp. 639-55.

Fang, J., Madhavan, S., Bosworth, W. and Alderman, M.H. 1998. 'Residential segregation and mortality in New York', *Social Science and Medicine*, 47, pp. 469-76.

Fiddle, S. 1967. *Portraits From a Shooting Gallery*. New York, Harper.

Finestone, H. 1957. 'Narcotics and criminality', *Law and Contemporary Problems*, 22, pp. 69-85.

Fishbein, D.H. and Perez, D.M. 2000. 'A regional study of risk factors for drug abuse and delinquency: Sex and racial differences', *Journal of Child and Family Studies*, 9(4), pp. 461-79.

Ford, A., Hauser, H. and Jackson, E. 1975. 'Use of drugs among persons admitted to a county jail', *Public Health Reports*, 90, pp. 504-8.

Foster, J. 2000. 'Social exclusion, crime and drugs', *Drugs: Education, Prevention and Policy*, 7, pp. 317-30.

Foucault, M. 1977. *Discipline and Punish: The Birth of the Prison*. London, Penguin.

Foucualt, M. 1979. *The History of Sexuality I: The Will to Knowledge*. London, Penguin.

Fraser, M.W. and Hawkins, J.D. 1984a. 'Social network analysis and drug misuse', *Social Services Review*, 58, pp. 81-97.

Fraser, M.W. and Hawkins, J.D. 1984b. 'The social networks of opoid abusers', *International Journal of Addiction*, 19, pp. 903-17.

Fuller, S. 2000. *The Governance of Science*. Buckingham, Open University Press.

Garb, S. and Crim, P. 1966. *Pharmacology and Patient Care*. New York: Springer.

Gearing, F.R. 1970. 'Evaluation of methadone maintenance treatment programme', *International Journal of the Addictions*, 5(3), pp. 517-43.

Giddens, A. 1991. *Modernity and Identity: Self and Society in the Late Modern Age*. Cambridge, Polity.

Glueck, S. and Glueck, E. 1950. *Juvenile Delinquents Grow Up*. New York, Commonwealth Fund.

Goffman, E. 1968. *Asylums: Essays on the Social Situation of Mental Patients and Other Inmates*. London, Penguin.

Goldstein, P.J. 1987. *Drug-Related Crime Analysis – Homicide: A Report to the National Institute of Justice*, July.

Golub, A.L. and Johnson, B.D. 1997. *Crack's Decline: Some Surprises Across US Cities*. Washington DC: US Department of Justice.

Goody, J. 1959. 'Death and social control among the LoDagaa', *Man*, 203, pp. 134-8.

Gordon, A.M. 1973. 'Patterns of delinquency in drug addiction', *British Journal of Psychiatry*, 122, pp. 205-10.

Gossop, M., Marsden, J. and Stewart, D. 1998. *NTORS: The National Treatment Outcome Research Study: Changes in Substance Use, Health and Criminal Behaviour One Year after Intake*. London: Department of Health.

Greenberg, M.A. and Adler, F. 1974. 'Crime and addiction: An empirical analysis of the literature 1920-1973', *Contemporary Drug Problems*, 3, pp. 221-70.

Grogger, J. and Willis, M. 2000. 'The emergence of crack cocaine and the rise in urban crime rates', *The Review of Economics and Statistics*, 82(4), pp. 519-29.

Hagell, A. and Newburn, T. 1994. *Persistent Young Offenders*. London: Policy Studies Institute.

Hammersley, R., Forsyth, A., Morrison, V. and Davies, J.B. 1989. 'The relationship between crime and opioid use', *British Journal of Addiction*, 84, pp. 1029-43.

Harding, S. 1991. *Whose Science? Whose Knowledge? Thinking from Women's Lives*. Milton Keynes, Open University Press.

Hawkesworth, M. 2001. 'Disabling Spatialities and the Regulation of a Visible Secret', *Urban Studies*, 38(2), pp. 299-318.

Heidegger, M. 1962. *Being and Time*. Translated by John Macquarrie and Edward Robinson. Oxford, Blackwell.

Heidegger, M. 1978. *Basic Writings (Edited by David Farrell Krell)*. London, Routledge.

Heidegger, M. 1985. *History of the Concept of Time: Prolegomena*. Translated by T. Kisiel. Bloomington, Indiana University Press.

Heidensohn, F. 1989. *Crime and Society*. Basingstoke, Palgrave.

Helmer, J. 1977. 'The connection between narcotics and crime', *Journal of Drugs Issues*, 7(4), pp. 405-18.

Hillyard, P. 2002. 'Invoking indignation: Reflections on future directions of socio-legal studies', *Journal of Law and Society*, 29(4), pp. 645-56.

Hillyard, P. and Sim, J. 1997. 'The political economy of socio-legal research', in Thomas, P.A. (ed.) *Socio-Legal Studies*. Aldershot, Dartmouth, pp. 45-75.

Hillyard, P., Pantazis, C., Tombs, S. and Gordon, D. 2004. (eds) *Beyond Criminology: Taking Harm Seriously*. London, Pluto.

Hillyard, P., Sim, J., Tombs, S. and Whyte, D. 2004. 'Leaving a stain on the silence: Contemporary criminology and the politics of dissent', *British Journal of Criminology*, 44, pp. 369-90.

Hobbs, D. 2001. 'Ethnography and The Study of Deviance', in Atkinson, P., Coffey, A., Delamont, S., Lofland, J. and Lofland, L. (eds) *Handbook of Ethnography*. London, Sage, pp. 204-19.

Hockey, J. 1990. *Experiences of Death*. Edinburgh, University Press.

Holloway, K. and Bennett, T. 2004. *The Results of the First Two Years of the NEW-ADAM Programme*. London, Home Office.

Holloway, K., Bennett, T. and Lower, C. 2004. *Trends in Drug Use and Offending: The Results of the NEW-ADAM Programme 1999-2002*. London, Home Office Findings 219.

Home Office. 2002. *Tackling Drugs as Part of Neighbourhood Renewal*. London, Home Office.

Home Office. 2004. *Drug Strategy Progress Report: Tackling Drugs – Changing Lives – Keeping Communities Safe from Drugs*. London, Home Office Drugs Strategy Directorate.

Horney, J., Osgood, W.D. and Marshall, I.II. 1995. 'Criminal careers in the short-term intra-individual variability in crime and its relation to local life circumstances', *American Sociological Review*, 60, pp. 655-73.

Horowitz, I.L. (ed.). 1967. *The Rise and Fall of Project Camelot: Studies in the Relationship Between Social Science and Practical Politics*. Cambridge MA: The MIT Press.

Hough, M. 1996. *Drug Misusers and the Criminal Justice System: A Review of the Literature*. London, Home Office Drug Prevention Initiative Paper 15.

Hough, M. and Mitchell, D. 2003. 'Drug Dependent Offenders and "*Justice for All*"', in Tonry, M. (ed.) *Confronting Crime.* Cullompton, Willan Publishing, pp. 26-50.

Hubbard, R.L., Marsden, M.E., Rachal, J.V., Harwood, H.J., Cavanaugh, E.R. and Ginzberg, H.M. 1989. *Drug Abuse Treatment: A National Study of Effectiveness*. Chapel Hill: University of North Carolina Press.

Hughes, B. 1999. 'The constitution of impairment: Modernity and the aesthetic of oppression', *Disability and Society*, 14(2), pp. 155-72.

Hughes, B. and Patterson, K. 1997. 'The social model of disability and the disappearing body: Towards a sociology of impairment', *Disability and Society*, 12(3), pp. 325-40.

Huizinga, D.H., Menard, S. and Elliot, D.S. 1989. 'Delinquency and drug use: temporal and developmental patterns', *Justice Quarterly*, 6, pp. 419-55.

Hunt, G. and Barker, J.C. 2001. 'Socio-cultural anthropology and alcohol and drug research: Towards a unified theory', *Social Science and Medicine*, 53, pp. 165-88.

Hunt, N. 2001. 'Reasoning and restricted choices within recreational repertoires', *International Journal of Drug Policy*, 12, pp. 425-8.

Inciardi, J.A. and Chambers, C.D. 1972. 'Unreported criminal involvement of narcotic addicts', *Journal of Drug Issues*, 2, pp. 57-64.

Jacobs, K., Kemeny, J. and Manzi, T. 2003. 'Power, discursive space and institutional practices in the construction of housing problems', *Housing Studies*, 18(4), pp. 429-46.

Jenkins, J.E. and Zunguze, S.T. 1998. 'The relationship of family structure to adolescent drug use, peer affiliation, and perception of peer acceptance of drug use', *Adolescence*, 33, pp. 811-22.

Johnson, B.D., Golstein, P.J., Preble, E., Schmeidler, J., Lipton, D.S., Spunt, B. and Miller, T. 1985. *Taking Care of Business: The Economics of Crime by Heroin Users*. Lexington MA: Lexington Books.

Johnson, B.D., Golub, A. and Fagan, J. 1995. 'Careers in crack, drug use, drug distribution and non drug criminality', *Crime and Delinquency*, 41, pp. 275-95.

Kandel, D.B. and Davis, M. 1991. 'Friendship networks, intimacy, and illicit drug use in young adulthood: a comparison of two competing theories', *Criminology*, 29, pp. 441-67.

Kemeny, J. 1992. *Housing and Social Theory.* London, Routledge.

Kemeny, J. 1995. *From Public Housing to the Social Market: Rental Policy in Comparative Perspective.* London, Routledge.

Kisiel, T. 2002. *Heidegger's Way of Thought: Critical and Interpretative Signposts.* London and New York, Continuum.

Kitchin, R. 1998. '"Out of place", "knowing one's place": Space, power and the exclusion of disabled people', *Disability and Society*, 13(3), pp. 343-56.

Kolb, L. 1925. 'Drug addiction and its relation to crime', *Mental Hygiene*, 9, pp. 74-89.

Kozel, N., Du Pont, R. and Brown, B. 1972. 'Narcotics and crime: A study of narcotic involvement in an offender population', *International Journal of the Addiction*, 7, pp. 443-50.

Kuhn, T. 1970. *The Structure of Scientific Revolutions.* Chicago, University of Chicago Press.

Lalander, P. 2003. *Hooked on Heroin: Drugs and Drifters in a Globalized World.* Oxford, Berg.

Lambert, S.F., Brown, T.L., Phillips, C.M. and Ialongo, N.S. 2004. 'The relationship between perceptions of neighbourhood characteristics and substance use among urban African American adolescents', *American Journal of Community Psychology*, 34(3/4), pp. 205-18.

Lane, M. and Henry, K. 2001. 'Community development, crime and violence: A case study', *Community Development Journal*, 36(3), pp. 212-22.

Lash, S. and Urry, J. 1987. *The End of Organised Capitalism.* Cambridge, Polity.

Lash, S. and Urry, J. 1994. *Economies of Signs and Space.* London, Sage.

Latkin, C., Mandell, W., Oziemkowska, M., Calentano, D., Vlahov, D., Ensminger, M. and Knowlton, A. 1995. 'Using social network analysis to study patterns of drug use among urban drug users at high risk for HIV/AIDS', *Drug and Alcohol Dependence*, 38, pp. 1-9.

Leder, D. 1990. *The Absent Body.* Chicago, Chicago University Press.

Lee, R. 1997. 'Socio-Legal Research – What's The Use?', in Thomas, P.A. (ed.) *Socio-Legal Studies.* Aldershot, Dartmouth, pp. 76-98.

Lindenberg, C.S., Reiskin, H.K. and Gendrop, S.C. 1994. 'The social stress model of substance abuse among childbearing-age women: A review of the literature', *Journal of Drug Education*, 24, pp. 253-68.

Lucas, P. 2002. 'Mind-forged manacles and habits of the soul: Foucault's debt to Heidegger', *Philosophy of the Social Sciences*, 32(3), pp. 310-28.

Lukoff, I.F. 1973. 'Issues in the Evaluation of Heroin Treatment', paper presented to the *Epidemiology of Drug Use Conference*, San Juan, Puerto Rico, February.

MacDonald, R. and Marsh, J. 2001. 'Disconnected youth', *Journal of Youth Studies*, 4(4), pp. 373-91.

MacDonald, R. and Marsh, J. 2002. 'Crossing the rubicon: Youth transitions, poverty, drugs and social exclusion', *International Journal of Drug Policy*, 13, pp. 27-38.

MacKenzie, D.L. and De Li, S. 2002. 'The impact of formal and informal social controls on the criminal activities of probationers', *Journal of Research in Crime and Delinquency*, 39(3), pp. 243-76.

Martin, A. and Stenner, P. 2004. 'Talking about drug use: What are we (and our participants) doing in qualitative research?', *International Journal of Drug Policy*, 15, pp. 395-405.

Massey, D. and Shibuya, K. 1995. 'Unravelling the tangle of pathology: The effect of spatially concentrated joblessness on the well-being of African Americans', *Social Science Research*, 24, pp. 352-66.

Mauss, A. 1991. 'Social science movements and cynicism: Appreciating the political context of sociological research in alcohol studies', in Roman, P.M. (ed.) *Alcohol: The Development of Sociological Perspectives on Use and Abuse*. New Brunswick NJ, Rutgers Center of Alcohol Studies, pp. 187-204.

May, T. 1996. *Situating Social Theory.* Buckingham, Open University Press.

McBride, D.C. 1976. 'The Relationships Between Type of Drug Use and Arrest Charge in an Arrested Population', in Research Triangle Institute (eds), *Drug Use and Crime.* Springfield VA: National Technical Information Service.

McBride, D.C. and McCoy, C.B. 1982. 'Crime and drugs: The issues and literature', *Journal of Drugs Issues*, 12(2), pp. 137-51.

Mead, G.H. 1934. *Mind, Self, and Society.* Chicago, University of Chicago Press.

Mellor, P. 1993. 'Death in high modernity: The contemporary presence and absence of death', in Clark, D. (ed.) *The Sociology of Death.* London, Blackwell, pp. 11-30.

Merleau-Ponty, M. 1962. *Phenomenology of Perception.* London, Routledge and Kegan Paul.

Merleau-Ponty, M. 1964. *The Primacy of Perception.* Evanston Illinois, Northwestern University Press.

Meyer, A.S. 1952. *Social and Psychological Factors in Opiate Addiction.* New York: Bureau of Applied Social Research.

Morris, T.P. 1957. *The Criminal Area.* London, Routledge and Kegan Paul.

Moyer, I.L. 2001. *Criminological Theories: Traditional and Nontraditional Voices and Themes.* London, Sage.

Mills, C.W. (1959) *The Sociological Imagination.* New York, Oxford University Press.

National Treatment Agency for Substance Misuse (2002) *Models of Care for the Treatment of Drug Misusers: Promoting quality, efficiency and effectiveness in drug misuse treatment services in England* (NTA: Department of Health). http://www.nta.nhs.uk/publications/MOCPART2/mocpart2_feb03.pdf.

National Treatment Agency for Substance Misuse (2002) *Models of Care for Treatment of Adult Drug Misusers: Framework for developing local systems of effective drug misuse treatment in England.* (NTA: Department of Health). http://www.nta.nhs.uk/publications/MOCPART2/mocpart2_feb03.pdf.

Newburn, T. 1999. 'Drug prevention and youth justice', *British Journal of Criminology*, 39(4), pp. 609-24.

Nurco, D.N., Ball, J.C., Shaffer, J.W. and Hanlon, T.E. 1985. 'The criminality of narcotics addicts', *The Journal of Nervous and Mental Disease*, 173(2), pp. 94-102.

Oetting, E.R., Donnermeyer, J.F., Trimble, J.E. and Beauvais, F. 1998. 'Primary socialisation theory: Culture, ethnicity, and cultural identification: the links between culture and substance use', *Substance Use and Misuse*, 33(10), pp. 2075-107.

Park, R.E. *The Crowd and the Public and Other Essays*. Chicago, University of Chicago Press.

Park, R.E., Burgess, E.W. and McKenzie, R.D. 1967 [1925]. *The City*. Chicago, University of Chicago Press.

Parker, H. 1974. *View from the Boys: A Sociology of Down Town Adolescents*. Newton Abbott, David and Charles.

Parker, H. and Newcombe, R. 1987. 'Heroin use and acquisitive crime in an English community', *British Journal of Sociology*, 38, pp. 331-50.

Parker, H., Bury, C. and Egginton, R. 1998. *New Heroin Outbreaks Amongst Young People in England and Wales*. London, Home Office, Crime Detection and Prevention Series Paper 92.

Parker, H., Williams, L. and Aldridge, J. 2002. 'The normalisation of "sensible" recreational drug use: Further evidence from the North West England Longitudinal Study', *Sociology*, 36(4), pp. 941-64.

Patch, V.D. 1972. 'Methadone maintenance in Boston', *Proceedings of the 4th National Conference on Methadone Treatment*, National Association for the Prevention of Addiction to Narcotics, Washington, DC, US Government Printing Office, pp. 507-10.

Patterson, K. and Hughes, B. 1999. 'Disability studies and phenomenology: The carnal politics of everyday life', *Disability and Society*, 14(5), pp. 597-610.

Pearson, G. 1987. *The New Heroin Users*. Oxford: Blackwell.

Pearson, G. 1999. 'Drugs at the end of the century', *British Journal of Criminology*, 39(4), pp. 477-87.

Pearson, G. 2001. 'Normal drug use: Ethnographic fieldwork among an adult network of recreational drug users in Inner London', *Substance Use and Misuse*, 36(1/2), pp. 167-200.

Pluddemann, A., Parry, C.D.H. and Flisher, A.J. 2004. *The Nature and Extent of Heroin Use in Cape Town: Part 2 – A Community Survey*. Cape Town, University of Cape Town.

Preble, E. and Casey, J. 1969. 'Taking care of business: The heroin user's life on the streets', *International Journal of the Addictions*, 4(1), pp. 1-24.

Prescor, M.J. 1938. 'A statistical analysis of the clinical records of hospitalised drug addicts', *Public Health Reports*, 43, pp. 1-23.

Prior, L. 1987. 'Policing the dead: A sociology of the mortuary', *Sociology*, 21(3), pp. 355-76.

Prior, L. 1989. *The Social Organisation of Death*. Basingstoke, Macmillan.

Quinney, R. 1970. *The Social Reality of Crime*. Boston, Little Brown.

Rai, A.A., Stanton, B., Wu, Y., Li, X., Galbraith, J., Cottcrell, L., Pack, R., Harris, C., D'Alessandri, D. and Burns, J. 2003. 'Relative influences of perceived parental monitoring and perceived peer involvement on adolescent risk behaviours: An analysis of six cross-sectional data sets', *Journal of Adolescent Health*, 33, pp. 108-18.

Ray, M.B. 1968. 'Abstinence cycles and heroin addicts', in Rubington, E. and Weinberg, M.S. (eds) *Deviance: The Interactionist Perspective*. London, MacMillan, pp. 486-92.

Resignato, A.J. 2000. 'Violent crime: A function of drug use of drug enforcement', *Applied Economics*, 32, pp. 681-8.

Rhodes, J. and Jason, L.A. 1990. 'A social stress model of substance abuse', *Journal of Consulting and Clinical Psychology*, 58, pp. 395-401.

Rosenthal, S.J. 1973. *Illicit Drug Use and its Relation to Crime: A Statistical Analysis of Self Reported Drug Use and Illegal Behaviour*. Philadelphia: Centre for Social Policy and Community Development, Temple University.

Rothbard, A., Alterman, A., Rutherford, M., Liu, M., Zelinski, S. and McKay, J. 1999. 'Revisiting the effectiveness of methadone treatment on crime reductions in the 1990s', *Journal of Substance Abuse Treatment*, 16(4), pp. 329-35.

Sampson, R. and Laub, J. 1993. *Crime in the Making: Pathways and Turning Points Through Life*. Cambridge MA: Harvard University Press.

Scheier, L.M., Botvin, G.J., and Miller, N.L. 1999. 'Life events, neighbourhood stress, psychosocial functioning, and alcohol use among urban minority youth', *Journal of Child and Adolescent Substance Abuse*, 9, pp. 19-50.

Scraton, P. and Chadwick, K. 1991. 'The theoretical and political priorities of critical criminology', in Stenson, K. and Cowell, D. (eds) *The Politics of Crime Control*. London, Sage, pp. 161-85.

Seamon, D. 1979. *A Geography of the Life World*. London, Croom Helm.

Shaw, C.R. and McKay, H.D. 1931. *Social Factors in Juvenile Delinquency*. Washington, National Commission on Law Observance and Enforcement.

Shaw, C.R. and McKay, H.D. 1942. *Juvenile Delinquency and Urban Areas*. Chicago, University of Chicago Press.

Shaw, C.R. and McKay, H.D. 1972. *Juvenile Delinquency and Urban Areas*. Chicago, University of Chicago Press.

Skeggs, B. 1997. *Formations of Class and Gender*. London, Sage.

Skeggs, B. 2004. *Class, Self, Culture*. London, Routledge.

Sprigings, N. and Allen, C. 2005. 'The communities we are regaining but need to lose: A critical commentary on community building in beyond-place societies', *Community, Work and Family*, 8(4), pp. 389-411.

Stephens, R.C. and Ellis, R.D. 1975. 'Narcotics addicts and crime: An analysis of recent trends', *Criminology*, 12, pp. 474-88.

Stewart, J.D. 2002. 'The doubtful polis: The question of politics in Heidegger's "Being and Time"', *History of Political Thought*, 23(4), pp. 670-86.

Storr, C.L., Arria, A.M., Workman, R.L. and Anthony, J.C. 2004. 'Neighbourhood environment and opportunity to try methamphetamine ("Ice") and marijuana: Evidence from Guam in the Western Pacific Region of Micronesia', *Substance Use and Misuse*, 39(2), pp. 253-76.

Strang, J., Finch, E., Hankinson, L., Farrell, M., Taylor, C. and Gossop, M. 1997. 'Methadone treatment for opiate addiction: Benefits in the first month', *Addiction Research*, 5, pp. 71-6.

Sutherland, E. 1937. *The Professional Thief*. Chicago, University of Chicago Press.

Thiele, L.P. 1995. *Timely Meditations: Martin Heidegger and Post modern Politics*. Princeton NJ, Princeton University Press.

Topalli, V., Wright, R. and Fornango, R. 2002. 'Drug dealers, robbery and retaliation', *British Journal of Criminology*, 42, pp. 337-51.

Turner, B.S. 1992. *Regulating Bodies; Essays in Medical Sociology*. London, Routledge.

University of Manchester. 2003. *'Both Sides of the Coin': An Insight into the Mind of a Street Robber – The Context of Street Robbery in South Manchester.* Manchester, University of Manchester, Department of Applied Social Science.

Valente, T.W., Gallaher, P. and Mouttapa, M. 2004. 'Using social networks to understand and prevent substance use: A transdisciplinary perspective', *Substance Use and Misuse*, 39(10-12), pp. 1685-712.

Valentine, G. 1999. 'What it means to be a man: The body, masculinities and disability', in Butler, R. and Parr, H. (eds) *Mind and Body Spaces: Geographies of Illness, Impairment and Disability.* London, Routledge, pp. 167-80.

Van Swaaningen, R. 1999. 'Reclaiming critical criminology: Social justice and the European tradition', *Theoretical Criminology*, 3(1), pp. 5-28.

Voss, H.L. and Stephens, R.C. 1973. 'Criminal history of narcotics addicts', *Drug Forum*, 2, pp. 191-202.

Waldorf, D., Reinarman, C. and Murphy, S. 1991. *Cocaine Changes.* Philadelphia PA, Temple University Press.

Walklate, S. 1998. *Understanding Criminology: Current Theoretical Debates.* Buckingham, Open University Press.

Walter, T. 1994. *The Revival of Death.* London, Routledge.

Walters, R. 2003. 'New modes of governance and the commodification of criminological knowledge', *Social and Legal Studies*, 12(1), pp. 5-26.

Webster, R.A., Hunter, M. and Keats, J.A. 1994. 'Personality and socio-demographic influences on adolescents' substance use: A path analysis', *International Journal of the Addictions*, 29, pp. 941-56.

Weisman, S., Mass, W. and Katsampes, P.L. 1976. 'Addiction and criminal behaviour: A continuing examination of criminal addicts', *Journal of Drug Issues*, 6, pp. 153-65.

White, H.R., Tice, P.C., Loeber, R. and Stouthamer-Loeber, M. 2002. 'Illegal acts committed by adolescents under the influence of alcohol and drugs', *Journal of Research in Crime and Delinquency*, 39(2), pp. 131-52.

Wilding, P. 1982. *Professional Power and Social Welfare.* London, Routledge and Kegan Paul.

Williams, L. and Parker, H. 2001. 'Alcohol, cannabis, ecstasy and cocaine: Drugs of reasoned choice amongst young adult recreational drug users in England', *International Journal of Drug Policy*, 12, pp. 397-413.

Willis, P. 1977. *Learning to Labour: How Working Class Kids Get Working Class Jobs.* London, Saxon House.

Willmott, H. 2000. 'Death. So what? Sociology, sequestration and emancipation', *The Sociological Review*, pp. 649-65.

Windle, M. 2000. 'Parental, sibling, and peer influences on adolescent substance use and alcohol problems', *Applied Developmental Science*, 4, pp. 98-110.

Woolgar, S. and Latour, S. 1979. *Laboratory Life: The Construction of Scientific Facts.* Princeton NJ, Princeton University Press.

Young, J. 1999. *The Exclusive Society: Social Exclusion, Crime and Difference in Late Modernity.* London, Sage.

Index

144 *Crime, Drugs and Social Theory*

symbolic interactionism 40
see also middle class; working class
cocaine 18-19, 25, 105
see also crack cocaine
coercion 2, 3, 126, 127, 129-30
Collins, J.J. 26
communication
articulatory authority 64-5
dominant pedagogic 7-8, 75-7
see also language
community development 31
'confirming encounters' 9, 85, 87-8, 91-2,
119
conflict theory 34, 43
Conservative government 130
constrained choice 52-3, 72-4
consumerism 51, 53
contract research 21, 22
control theory 33, 49, 50
Cooley, Charles Horton 40, 42
coping model 33
crack cocaine 19, 83, 94, 98
'physiological low points' 121
violent crime 26-7, 104-5
Crim, P. 26
crime
Chicago School 34, 38, 53
consequences of becoming/being a
problematic user 101-12
ecological approaches 38-40, 53
epistemological distance of theory 5-6,
54, 55-60, 68, 72, 127-8
growth of 128
post-modern theory 51-3, 54
practical 'point of view' 76-82
'recreational' 70, 105, 109, 128
social bonds 118-20
social constructionism 34-7
social network theory 48-50, 53
social science 'point of view' 70, 71-4
subcultural theory 43, 44, 53
symbolic interactionism 40, 49-50, 53
see also property crime; shoplifting;
street robbery
crime-drugs link 3, 11-12, 24-30, 130
hypothetico-deductive research 3, 5, 17-
18, 19, 24, 30, 31-2
increased involvement in crime 28-9
statistical associations 25-7
third variables 30-31

criminology 3, 4, 9, 20-24, 33
crime-drugs link 18, 24-5, 27, 30-31
critical 18, 23, 34-7
educational issues 76-7
cultural reproduction 7, 75
Cuskey, W. 28

Dai, B. 38
Dasein
'being-in-the-world' 58, 60, 61, 62, 67,
75, 87-8
bereavement 96
'disturbing encounters' 98, 119-20
de-industrialisation 38, 39, 51, 54
dealers 36
death 11, 12, 86, 95-8
see also bereavement
'decency codes' 52
decriminalisation 37
delinquency 30, 31
Chicago School 38
peer influences 49
perceptions of neighbourhood context 48
symbolic interactionism 40
depression 11
Desimone, J. 104, 105
detoxification
'being-against-care' 114, 121, 124
'being-towards-care' 113, 116, 118, 123
care planning 115
crime-drugs link 27
deviance 28, 29, 33
Chicago School 37-8
ethnography 43
social network theory 53-4
symbolic interactionism 42
differential association 33, 46
'disturbing encounters' 13, 67, 88-9, 91-2,
98-9, 115
'disturbing episodes' distinction 95
existential basis 9-10, 85-6
social bonds 119-20
Dole, V.P. 27
domination 7, 60n1, 70, 75, 76, 80
see also power
doxa 61n2, 62, 64, 71, 75, 80
Drug Intervention Programme 2
drug use
becoming a problematic user 85-99,
101, 102-4
bereavement 11, 95-8